## Scribe Publications
## THE HOUSE OF FICTION

Susan Swingler was born in Birmingham, and now lives in Gloucestershire. Her jobs have ranged from freelance photographer to gardener, university lecturer to curator and researcher. She and her husband travel widely, and have made regular visits to Australia since the late 1970s.

*For Rebecca and Lucy*

# *The House of Fiction*

Leonard, Susan, and Elizabeth Jolley

{a memoir}

# SUSAN SWINGLER

SCRIBE

*Melbourne · London*

Scribe Publication Pty Ltd
18–20 Edward St, Brunswick, Victoria 3056, Australia
50A Kingsway Place, Sans Walk, London, EC1R 0LU, United Kingdom

Originally published by Fremantle Press 2012
This edition (with minor corrections) first published by Scribe 2014
This impression no. 2 reprinted in 2014

Typeset in 10.5/14 pt Mercury by the publishers

Printed and bound by CPI Group (UK) Ltd, Croydon, CR0 4YY

National Library of Australia
Cataloguing-in-Publication entry

Swingler, Susan, author.

The House of Fiction: Leonard, Susan, and Elizabeth Jolley / Susan Swingler.

9781922247292 (paperback)

1. Jolley, Susan–Family.  2. Jolley, Leonard, 1914–1994.  3. Jolley, Elizabeth, 1923–2007.  4. Family secrets.

920.720994

scribepublications.com.au
scribepublications.co.uk

# CONTENTS

Chapter 1 ..................................................................................... 1

Chapter 2 .................................................................................. 18

Chapter 3 .................................................................................. 37

Chapter 4 .................................................................................. 51

Chapter 5 .................................................................................. 67

Chapter 6 .................................................................................. 85

Chapter 7 .................................................................................. 105

Chapter 8 .................................................................................. 113

Chapter 9 .................................................................................. 130

Chapter 10 ................................................................................ 153

Chapter 11 ................................................................................ 160

Chapter 12 ................................................................................ 173

Chapter 13 ................................................................................ 189

Chapter 14 ................................................................................ 212

Chapter 15 ................................................................................ 229

Chapter 16 ................................................................................ 250

Chapter 17 ................................................................................ 273

Chapter 18 ................................................................................ 287

Afterword ................................................................................. 395

Acknowledgements ................................................................. 311

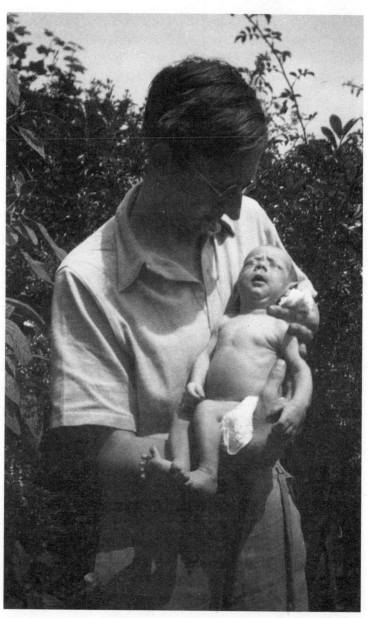

*Leonard with Susan, June 1946*

# CHAPTER 1

*Everything should not be told, it is better to keep some things to yourself.*
– Elizabeth Jolley

A beginning for this story might be in 1940 when my father, Leonard Jolley, fell ill and was nursed by a young woman called Monica Knight; this meeting changed their lives, and ultimately mine, although I wasn't yet born. But that was the start of their story, not mine. I've decided to start in 1967 when I was twenty-one and two people stepped into my life to present me with a version of my past I didn't recognise. This was when I began my quest to unpick the strands of an elaborate and long-lasting deception: too much had been kept from me.

It was the summer of love. I wore a flower in my hair and we danced to *Sgt Pepper*. But far from dropping out and turning on, following the hippie trail or even merely moving in with my boyfriend, I was planning to get married, just as soon as my university finals were over. At that time the age of consent was twenty-one, and as my twenty-first birthday would fall in the middle of the exams, my mother signed the consent form for my marriage and I concentrated on revising.

A week later the form was returned to me. My mother's

consent wouldn't do as she was not my legal guardian.

Armed with a pocket full of coins I hurried to the nearest phone box to call the register office in Exeter. The registrar had someone with him, and I was put on hold. Every few seconds the peeps went and I dropped another coin into the box; they were running out fast. At last I was put through.

The registrar explained, not unkindly: 'You're a minor. Your father is your legal guardian and I'm afraid your mother does not have the right to consent to your marriage.'

'But why? I haven't seen my father for years and he gave up sending my mum any money for my maintenance ages ago.'

'That's beside the point. The law's the law. Unless your parents had made specific arrangements for your guardianship when they divorced, your father remains your legal guardian. And as far as I can see, there was no such arrangement made. You'll just have to get his signature on the consent form or wait until after you're twenty-one.'

'Please ... listen. My father lives in Australia. I haven't heard from him for — I can't remember the last time he wrote. Two years ago? There isn't time to get the papers to him. He might not even be at the address I have for him.'

'You could always try the telephone — check if he's there.'

I looked at the diminishing pile of coins in despair. Telephone? It would cost a fortune. I didn't have his number. His wife would answer. He'd refuse to speak to me. We hadn't exchanged a single spoken word since I was four. Didn't the man whose fingers I could sense tapping on his desk realise how impossible a telephone conversation would be? I tried another tack: 'The passport office let me have a new passport without his signature.'

The registrar didn't seem to believe me, and I had to admit that they'd only given me a three-month extension so I could try to track him down.

'Which you presumably did.'

'Yes, he was in America, on some kind of sabbatical or a lecture tour or something. He's probably back in Australia now, but I don't know for certain and I haven't got three months. I want to get married in July, and the invitations have gone out and I've got my finals, and ... Please. I don't see why my mother's signature won't do. She's signed consent forms for operations. My father has had nothing to do with me for years.' I was almost crying in frustration.

'I'm sorry, my dear. But that's the law. Once you're an adult—once you have celebrated your twenty-first birthday—you can sign the banns yourself.'

'But I'll be in the middle of my exams.'

A pause, an almost audible shrug from the other end of the line.

I had an idea. 'How about my stepfather? If it has to be a man, won't he do?'

'Your father, or yourself once you've reached your majority.'

I slammed the phone down and trudged back to the flat. Men. I didn't know why I was even bothering to marry one of them in the first place.

But I was. We'd planned it and were looking forward to it—not a church wedding, just the register office and a party at my parents' home afterwards. My mother Joyce and stepfather Mick would organise the food and drink, and the boy next door would take the photographs. I would wear an ivory silk dress (made by Joyce) with red flowers in my hair and strappy, red patent-leather shoes on my feet.

On the morning of my twenty-first birthday I sat in the main hall of the Wills Memorial Building at Bristol University and tried to focus on the exam paper in front of me. As soon as we were let out, rather than slope over to the Berkeley Café with my friends for the exam post-mortem, I leapt on a bus to the train station and got to the register office in Exeter in time to sign my own consent form, then straight back to Bristol to prepare for the next day's exams. It wasn't such a big deal in the end, but nevertheless I was still angry at the ridiculousness of a situation where a man who happened to be my father, but who had taken no interest in me or responsibility for me, had such power over me, whereas my mother, who had taken total responsibility for my upbringing, wasn't even allowed to say whether I could get married.

*Gordon and Susan on their wedding day, July 1967*

The wedding went ahead on the day we'd planned. The sun shone, the guests crowded the rooms of my parents' cottage and spilled into the garden. There were lots of friends and a good smattering of Gordon's family, but only one relation from mine: my mother's cousin, Gwen, the only one who had not followed the rest of the extended Exclusive Brethren family when they severed all contact with us long ago.

We went on our honeymoon and then we were back to being students again (I had begun a postgrad course, and Gordon was still an undergraduate), and it was the first week of term. I stood on the bus coming home from college, my left hand casually resting on the back of a seat, and admired my wedding ring, bright gold against my sun-tanned skin. I wiggled my fingers so that it flashed in the light, and I smiled to myself. I was thrilled with my new status as a grown-up married woman. Our home was a tiny cottage, romantically called Thyme Cottage, with a big garden. I picked white asters and bronze chrysanthemums from the garden, and stuffed them in jam jars on the window sills. We'd even got a tabby kitten.

I threw my bags on the floor and picked up the post — two envelopes to Mrs Susan Swingler. I didn't recognise the handwriting. I tore them open to find cards congratulating me on my marriage, accompanied by cheques from people I had never heard of before: Laura and Stanley Welton, and Harry Jolley. Each cheque was for £50 — a lot of money then. A note accompanied Laura's card: she was delighted to discover where I was living, and she asked for news of my mother, Joyce, whom she appeared to know. Harry Jolley had merely signed his name. He was obviously something to do with my father. A brother? A cousin? My grandfather? I knew Grandpa's name was Henry, but surely he'd be dead by now — although the handwriting did look like that of an old man ...

Later that evening I phoned my mother. She seemed both pleased and astonished that they'd written. 'Laura's your father's sister, and Harry's his elder brother.' But why had I never heard of them before? She didn't say anything for a moment and then she said, 'It was a promise I made. You see ...' She hesitated. 'When Daddy ... Leonard ... and I separated, he asked me not to contact his father or any of his family.'

'But why? What difference would it make to them?'

My mother sighed. 'I promised. He was in a terrible state, so I promised. And I've kept my word. But I'm so glad they've found you. I've no idea how.'

I wrote to thank my new-found relations for their generous wedding presents, and told Laura how pleased Joyce was that she could now write to her, which she'd be doing soon. Laura wrote back immediately inviting me to go up to London and visit. I couldn't wait.

The Weltons' house was a 1930s semi on a wide, tree-lined street. The front garden was a mass of brightly coloured flowers, and the front step and doorknocker gleamed. The person who answered the door was much smaller than I'd imagined. I had never seen a photograph of Laura and had assumed she'd look like my father, whom I remembered as tall and imposing. But I had been only four years old when I last saw him, and all grown-ups seemed like giants. Apart from my memories, the only other image I had of Leonard was a photograph that showed him propped up on his elbows, bare-chested, playing chess. But rather than sitting at a table, he was lying down, his legs encased in a kind of plaster cast and resting on an steeply sloping plank or bed. My mother told me that this was when he was in hospital, before I was born, and that he was suffering from rheumatoid arthritis. This immobilisation was the way they treated his condition

*Leonard in hospital, 1940*

at that time. I had never asked my mother if there were any other pictures of him, or why she'd chosen to keep this one.

My husband, Gordon, and I sat on the sofa, with Laura in an armchair opposite. Her husband, Stanley, came in to meet us and then retreated to the garden. Laura made tea, and we drank it from fine bone china.

'This was your grandmother's best china — I think she'd be pleased if you were to have it, now you're setting up a home.' I glanced down at the cup, rimmed with a thin band of gold and decorated with a pattern of pale-blue clematis and ivy, and twisted my legs around one another at the knees and ankles. I couldn't think of anything to say. The more I felt Laura scrutinising my face, the tighter I twisted my legs and the harder I studied the pattern on the cup. Bone china tea sets weren't really our style. Thick, muddy green and brown hand-thrown mugs hung from the hooks on our kitchen shelves. But it would be rude to refuse her offer; she obviously cared very much about the best china. I smiled and mumbled a thank-you.

'You won't remember your grandmother, of course,' Laura said.

But I did. I remembered both the woman and her house: the steep flight of steps that led to a front door, its brown blistering paint, and behind that a gloomy hall, an umbrella stand holding knobbly sticks; one that impressed me had a bird's head handle. Grandma Jolley looked like a bird with her long nose and small, bright eyes.

'I remember going there once,' I told Laura.

Laura raised her eyebrows. 'You must have been very young.'

'But I remember it clearly. Grandma was in bed — a high bed with a carved wooden bedhead.' I remembered how dark it was in the bedroom, the curtains shut against the bright sunlight; green curtains, possibly, or black. I looked around Laura's sun-filled room, a jug of late roses on the pale-wood coffee table between us. 'She was propped up with pillows and bolsters, and looked very frail. She wore a knitted bed jacket — dove-grey, lacy.' I remembered her fingers, long and bent; they reminded me of an illustration of the witch in the story of Hansel and Gretel. In truth I had been frightened of this old lady, but I couldn't possibly say so to her daughter.

'Go on,' Laura urged.

'I think she must have told me to get into the bed with her, under the eiderdown.' The eiderdown was pink and slippery, and she pulled it up over my legs with her twisted hands. I suppose I was still wearing my shoes. 'That's all I remember. Just her propped up in her bed, and the room.' Except, no, I remembered more — an unpleasant, throat-catching smell hung in the room, which I now realised was probably a mixture of stale urine from a pot under the bed and lavender water sprinkled on a handkerchief or sheets. That thought reminded me of the outside lavatory with a high wooden seat and next to it a shelf with squares of newspaper, and beyond that, a garden. I caught at the memory of a garden. 'There was a lovely garden out at the back. It was walled, full of tall spikes of flowers, peppery-smelling — they must have been lupins.'

Laura was delighted that I'd remembered the lupins. 'That garden was your grandfather's pride and joy. Oh, how he looked after those lupins! As if they were his own children. He patrolled the garden at night with a torch to collect slugs and snails. And delphiniums — he grew enormous delphiniums.'

I was warming to this memory of a garden. 'Didn't he have snapdragons, too?'

'Probably. He liked all the old-fashioned cottage garden plants. He was determined to bring the countryside to Hackney. Your great-grandfather was a gardener, too. It was his job. We're all gardeners, we Jolleys. I am, and my brother Harry, too. We've all won prizes — Harry's are for orchids. And your father loved gardening. Well, you know that, don't you.'

I had no idea if Leonard was a keen gardener. I was still scanning my memory for pictures of a London garden of the late 1940s. 'There was a birdbath, too. I remember that.'

Laura smiled. 'There was, and we have it now — it's in the back garden. You must have a look later. I'm surprised you remember so much. You couldn't have been more than three, because Mother died soon afterwards and your grandfather never saw you again. It saddened him that you moved so far away and he wasn't able to see you grow up. But we had letters, of course, and pictures.' She turned to Gordon. 'Do you like gardening?' At the time Gordon had absolutely no interest in gardening, but he said something polite, like he was looking forward to growing some vegetables in the garden of the cottage we were renting.

Laura was inspecting me again, with that penetrating, analytical look which I later got used to, but on this first meeting found unnerving. 'You look so like him. Not your features so much, as the way you hold your head and the way you use your hands.' I looked at my hands. I hadn't been aware that I was using them in any particular way. 'And your voice. There's something about your voice.' She frowned. 'I have to say, I was expecting you to have an accent.'

An accent? Why would I have an accent? Did she mean a Devonshire burr?

Gordon was clearly getting fed up with our wanderings down memory lane. What he wanted to know was why this aunt and her brother had suddenly appeared out of the blue. So he asked her. She explained that Harry's wife had died earlier in the year, in June; lonely and bereaved, Harry had decided to go to Australia to visit his daughter and her family in Canberra and, as he would be unlikely to travel so far again, he arranged to see his brother and his family in Perth.

Laura leaned forward. 'You can imagine his surprise when, instead of Joyce, a total stranger greeted him at the airport and introduced herself as Leonard's wife. He'd known Joyce well when we were young — she was a bridesmaid at his wedding — and none of us had even heard of this woman before. Her name was Elizabeth, and she was perfectly nice, but as he told me when he came home, he was totally unprepared. He called her 'the wrong wife', and the epithet has stuck. He didn't ask all the questions I would have asked, but at least he got your address from Leonard, who also told us you were getting married.'

She turned to me. 'When did you and Joyce come back to England?'

'What do you mean? Come back from where?'

'From Australia, of course.'

I stared at her. I was beginning to feel lost in Laura's account of what had led to our being here, in her house, sipping tea from my grandmother's china. 'I've never been to Australia.'

'But ... we have pictures of you ... photos ... There's one over here, I put it in a frame.' She took down a photo from the top of a bureau in the corner of the room and handed it to me. Gordon leaned to look over my shoulder.

The picture was slightly out of focus. A girl of about fifteen stood by a gate, her eyes hidden by glasses. I wore glasses, too; she was slim, like me, and again, like me, had straight hair. Could that girl be me? I had the strange sense of being in a dream, out of touch with reality. I tried to focus on the girl's face, but it was blurred. Had I been there, wherever it was, and been photographed and then forgotten all about it? Laura didn't seem to doubt that I was the girl, and yet the photo had been sent from Australia.

'That's not Sue,' Gordon said.

'But ...' Laura began.

I clung to Gordon's certainty. It most definitely wasn't me. I'd recognise a picture of myself, wouldn't I? I handed her the photograph. 'It's not me.'

She frowned at it, then at me. 'Then who is it?'

'Perhaps it's one of their other children. But it's definitely not me.'

'And you say you've *never* been to Australia?'

'Never.' I said it with more conviction than I felt.

'Stay there. I just want to get something,' Laura said and left the room.

Gordon picked up the photo from the coffee table. 'It could be you.'

'Well, it's not, is it? I'd remember, and I've never seen it before in my life.' I took it back to place it on top of the bureau and glanced at the other photos displayed. There were a couple of Laura and her husband and one of a family group: a man and woman and three children. It was a studio portrait, sepia tinted. The man wore a dark suit and a moustache, and his hand rested on the back of a chair on which a very sad-looking woman sat. Her hair was swept up from her high forehead, and I immediately recognised her hands — even then, the fingers were bent and arthritic: Grandma Jolley. So the moustachioed man was my grandfather, and that little boy with sticking-out ears and a surprised expression my father. I'd never thought of him as a little boy; for me he was fixed forever at the age I'd known him — his mid-thirties.

*Henry, Bertha, Harry, Leonard, and Laura Jolley, 1922*

Laura came back into the room carrying two shoeboxes. She set them down on the coffee table. 'You never went to Australia, you say.'

For a moment I felt as if my memory must be playing tricks on me and there in those boxes was evidence that I had lived in Australia. I'd somehow blanked it out of my mind.

'Honestly, the furthest I've ever been is Greece, where we went for our honeymoon.'

Laura was rifling through one of the shoeboxes. She pulled out a wallet of photos, selected one, and pushed it across the table to me.

'And this isn't you and your brother and sister?'

Three children were lined up on a beach in their swimming costumes, snorkels and masks spread out for inspection in front of them.

'I'm an only child.'

She hastily pushed the photo back into the wallet.

Silence; each of us absorbed in our own thoughts. Had Laura been told, or merely assumed, that the girl in the photo was me? Was she the oldest of the three children on the beach? Laura had put the lid on the box, and I didn't feel able to ask her for another look. Had this girl stolen my identity? Or had she — who even Gordon agreed resembled me — been given my name? Was there a second Susan Jolley? But why, when Leonard already had one daughter called Susan? Perhaps a simpler solution was that she was Elizabeth's daughter by an earlier marriage. Susan was a popular name, after all.

At last, Laura spoke. 'So these are his wife's children, not Joyce's?' She sounded weary.

'I suppose they must be. I know he has other children. Elizabeth wrote and told me. That girl, in the photo over there, the one you've framed, must be one of them.'

'His wife writes to you?'

'Yes, every now and then.' I didn't want to go into the story about how I'd written to Leonard when I started at university and was feeling lonely and insecure, and how it was a woman called Elizabeth, apparently his wife, who replied, telling me he didn't take much notice of any of his children, but was proud of me. She had enclosed a money order. Blood money I'd called it, yet happily spent it on some new clothes.

'Are you going to tell me now that you've never been to Scotland either?'

This was beginning to feel like a cross-examination and I was being accused of something, but my crime wasn't clear to me.

'I went with Mum and Mick to the Edinburgh Festival when I was about seventeen, but that was the first time.'

'You know, I could never understand why Joyce didn't write, and when she finally did, why the handwriting didn't look right.' Laura spoke quietly now, and hurt puzzlement replaced the school-teacherly sharpness of her voice. 'I told Harry and Father, that's not Joyce's handwriting, but they said I was imagining things, that people's handwriting changes. I *knew* something was wrong. Why didn't I act on it?' She suddenly looked old. 'You've never lived in either Scotland or Australia.'

I felt for Gordon's hand. Tears pricked at my eyelids. I swallowed. 'I told you. Don't you believe me?'

'I'm sorry,' Laura said. 'I don't know what to believe any more. You see, your grandfather and I went to see you off when you left for Australia. We went down to Tilbury, and when we got there, they told us we must have got the date wrong. The *Orion* — I remember the name of the ship — the *Orion* had sailed the previous week.'

'You and my grandpa thought we were sailing to Australia? Why? I don't understand ...'

Laura shook her head and looked away, out of the window into the garden beyond. I wanted to comfort her, but didn't know how to. I didn't know this woman, and she didn't seem to be the sort of person to take kindly to a hug from someone she'd only just met.

'Why did you think we'd be on the *Orion*?' My voice sounded small.

*Leonard, Laura, and Stanley, 1930s*

She turned back to face me and Gordon. 'Your grandfather had seen Leonard a week or so before, while you were visiting your mother's family in Kent.' She frowned. 'Or so he said. He told Father that you'd be sailing on such a date, and if we wanted to see you and say goodbye, to come to the dock. So when Father told me about it, I arranged to take the day off work to go down to Tilbury with him to say our goodbyes.

But the ship had already sailed. It didn't make sense. Father insisted that Leonard had told him you'd be leaving a week after his visit. I thought he must have misheard.' She took a hanky from her sleeve and blew her nose. 'He deliberately misled us. What could have possessed him? To be so ... so cruel?

Laura's husband, Stanley, came in, and with him a welcome atmosphere of normality. He showed us round the garden while Laura made us something to eat. Over high tea they asked me about my mother and Mick, their home and their jobs, and we told them about ourselves. Nothing further was said about letters and photographs.

However, just before we left, Laura asked, partly ironically, I suspect, 'When did you last see your father?'

'September 1950.'

Gordon and I walked back down the suburban street.

'Are you okay?' he asked.

'Fine.' I glanced back towards Laura's house, but I didn't feel fine. I felt strange and disorientated. 'Except ... I don't think she believed me.'

'I think she did in the end. It was quite a lot for her to take in.'

I wasn't convinced. 'You know, I don't know what to believe any more. That photo — the girl looked just like me.'

'But she wasn't you. I could see it straight away.'

'But you said she could be me.'

'I was joking. Like you, granted, but not you. Really.'

He squeezed my shoulder. 'Hey, don't get all upset. You've got a new aunt and uncle. And a cousin in Australia. You've always complained that you don't have a family.'

I glanced back once again down towards Laura's house, thinking I maybe should go back there and ask more questions, sort it all out. Gordon pulled at my hand, hurrying us along towards the bus stop.

'Why do you think your mum promised not to contact them?'

'You know what she said — Leonard was in a bad way. Maybe she was scared he'd kill himself. I don't know.'

'But to keep quiet for so long?'

'Seventeen years ... but I suppose if she'd made a promise ...'

'Do you think it was to do with the Brethren?'

The Brethren were the Exclusive Brethren, an extreme religious sect that my mother's family belonged to and who, in the early 1960s, following the instructions of a particularly hard-line leader, James Taylor Junior, had cut off all contact with us because we were not believers. We were dubbed 'worldlies', sinful people who would contaminate the true believers if we had anything to do with them. Gwen, Joyce's cousin who came to our wedding, was the only other member of the family to leave the Exclusives at that point.

'Joyce is a woman of her word,' I replied. 'I don't think it's anything to do with the Brethren. She stopped going to meetings when she was a student, years before she got married, let alone divorced.'

Whatever her reasons for maintaining such a long silence, I couldn't help but feel let down in some way by my mother. I'd always felt so close to her, so why had she kept things from me? Why had she made such a rash promise to my father? Why had she not got in touch with Laura later, when Leonard was married and living in Australia, or when she married Mick, my stepfather?

I felt at a loss to begin to find the answers to these questions, and then others pushed themselves forward. Why had my father lied to his sister and father about us sailing to Australia? And who was the girl in the photograph?

# CHAPTER 2

During the weeks that followed this trip to London, I was caught up in the excitement of making Thyme Cottage our home and in the demands of a new course. I was aware that Joyce and Laura had corresponded since the weekend when Gordon and I had visited Laura, but I didn't pursue the questions that still hung in the air around the identity of the other Susan. An even more difficult question to ask was why my mother had kept me in the dark about my father's family. I'd asked, often enough when I was a teenager, if I could see my grandfather again, whom I remembered, but was told that he would be very old by now and that he had probably died.

My father had maintained contact with me throughout most of those seventeen years, sending the occasional letter or card and presents for birthdays and Christmas, although he refused ever to see me, despite my frequent requests before he left the United Kingdom for Australia. I'm not sure now why I didn't write to him and ask for my grandfather's address. But I didn't. I suppose that I felt that it wasn't my place (although I wouldn't have put it like that at the time), and that if Grandpa wanted to get in touch with me, he could get my address from my father. Little did I know that he had written to me, as had Laura. But it would seem that it was the other 'Susan' who received the cards and letters, and this other girl had lived in

Scotland, and was now, I assumed, living in Australia. It was the other 'Susan' and the other 'Joyce' whose letters had been put in those two shoeboxes that Laura kept.

I would have to wait until I saw my mother in person before I could even begin to talk about these things, and this wouldn't be until Christmas.

I kept thinking about my new-found aunt, and how devastated she had been when she realised that her younger brother had lied to her so consistently for such a long time. Gordon and I speculated as to what had really been going on for all these years, but we couldn't begin to unravel the motives of the older generation. I told him as much as I knew about my parents' families; but of the third person in this story, my father's new wife, I knew nothing other than the few things my mother had told me when I'd asked. I didn't know what part she had played, if any, in the long-running deception.

In the autumn of 1967 this is what I knew. Leonard was the youngest of three children. His father, Henry, came from Diss, in Norfolk, from a poor rural background. Henry had left, like many a young man, to seek his fortune in London; the family story, according to my mother, was that he'd walked all the way. He settled in Bow, married, and dedicated himself to self-improvement through education. My mother was clearly in awe of her father-in-law's determination: he studied Greek and Latin and theology, and became a lay preacher working for the London City Mission as a kind of social worker. He was ambitious for his children, determined that they should reap the benefits of education. All three won scholarships to guild schools, and eventually went on to London University. Leonard won an open scholarship to University College to read English, and it was here that he met Joyce, another open-scholarship student.

My mother's father was a convert to the Exclusive Brethren, and a stickler for keeping to the rules — no trips to the cinema or the theatre, religious 'meetings' several times on Sundays — no deviation tolerated from the straight and narrow path of 'the true light'. Joyce was a bit of a rebel, and had no intention of settling for a shop job and early marriage to an Exclusive Brethren brother; she would leave home, see more of the world, and achieve something with her life.

Because she knew that her father wouldn't support her application to university, she did it secretly, with the help of her headmistress at Dover High School, and also managed to secure a maintenance loan from Kent County Council so that she could live independently in London.

So Joyce and Leonard met at Gower Street, and started going out. As well as sharing equally fervent religious backgrounds, they shared left-wing political ideals and had spent long periods of their adolescence steeping themselves in books. Joyce had had a long-distance passion for drama — she read lots of plays, but until she went to university she had been able only to imagine them staged.

Leonard had been a sickly child, and although he was a good swimmer and keen cyclist, he became severely ill with rheumatoid arthritis when he was in his twenties. It was while he was in hospital — and he was bedridden for over a

*Joyce and Leonard*

year — around the beginning of the war, that he met Monica (later known as Elizabeth), a young trainee nurse. Her family were Quakers (a religion he had become interested in), and he and she shared a love of music. Joyce got to know her, too. After he was discharged from hospital, Leonard joined a Quaker pacifist commune and appeared before a tribunal in order to be registered as a conscientious objector.

He got a job as a librarian in Birmingham, and my parents married (in a Quaker ceremony) around 1942. Then Monica (Elizabeth) moved to Birmingham — or perhaps she was already there. She and Leonard met up again, and Joyce, Leonard, and Monica were friends, spending a lot of time together. Then I was born. And four years later the marriage was over, and my mother and I set off for a life without Leonard. He lied to Joyce about the identity of his lover, but later she discovered he was with Monica.

I now understood that his family knew nothing about Monica; even after Harry turned up in Australia at their home, they didn't know that Leonard's new wife had ever been called anything other than Elizabeth. I had shown my mother the letter Elizabeth had written to me accompanied by a money order, and this was when I learned that this Elizabeth was the same person as Monica. She had changed her name by deed poll from Monica Elizabeth Knight to Monica Elizabeth Jolley in September 1950, just a few weeks after Leonard left us, and long before my mother and father were divorced and Elizabeth and Leonard married (December 1952). It was at this time she began to use the name Elizabeth instead of Monica. Years later I discovered in a biography of Elizabeth (*Doing Life* by Brian Dibble) that this was not the only time she had changed her name: she'd changed it from Monica Knight to Monica Fielding in 1949. Why would a person change her name twice in a couple of years?

As well as talking myself into circles, asking myself unanswerable questions, I began to make a conscious effort to remember, just in case there were clues that as a young child I had missed, or misinterpreted. As far as I could remember, the atmosphere in our Birmingham home was happy. I didn't recall any rows or arguments, and my memory of my early childhood is sharp, possibly because my circumstances changed radically after my parents separated. I spent a lot of time thinking back to how things had been before my father left, and how happy I'd been.

*Susan at Deal, May 1949*

For me, the summer of 1950 was filled with sunshine: from early morning until teatime and later, children played out on the street, and sometimes I'd be allowed to join them, if the girl next door kept an eye on me. School would be starting soon. I was excited, as this year I, too, would be starting school. Earlier in the summer, around the time of my fourth birthday, Leonard had taken me on an outing on the back of his bike. I wore new red sandals, and he tucked me into my seat and told me to hold on tight. I did, wrapping my arms around his waist, feeling the rough texture of his tweed jacket on my bare arms and against my face. As we crossed the bumpy paths of the allotments, red bean flowers swayed around my head, and I stuck my feet out so as not to spoil the red sandals (and to avoid us tumbling into patches of potatoes and rows of leeks). We were on our way to a fete at the nursery school. 'You'll be starting there after the summer,' he told me.

But it didn't happen like that. After that summer, I didn't see the house, the street, the allotments, the children, or my father again. For me, the nursery school, with its rows of pegs where you would hang your coat, your name on a card above it, and the sun-filled playground with a sandpit in the far corner, would remain a dream, a possible future beyond my grasp.

When it came to saying goodbye to my father for the last time, I had no sense of anything irrevocable happening. Daddy was going to a place called Scotland because he'd got a new job and needed to find another house for us to live in. Mummy and I would join him soon.

Leonard saw us off at the station, and that was my last memory of him. It was busy and noisy. He hauled the cases into the carriage and then lifted me up to give me a kiss before placing me in the carriage next to my mother. He slammed the door shut and stood back, still looking up at me. The guard blew his whistle, and the train drew away. My father began to run after the train and I, held tight by my mother, leaned out as far as I could to wave until he slowed down as the train gathered speed and he disappeared in a cloud of smuts and steam.

We were on our way to a school near a city called Bristol. My mother would teach the big children, and I would have lessons with some younger ones and soon learn to write my name properly and read books all on my own. We would sleep at the school and eat all our meals there, and I would have friends and the countryside to play in. It wouldn't be for long — just while Daddy found us the new house. My mother tried to make it sound exciting, but I wanted to stay at home and go to the local nursery school. I didn't like the idea of having to stay somewhere I didn't know and where I wouldn't know anyone. Also I didn't understand why we had to go away to school in order for my father to find us a house, but then lots of things grown-ups did were a mystery. I had very little idea what school meant; after all, the only one I'd ever seen was the nursery that I wasn't going to attend.

After a long journey we were met at the station by a woman who hugged me and told me to call her Jo. She had golden curls and bright-red lipstick, and she smelled of cigarettes and perfume. Our cases were tossed into the back of a rusting and dented shooting brake. Moss grew on the window ledges. My luggage was a brown cardboard attaché case, and I carried my doll Jill and my teddy, not wanting them to be squashed up in a suitcase; my mother's case was dark blue, and the locks were rusty. My mother and Jo sat in the front of the car and talked. The smell of oil, wet dogs, and stale tobacco made me feel sick. I wanted to go home, and said so. Jo turned round to smile encouragingly at me as I huddled on the back seat. She had a little boy just a bit older than me, she said; his name was Melville, and he was looking forward to seeing me. I held my toys tight and glared out of the window. We drove through lamplit streets and finally out into the countryside. It was getting dark.

A driveway curved past a battered cedar tree set in a wide sweep of lawn, and we drew up in front of the biggest house I had ever seen. Grey stone walls rose above us, pierced by high windows and a huge oak door. This was a castle, dark, forbidding—a fortress. There was even a tower, with crenellations. This didn't look at all like a school. It was a witch's castle.

*St Catherine's School, previously known as Knole Park*

School life was noisy: there was always someone shouting at someone else, or a piano being thumped, or kids thundering up and down stairs, along corridors with no carpets or curtains to absorb the sound, and rarely the quiet of concentration in a classroom. I wasn't used to living with other people, and neither was Joyce. During the day we hardly saw each other — she was teaching in the main school, and I had lessons in a separate building in the grounds called The Juniors Hut. The other children under six were Melville and two other boys: the cook's son Laurie, and my teacher's son Andrew. Like the principal, my teacher's name was Jo — Jo Merchant. Andrew went home with his mother every night after school, and Laurie slept in a room in the tower with his mother. He was a small, weak child, a natural victim who would crumple in tears when taunted by the other children. I soon grew a thicker skin than Laurie's and learned to keep out of the way, or, when necessary, join in the bad behaviour.

I saw my mother at night-time when she would bath me, usually with one or two of the other younger children, and then she and I would go up to our attic bedroom for a story — the best bit of the day, because I didn't have to share her with anyone else, and I could call her Mummy, rather than Mrs Jolley, or Joyce. That room was our haven; it wasn't very homely — no rugs on the bare wooden boards and no curtains at the window, but it was ours, and nobody else would barge in. We had two narrow beds and a trunk with metal bands around it, which was placed between the beds. The trunk held

*Joyce at St Catherine's*

the few things — clothes, mainly — that she had packed up to bring with us to the school. A bedside lamp sat on top of it, and a collection of my books and her own reading.

That first autumn, when at night rain lashed against the dark window of our bedroom and wind moaned in the tower, I would sometimes work myself up into a panic. The house was haunted — everyone knew it. The ghost was known as the White Lady; she had been the wife of the Lord of the Manor, who had lived in the house hundreds of years ago, when it wasn't a school but a grand manor house that used to be called Knole Park. She had met an untimely end in the tower — had she been murdered? Or leapt in despair to her death from the parapet? Years later, I was told that she had been shot by her jealous husband, the Lord of the Manor, for having an affair. Her favourite haunt, one of the older girls told me, was the top corridor, the one outside the room where I lay, hardly daring to breathe, clutching my doll and teddy tightly to my chest. Sometimes, on nights like this, as I waited for the hideous form to reveal itself, and longed to be back home with my father in a proper house that wasn't haunted, I'd summon the courage to get up and find my mother.

The White Lady always kept herself hidden, but I could feel her watching me as I crept along the dimly lit corridors, keeping close to the walls, tiptoed down the long flights of stairs in bare feet, through the dining room, where the trestle tables were already laid for breakfast the next morning, along another corridor until, at last, with a wonderful sense of achievement, I burst into the bright cosiness of the kitchen.

The kitchen was the one warm place in the house. Elsewhere there were oil stoves that were hot when you held your hands over them, and they made patterns on the ceilings, but barely took the chill off the cavernous rooms. The kitchen smelled of baking and pipe smoke — the pipe belonged to Ralph, the headmaster. A bank of cream Agas threw out heat. Joyce would be sitting at the scrubbed wooden table, drinking cocoa or beer with the other staff. There was a lot of laughter and a lot of discussion. I didn't get told off for this intrusion into the grown-up world. She'd scoop me up onto her knee, and I'd be allowed to snuggle there for a while until, in the heat of the room and the comfort of her arms, I'd begin to feel sleepy, and then she'd carry me up to our room, where she'd tuck me in bed and, if I was lucky, read me an extra story. When are we going to see Daddy again? I'd ask as she pulled the sheet up to my chin and tucked Jill and Ted either side of me. Soon, darling, soon, she'd whisper as she stroked my hair, and I would drift off to sleep.

Most of the time during that first term I didn't understand what was going on. I didn't know how to behave, and veered from being a baby to a 'little tyke'. I played with Melville and Andrew, and an older boy called Billy. I rapidly became wary of Tom, a boy who would be your best friend one minute and a violent and mean enemy the next. I soon learned to swear and to be rude about the teachers, but what I really wanted was to be a nice little girl, and to go back to our house in Birmingham. At night I imagined myself there. I recalled every detail of the layout of the house and its furniture. I remembered my own bedroom with the yellow and green wooden boxes where my toys were kept. Now they were all put 'into store' waiting, like me, for Daddy to find our new house.

As I lay in bed high up near the roof of the manor, I tried to work it out — we'd been here for ages, so why didn't my daddy come and fetch us? I knew that some of the children were very naughty and got into trouble with the police, and sometimes they ran away and had to be brought back. The lady in the post office called the school a borstal (which was far from the case).

I later learned that it was called a progressive school, and that it took some pupils with behavioural and emotional problems. But at the time, I was too young to understand. I knew that there were children who stole sweets from Woolworths on a Saturday when we went into Bristol to spend our pocket money and had been caught 'scrumping' apples from a garden in the village in the autumn. But I wasn't naughty, not really naughty, although I had eaten the apples. I hadn't been arrested by the police or appeared in court. For along with swear words, other words like 'court' and 'magistrate' entered my vocabulary. Daddy would come and fetch me. He'd promised. Had I known that when someone made a promise they were supposed to say 'cut my throat and hope to die', I'd have asked him to say it and draw his finger across his throat. Then I'd know for sure he'd be coming. Any day now.

Tom was about nine or ten; I was now nearly four and a half. One morning, he and I were alone in what was called the KG, a big, airy room which opened out into a glazed area, which must at one time have been a conservatory and now held tottering piles of wooden benches and chairs that would be dragged out and arranged in rows if the whole school had to be called together, for assemblies or performances. Mostly, though, the floor of the KG was kept clear of furniture, and this was where we'd listen to the radio and do 'music and movement', or sit on the floor and learn about 'how things began'.

Had Tom and I arrived early for a lesson on this occasion? Unlikely, but whatever the reason there were just the two of us there that morning. Wintry sunshine filtered through the glass panels and made lozenges of light on the floor. Tom had pulled out a chair and was sitting on it the wrong way round, leaning over the back and rocking to and fro.

'My dad was a soldier in the war. He got loads of medals,' Tom bragged.

'My daddy's going to come and get me. In a car.'

'Liar. Bet he's buggered off.'

Lots of the fathers had buggered off or were in prison. And I was telling a fib about the car, but perhaps my dad did have one now, and one of these fine winter mornings he'd come and pick up me and my mother, and drive off with us up to Scotland to our new house. And if he did have a car now, it would be nicer than the school shooting brake, I was sure of that.

It was hard to know when kids were joking or serious, but Tom's dad had definitely buggered off. He'd told me so. But why did I believe that and not the war medals? I knew one thing for sure about my own father—he would come back, and even if at times my certainty wobbled, I wasn't going to let Tom know.

'He is, so there. He's going to come and fetch me. We're going to live in Scotland.'

'Oh yeah, why d'you come here in the first place, then?'

That was the question. I stood on the outside edges of my feet and stared at the worn wooden floorboards.

'He's buggered off, your dad. He'll never roll up in his big black car. Fucking Scotland, my arse.'

'Shut up.'

'Shut up,' he mimicked. 'What you gonna do then, run and tell Mummy? Go on, I dare you to tell. You tell, and see what happens. Squirt.'

I glared at the boy and turned away. Daddy had gone to Scotland, and he was looking for a house for us. He'd told me so. That night I said to my mother, 'Daddy's gone to Scotland to look for a house for us, hasn't he? Tom said I was lying.' She said something like, 'Don't take any notice of what Tom says,' but she didn't give me a clear answer.

Now I realise how hard it must have been for her, trying to protect me from the reality of Leonard leaving us. Perhaps, like me, she held out hope that it wouldn't be forever. Because she *didn't* say we *weren't* going to Scotland, I believed we would. And surely it would be soon.

I gradually got used to life at St Catherine's School. Despite its name, the school was not religious. A member of staff would take children whose parents wished them to attend church to the village church in Almondsbury, but for the rest of us there was no religious ceremony and, as far as I remember, no religious instruction. The lessons I did have — reading, writing, stories, art, needlework, nature study, music, dance, and even elocution — I enjoyed enormously. Outside lesson time, we had a great deal of freedom to play in the grounds and woods and farmland that surrounded the school.

Apart from the boys, I had one other good friend, Beryl. Beryl was much older than me, shy and timid with children her own age, but she was kind, and I was no threat to her. She let me decide on our games that involved dolls and dens. I was physically more adept than Beryl, with her hunched shoulders and thick glasses. I was very good at climbing trees, and would perch on a branch above her head and say, come on Beryl, don't be weedy. This gave me particular pleasure, as I was known as Weed or Squirt to the likes of Tom.

Mainly we played cowboys and Indians, hide-and-seek, making dens or climbing trees, or fishing for newts and sticklebacks in Turk's pond down the hill beyond the woods. But at one point during my first year there, we had a craze for a rather grisly game called funerals. We made our own graveyard under a line of yew trees that led from The Hut to a rusting gate into the woods. Most of the bodies we buried were dead birds and the skeletons of unnamed small creatures we found in the woods. Spiders were killed and flies scooped up by the dozen. Tom trapped mice, and once got a drowned kitten from somewhere. It was my job to collect green and pink marble chips from the graves in the village churchyard. Whenever I filled my pockets with such loot, I whispered my apology to the dead person in the ground beneath. Beryl came with me as the under-tens were allowed to go to the village only if they were accompanied by older children, and if the member of staff on duty was told where we were going and when we'd be back. Whether my pockets bulged with marble chips stolen from strangers' graves, or cigarette ends picked up from the pavements for the older boys, I was never questioned by the teachers. Perhaps they thought I wouldn't do such things.

Back in our own graveyard, we would conduct services under the yew trees, singing 'There Is a Green Hill Far Away',

*Beryl and Susan in the grounds of St Catherine's, October 1951*

or 'God Is Working His Purpose Out'. On winter evenings I remember looking up through the sooty branches and seeing the moon hanging in a clear sky and humming to myself the tune of a popular song of the time, *I see the moon / The moon sees me / Under the shade of the old oak tree / Please let the moon that shines on me / Shine on the one I love.* Daddy. Leonard.

It was only much later when my mother and I talked about St Catherine's that I came to understand why she chose to live and work there. It had been an unusual introduction to school life for me, and as I grew up and told my friends about it, they generally thought I was exaggerating — it was all so distant from their own experiences of infant and primary school. The older I got, the more I appreciated the kind of education I'd received. When I asked why she applied for the job in the first place, her answers were absolutely clear. First of all, she said, she wasn't ready to live on her own with just me, or with any of her relatives: her mother, sister, and cousin apparently all offered us a home, but she wasn't prepared to compromise her independence. St Catherine's would provide us with not only a place to live, but a community to live amongst, and give her a purpose other than the basic need to earn money. The school espoused the kind of education that mirrored her own ideals. She had experienced something of the kind when she had visited Leonard at the Quaker commune where he lived for a while during the war. Also, on a more direct personal level, she had warmed to the principals, Jo and Ralph Cooper, when she was interviewed for the job. She knew, she told me, that there would be a number of 'problem' children, supported financially by their local authorities, but the majority would be private pupils whose parents paid fees. However, what was underplayed at her interview was quite how many difficult and troubled children there would be to teach. They wanted an experienced and well-qualified teacher, she said, who supported the ethos of the school and could manage disruptive children. In addition to the educational principles, this ethos involved very low pay. All staff received the same wage, whether a cook or a matron, a boilerman or a teacher.

When it came to the Christmas holidays at the end of our first term, I was very excited — not only because I fully expected Father Christmas to bring me the presents I'd asked him for (Beryl had helped me write him a letter), but also because I was sure that we would be going to Scotland, and was worried as to whether he would know which chimney to come down.

In the event, Father Christmas did find me, but at my mother's cousin, Auntie Gwen's, in High Wycombe. The disappointment of not seeing either my father or our new house in Scotland was softened by having a cousin to play with, and at last being considered by him as a person who could be played with, rather than merely tolerated. Ally was about eight, and, whether it was my new and impressive knowledge of swear words, or just the fact that I was now at school, I was allowed to be his assistant, sorting out the red and green strips of Meccano and putting the nuts and the bolts into tobacco tins so that he could build complicated motorised machines. Just before Christmas, we went to see Auntie Gwen's brother who lived nearby, and it was he who would provide our Christmas dinner chicken. I watched, fascinated, as Ally's uncle chased the chosen chicken round the coop while Ally and I cheered him on. The uncle made a big game of this, and then, when he finally caught the victim and wrung its neck, I was horrified. While Ally laughed at its twitching yellow chicken legs, I cried and resolved not to eat the poor little thing. Of course, once it was roasted and surrounded by potatoes and sausages, I quickly changed my mind.

It was during this Christmas holiday that my mother finally told me that there would be no house in Scotland for us: we would return to St Catherine's after the holiday. As far as I remember, Ally and I had been playing in the attic, and he pulled from a box a gasmask that he'd had as a toddler in the war. It had a face like Mickey Mouse, with red rubber ears and a blue can instead of a nose. He blew raspberries in it, and we were both convulsed with giggles. We took it downstairs to show our mothers.

'I'm going to get my toys soon, aren't I?' I said. 'They're in store, now, but Daddy's looking for a house for us to live in, and then I'll get them all back.'

Auntie Gwen and my mother looked at each other. And then she told me — gently, I'm sure, but I didn't want to believe her, and I shouted and hit out at her.

I ran upstairs and buried myself under the eiderdown in Ally's bedroom. Later, when I'd calmed down, Ally told me he'd heard our mums talking about it, and his mum called my dad a bastard, and he'd never heard her swear before. That convinced me.

The realisation that grown-ups could tell lies came as a profound shock. They lied as much as the children at school, only it was worse, because we children knew that things were never as rosy as we painted them to each other. If they were, why didn't we live in normal houses with our mums and dads and go to a day school, like Ally did?

I boiled with anger, and in my mind shouted at my father. I wanted to hit him. Not only did grown-ups tell lies, but they broke promises. Daddy had promised. He'd lifted me up in his arms and kissed me goodbye and promised — he'd promised it wouldn't be for long, that we'd be seeing each other again soon, really soon.

Years later, when I asked Joyce again, why did you lie to

me, why not tell me what was going on, she said it was to avoid my devastation, which she wouldn't have been able to cope with, and to protect Leonard. But she added that at times she felt like taking me in her arms and saying, he doesn't want to see either of us, so try not to think about it. Perhaps she should have; perhaps I would have been angry and done my best to forget him. But she didn't criticise him, and I chose to believe that one day — not next week or the week after, but some time, say, at the end of the Easter term — he'd fetch me from school, and we'd live together and be happy, like we were before.

But here I was, seventeen years later, and I had neither seen nor spoken to my father since he had disappeared into that cloud of smuts and steam so long before. I had received letters and books and sweets and promises of yes, you can see me when you're old enough, but the promises were never fulfilled. When I was thirteen he moved to Australia, and as far as I was aware had not returned to England since. In fact, he had, once, for an extended period, but he had always been careful not to let me or my mother know. The truth, it seems, was that he had no intention of seeing or speaking to me ever again.

In the autumn of 1967 I was still ignorant of much that had happened in the past, but I would be seeing my mother and Mick in a few weeks, at Christmas, when I'd be able to ask my questions. In the meantime, I was spending a lot of my college time with children, as I'd decided to do my dissertation on child art; reading books on child psychology and art theory intensified my own memories, which came back to me at night, so vividly that I could almost smell them. With the memories came the increasing feeling that Leonard had not only betrayed Joyce (which I'd already known about), but that he'd betrayed me, his father, and his brother and sister, too.

# CHAPTER 3

Perhaps my father was missing me, or feeling guilty, because Leonard sent me some very nice presents for the Christmas of 1950, including a new doll who had her own little bed with a real mattress and lace-edged pillow. Once back at school, I asked if I could move out of the bedroom I shared with my mother and into a dormitory. I was four and a half, and I didn't want to be different from the other children. I took the doll with me, but left her bed in my mother's room. 'It'll be safer here,' she said.

I very quickly learned that life in a dormitory wasn't necessarily easy. One morning, soon after the beginning of term, I made my bed and tucked Jill, Ted and the new doll — as yet unnamed — in the bed. When bedtime came, the new doll was missing. One of the bigger girls, Christine, was playing with it. I asked for it, but she refused. I had a doll already, she argued, and she didn't. I grabbed it from her. She was bigger and stronger than me, and pulled its arm until I thought it would snap off. I let go, saying I'd tell on her (not a strategy I had used before). She threw the doll on my bed and swept out of the room, hissing, 'You'll be sorry.' I was amazed it was so easy to get my way.

When the teacher on duty came to turn the lights out, Christine was still missing. It was a very cold, dark night, and it had been raining hard. I began to get anxious: they'd have to go and look for her. Children often tried to run away, and as we weren't locked in, it was easy. All you had to do was walk to the main road and get a lift. The problem was where to go. I panicked. Christine had been taken off by a stranger, or knocked down by a car—she was lying at the roadside, bleeding to death. She said I'd be sorry, and I already was.

But she hadn't tried to run away. She walked back into the dormitory, black hair streaked over her white face, mud all down her sodden pyjamas. She stood at the end of my bed. 'Look what you made me do.' She thrust out her hand towards me. Shards of glass stuck out from her palm, crimson blood welling and then dripping through her open fingers on to the bare floorboards. 'It's your fault. You made me do it.'

What had I done to 'make' her harm herself so violently? I'd only asked her to give me back my doll. But I was in no position to argue. Her blood was dripping onto the floor, and she said it was my fault! I was appalled. 'You can have it. Go on, take it. I don't want the stupid doll.' And I threw my lovely new doll onto her bed.

A smile of triumph spread over her face. She knew I wouldn't tell on her. I realise now that this kind of psychological bullying is not so unusual in disturbed children, but at the time all I knew was that it wouldn't be a good idea for me to go to any grown-up and tell them what had happened.

When it snowed, we spent most of the day outside, and the thrill of speeding down Pigs Hill on a toboggan, screeching as loud as I could, made up for Christine's meanness. The freedom to run in the woods and to climb trees was exhilarating, especially as in Birmingham I'd never been allowed to go anywhere on my own. Here you could disappear for hours and nobody would fuss. I suspect that my mother found adjusting to the life at St Catherine's harder than I did — not only were the children more difficult than she'd been led to believe, but I think she worried about my safety and possibly the influence of some of the naughtier children. For me, though, apart from missing my father and our house, I had friends and we had fun, and what's more I enjoyed my lessons.

For the Easter holidays we went to Deal in Kent, to stay with my mother's mother, Grandma Hancock. The last time I had been there was the previous summer, when I was just four years old. Leonard had seen us off at New Street Station in Birmingham. I now wonder if he saw this as some kind of rehearsal for his eventual final farewell — he was definitely planning it at that time. I was always happy to go and see Grandma and her sister, tiny Great Auntie Millie, who lived with her. Sometimes Leonard came with us, but usually it was just me and my mother. The sun always seemed to shine in Deal, and I went swimming in the sea with my cousins and ate ice-creams. At that time, although Joyce had long since left the Brethren, we were always welcome to stay with our Brethren relations, and my mother's sisters' children often stayed with our grandmother at Easter and during the summer holidays.

*David, Susan, and Ally on the beach at Deal*

There was a distancing between Joyce and her sisters' families in the early 1960s when James Taylor Junior began to exert his rule, and the big split came some years later, in 1970. But at the time we were living at St Catherine's there was no real dissent in the family: Joyce's relations accepted us and our different way of life.

When I was at Grandma's (or indeed staying with my Auntie Gwen or either of my mother's sisters), I attended Brethren meetings, which I found boring, but then afterwards we'd eat delicious cakes or roast dinners, and Auntie Millie would tell us — the cousins — stories of when she was little, and how she had to eat minced-up bones and blood to make her grow. But it didn't work because she was still very small.

At Grandma's everyone made a fuss of me, which was quite the opposite of what happened at school, and I enjoyed it. This might of course have been because they felt sorry for the situation I was in — virtually homeless — and I was aware that Grandma didn't like the idea of my being brought up in such a godless place as St Catherine's.

Here, I was careful to mind my Ps and Qs, and Grandma enjoyed dressing me in nice clothes (she had worked as a seamstress and she made me flowery dresses with smocking). At the top of her wardrobe was a cardboard box, and in it, folded under a layer of tissue paper, was a sailor dress and a pair of patent-leather shoes with ankle straps. I was waiting to grow big enough to wear them. Leonard had brought these back from America when I was three, but when I tried them on, the dress drowned me and the shoes were like boats. I tried them on again this Easter, and again they went back into the box. You need a diet of blood and bones, Auntie Millie teased, then you'll fit your frock. He'd also brought back for me two little dolls, but they weren't with the dress in its box; they, along with my doll's house and doll's pram, were in store.

I was happy at Deal, and had my mother even hinted to me that Grandma had invited us to live with her, I wouldn't have stopped nagging her to do it. As it was, I probably would have rebelled against the strictness of the Brethren life within a very short time, and certainly Joyce would have hated it. She had made an enormous step when she defied her parents and the Brethren by applying to go to university without their knowledge. For her, to go back would have been impossible. But I was unaware of any of this, and embraced the ways of my grandmother's house unquestioningly. When staying in Deal, at night, after hot milk and malt, I knelt by the side of the bed and said my prayers. I was allowed to have one story, and then the gas light was turned down, a candle lit, and I fell asleep to the sound of waves crashing on the pebbly beach.

It was the soothing predictability of daily life in Deal that I relished. Routine, rules, and religion gave structure to our lives and defined our parameters. Here there was just one set of rules — not several, as there seemed to be at St Catherine's, depending on who you were with. Here you just *knew* the rules — whether it was saying grace, not taking things without asking, wearing a hat, and going to meetings — twice on Sundays. We trouped in, everyone wearing their good clothes, all the women in hats. Chairs were arranged in a square around a central table. The men sat on the front rows of chairs; women and children, further back. No women ever seemed to speak, and sometimes there were long silences when one of the men waited for the Lord to move them to pray or to preach. I dreaded my tummy rumbling in the silence broken only by a ticking clock. The grown-ups passed around a cup of wine and a plate of bread, which I was told were the blood and the flesh of Jesus, but the children were not offered any. In any case, I didn't like the idea of drinking Jesus' blood. We were given pennies to put in a collection bag.

There were, of course, many more rules associated with the Exclusive Brethren to do with articles of faith, but they didn't impact on me; and in future years, when the leadership of the sect was taken over by James Taylor Junior, who considered himself the voice of God on earth, new and increasingly draconian rules would tear my family apart. But in the 1950s, rules such as no television, no visits to the theatre or cinema, no radio, girls having to have long hair and wear a hat when they went out — these things didn't rankle. It was just what you did, or didn't do, at Grandma's. What was comforting was to know that things were always the same there. The same people at the Meeting Room, people who always seemed astonished that you'd grown, the same food on the table, the same hymns sung around the piano at night-time, the same flowers always growing in the garden — marigolds and hollyhocks.

The routine was as predictable as in The Scaffold song of the 1960s, 'Today's Monday'. Naturally, Monday was washing day, when the kitchen filled with steam from the copper, and Auntie Millie struggled with the mangle, the wrung water making a satisfying hiss as it hit the metal bucket. If it was fine, the sheets flapped on the line in the garden, or if it rained, they'd hang on a wooden clothes horse in the back room. This clothes horse also served as the frame for making indoor dens.

At St Catherine's, every day was washing day — bedwetters had to take their sheets to the bathroom to be rinsed. I don't know what happened to them after that, as I didn't wet the bed, so I never had to strip my bed. Some kids said they wet themselves on purpose so that the bed would be nice and warm. I wasn't convinced. I reckoned it must get really cold and smelly soon after, and you'd have to stay there all night. I suppose the bed stripping and carrying of the sheets to the bathroom was thought of as a kind of aversion therapy. If so, it didn't work.

Back at school after Easter, I quickly adapted to school life. As the days lengthened there was more time for playing outside. On warm summer nights we slept under the stars. There was a small concrete swimming pool down by The Hut, and I learned to swim. After lessons we'd go fishing in Turk's pond, play ball on the tennis courts, or make dens in the woods. I loved climbing trees, and as I was so light the thinnest branch would take my weight; I could even run across the mat of small branches between the yew trees. I also became expert at hiding: I could make myself invisible, lying along branches of trees, pressing myself into shadows, and for someone as fidgety as I was, I managed to remain very still and very quiet when I wanted to — a result of having to sit still and quiet in long meetings, which could be totally eventless and as quiet as the grave if nobody was moved by God to speak.

During the summer holidays, those children who didn't have homes to go to stayed at school. The high point of the summer was going to Cornwall for a month's holiday at Menabilly Barton, near Fowey. Jo Cooper had known the writer Daphne du Maurier when they were in school in Paris together, and Daphne let us stay in one of the fields near Menabilly. There were about sixty children at school, and roughly a third came to camp each year. We slept in heavy ex-army sleeping bags that laced up the front. (I wonder now what happened to the bedwetters there.) There was one big tent for the girls and one for the boys. The staff slept in smaller individual tents, with canvas camp beds. We ate all our meals sitting or lying on the grass, and somehow the food tasted better.

Possibly because the sea was so close and I always felt safe near the sea, I loved being at Menabilly — the bell tents, smelling of damp and yet cosy with a farty fug, burying myself deep in my sleeping bag so that the chatter of the older

*Joyce and Jo Cooper with two of the older children at*
*St Catherine's school camp in Cornwall*

children became a comforting hum. On sunny days I was intensely happy lying stretched out on hot grey rocks, gazing into a deep square pool that appeared gradually as the tide receded, revealing maps of pink and yellow lichens, blood-red sea anemones which swayed to an unheard tune on a ledge in the pool, small round yellow and brown shells swept by the current into piles in the corners, and scuttling hermit crabs. The sun sizzled on my back, my legs stung from the salt drying on my skin, and my face, inches above the surface of the water in the pool, was reflected back at me — seaweedy straggles of hair, a face breaking up and then rearranging itself in moving patterns as the water shivered and shimmered in the bright light. I knew my mother was near, leaning against the rocks of the slate cliff, reading, and that perhaps later we'd make a fire on the beach and cook winkles in a tin can. I made friends with the gamekeeper's daughter, and we'd run through the rhododendron woods and play at house in a deserted little wooden hut, rather like a gardener's shed, but miles from any formal gardens; it was hidden in the valley that ran inland from the beach, and was furnished with shelves and cup hooks and an old table. I imagine that at one time, years before, it had been a kind of folly associated with the big house.

It didn't last, though, this summer idyll. Back at school, more children with problems arrived, and more staff left, exhausted by the endless emotional and physical demands of the job. Even at five years of age, I realised how hard it was for my mother, and I knew when I was being naughty and hurtful; I sometimes felt remorseful, but the feeling never lasted long. I had absolute confidence in her love for me, and was convinced that one day Leonard would come back to us. We'd just have to wait.

In the meantime, though, some unpleasant things happened. One event in particular stayed with me for years. There was an Irish girl, Maureen, a big adolescent, possibly around seventeen years old. She shot dark looks at you if you dared so much as glance at her, and then she'd ask what the fuck you were staring at. She had red skin and a wild temper. I avoided her. Or if she picked on me, I'd do exactly what she told me to.

It was night-time and we'd all been watching television in the room called the office, where Ralph had his desk. The older children sprawled over old leather sofas and chairs—much of the furniture scarred from being hacked about with pen knives—and the younger children sat on cushions on the floor close to the small television set. Cocoa and bed followed. I was on my way from the bathroom to the junior dormitory when I heard my mother's voice on the half-landing above. She was asking Maureen to do something—I don't remember what—but whatever it was, Maureen didn't want to do it. Joyce asked her again. I ran up to see what was

*Melville and Susan hold the rope for the high jump*

happening. With a burst of fury the girl lunged at my mother, knocking her glasses off her nose and then smashing her fist back into her face so that she bled. I was terrified, unable to move. Maureen looked down. I thought she'd go for me, but she merely ground her foot into the glasses lying on the floor. And before my mother could do anything, the girl was clumping down the stairs, snarling at the group of gaping kids who were drawn by the sound of an argument, and the door of the senior girls' dorm slammed behind her. Did I go and give my mum a cuddle? I fled to my dormitory and hid my head under my pillow. Soon my mother came to find me, to reassure me she was all right and to tell me not to worry.

Other frightening things happened: on one occasion, Tom locked me and Melville in the cellars, hitting me over the head with a large lump of wood; on another, he attacked one of the younger boys. Like most bullies, Tom picked on the vulnerable. It was a wet weekend afternoon, and we were messing about in the dormitory. The boy must have said or done something to upset Tom, because quite suddenly Tom threw him onto a bed, yanked down the boy's shorts and underpants, and grabbed hold of his penis. He then whipped his mousetrap from a pocket and snapped it over the boy's penis. He screamed until he was choking while Tom laughed. Then, bored, or possibly frightened by the extreme pain he was causing, Tom released his victim and swaggered out of the dormitory, leaving the child curled up on the bed, his hands held to his crotch, sobbing juddering snotty tears.

Years later, I was talking to my ex-teacher, Jo Merchant, about our time at St Catherine's, and recounted this incident. Neither the victim nor any of the onlookers had reported Tom to the staff—we were too scared of what he might do next. Our silence had saddened but not surprised Jo: she told me that he was known to have severe mental-health problems and she had taken him up to London for a series of appointments with a child psychiatrist at the Maudsley. 'They described his behaviour as psychotic. God only knows what happened to him in the end.' Despite his frightening behaviour, I liked Tom. Maybe because he was charming or promised excitement and adventure—he thought of good games, like the funeral game, and he could make me laugh, imitating the teachers (particularly our elocution teacher). When we were down in Cornwall, he once took me and Melville on an adventure to find pirates' treasure. We clambered over rocks, gradually making our way further and further along the coast away from the safety of the cove at Menabilly, collecting shells and rusty bits of metal in a bucket, and then quite suddenly we realised our route back had been cut off by the tide. Tom helped me and Melville climb up a steep cliff to escape the incoming water, and our safe return to camp across the cliff top was a shared triumph.

Two years after we first arrived, and now six years old, I still missed my father, and now that I could write, I wrote to him weekly, asking when I could see him again. When he did answer, it was mainly in the form of sweet parcels. I looked forward to receiving those parcels with Scottish stamps on them — particularly the boxes of Edinburgh rock, with a picture of Edinburgh Castle on the lid. When you opened it there was a sugar-dusted sheet of paper, under which were sticks of crumbly coloured sugar lying on corrugated wax paper. My favourite flavour was ginger, but the colour was a dull beige. I enjoyed the power of choosing who might be lucky enough to get a stick of my rock. Nobody else got Edinburgh rock.

It wasn't until much later that I was told that my parents were divorced. In fact, the divorce went through in the late summer of 1952. Divorce was a messy and, at that time, to many, a shameful thing. My mother told me later how the whole process had left her feeling wrung out. She needed to get right away, from England, from her family and from everything that might remind her of Leonard and his new wife. She needed the time and space to recover herself and think about her future life as a single woman. In order to do this, she needed to find another job where she could take a small child.

At the end of the summer term of 1952, when I was just six, I was told that after the holidays we were going to move to another country. Not Scotland, but France.

Before that, though, I would have a holiday with my grandma. My mother was going abroad for a short time on her own. I clung to her hand, begging her not to leave me behind, but she told me not to be a silly goose, that she'd be back in no time and then we'd go away together. It must have been a huge relief for her to leave for a holiday without me (and with an Austrian friend — a man — called Toni), with her divorce completed and the knowledge that she had a job to go to and a place for us both to live. This, she told me, would be another boarding school, but it wouldn't be the same as St

*Jo Merchant and Joyce, c.1960*

Catherine's. For a start, nobody would speak English — they'd speak another language, French. And there wouldn't be any boys there.

This wasn't good news. I liked boys, and Melville and Andrew and Billy were my best friends. My mother explained that the school in France was a convent, which I understood was just another boarding school but with only girls as pupils, and the teachers were all women who were called mothers or sisters, even though none of them had children and they weren't really sisters. The school was called Maison Notre Dame, which meant House of Our Lady, and was in a little village in the mountains. During my last term at St Catherine's there was a man from Switzerland called Eric on the staff, and he had a girlfriend called Erica who sometimes came and stayed with him. I liked Eric and Erica a lot. Eric told me about France and how there would be mountains covered in snow, and he'd see us there in the mountains next Christmas. He also taught me some French phrases: *'je m'appelle Suzanne'*, *'je suis anglaise'* and *'j'ai six ans'*.

# CHAPTER 4

Paris, France, September 1952:

'Eat up, Susan.'

My lips remained glued together and my teeth clenched. This food was horrible. And so was my mother, to bring me here. This place wasn't like the cafés at home where you'd have a tall glass of milkshake with a straw and a bun while the grown-ups drank tea and had perhaps a Danish pastry or a toasted tea cake; it wasn't like a café at all.

'Please, darling.'

I clutched Ted and Jill on my lap. They didn't want to be here either. Gobs of fat floated in grey water, and grey sludge had settled at the bottom of the bowl in front of me. Around us were other tables where grown-ups jabbered at each other, and choking cigarette smoke drifted through the air. I missed Ralph's pipe smoke.

'Just try it. It's only potatoes and some onions.'

A lump of yellow bread rested on the red-and-white check tablecloth next to the bowl of grey liquid. I was hungry, but nothing would make me eat this muck.

Joyce shrugged. 'There isn't anything else. You'll go to bed hungry if you don't eat. Go on. Just a spoonful. It's nice.'

'I don't care.' I didn't want to go to bed in this foreign, smelly, noisy city. I'd formed my opinion of Paris as soon as we got on the Metro, pressed on all sides by people who smelled horrible, and *looked* at me. Joyce heaved the battered blue suitcase along a dark street towards the hotel where we were to spend the night; I trailed after her, Jill tucked into the front of my mac, Ted in one hand and my brown attaché case in the other. I had never been to a hotel before, and was expecting somewhere grand with a chandelier and possibly men in uniforms, like Carwardine's tearooms in Bristol, which had a wide, sweeping staircase leading to an upper floor where waiters brought you ice-cream in a shallow glass dish; but the staircase that led to our room was steep and narrow, and the old man who carried our cases up wasn't in a smart uniform. Our bedroom had a small window that looked out over rooftops, a dark cupboard, and a high bed with a bolster like a spare body lying across the top of it instead of plump pillows. There was a washstand and a jug of water.

I lay in bed, my back turned towards my mother. I was cold and wanted a cuddle, but wouldn't ask for one. I thought about where I'd slept the previous night — in the soft, warm feather bed at Grandma's, with the sound of the waves lulling me to sleep. That's where I wanted to be. Not here.

It was a long, slow journey from Paris across France. Late in the afternoon we changed trains. Not far now, my mother said. We were on a small local train, where old women dressed in black jostled for space on wooden benches, spreading their skirts wide. A yellow light flickered above our heads. One old lady had some live hens in a basket wedged between her knees. With each hour that passed I felt I was being dragged further and further away from what I liked, from England and from all things familiar and understandable. Finally I fell asleep with my mother's arm around me, the toys wedged between us.

We had arrived. Or at least we'd got off the train. A woman met us: she, too, was in black, her long-skirted dress billowing in the wind and a black scarf framing a white face with pale eyes. She bent over to hold my face between her hands, and smiled at me. I wriggled free. The air smelled of rain and the countryside. The woman, a nun apparently, had a bicycle. A man was waiting outside the station, the bicycle was put in the back of a van with our suitcases, and we squashed into the front seat. After a short drive, the van stopped, and the nun, my mother, and I got out, the bicycle was taken from the back of the van, and the nun balanced the blue case on its seat. I carried my attaché case and Jill and Ted, and we set off into the gusty night, wet leaves underfoot, the feeble light of the bicycle showing the way.

We came to high metal gates; the nun pulled a lever, and in the distance I heard a bell clang. The gates opened by themselves and we entered. A long drive opened out into a gravelled area and I had my first sight of the school. St Catherine's had appeared as a castle when I first saw it. This place was even more imposing — it was a church, with high, arched windows. I'd often played in the graveyard of the village church down the hill from St Catherine's, climbing over the tombstones, collecting the chips of coloured marble with Beryl. I knew from stories told in the dormitory that it was somewhere you should never go to at night because of the ghosts; but here we were in the company of a strange woman who looked more like a witch than anyone I'd ever seen before, approaching a church on a dark, wet, and windy night. My mother seemed unaware of the danger we were in — she was busy talking to the witch, and I didn't understand a word of their jabber. My panic eased as we passed the church without entering. And we didn't enter the building next to the church either, but veered away from it and followed the wavering bicycle light down a path to a second smaller house with rows of lighted windows. St Catherine's was stony and grey, with ivy twisted over broken-down walls. This house was square and tidy.

The bathroom, too, was tidy. No peeling paint and hissing geyser in this clean white space. Wash basins lined three of the walls, and bathroom cubicles the fourth. My mother and the nun in black had disappeared, and I was now with another nun, this one wearing white. She had a kind face, pink cheeks, and grey eyes. A wooden cross hung from her waist. Another little girl appeared; they spoke, and she grinned at me. Hot water gushed into the bath. The sister pointed to the other girl, who had started to undress, so I copied her: I tugged my jumper over my head and stepped out of my skirt, but as soon as I got down to my knickers and started to pull them down, they were sharply pulled up again and the nun pointed at the full bath. I was to get in. In my knickers? Puzzled, I began once again to pull them down. But the nun yanked them up and

*Maison Notre Dame, Mattaincourt, France*

immediately lifted me up and plonked me in the bath. With my knickers on! Then the other little girl got in at the other end of the bath, and she, too, had her knickers on.

Paris, the bowl of grey soup, the hens poking their heads out of the basket between an old lady's black-stockinged legs, a nun in black, another in white, a church, and now bathing in knickers? I began to cry. Apparently I continued to cry for three days. It was my teacher, Mère Marie Geneviève, who told me, just a few years ago, that I cried for three days, *sans cesse*. My mother wasn't allowed to leave her classes to come and see me, so Mère Marie Geneviève, who didn't speak any English, would hold me in her arms and try to comfort me, but nothing she could do would stem the flow of tears. I don't remember this outpouring of grief. I do remember how much I loved her.

My mother and I shared a bedroom. To reach it you walked through a dormitory, a row of iron bedsteads against either wall of the room, each bed neatly made with a nightdress folded on the pillow. There was none of the chaos of St Catherine's. And certainly no bedwetting. Our room was in the top corner of the house with windows on two walls; it was big and bare and very cold. At night you shut the shutters against the cold winds of the Vosges mountains, but still the snow got through to the inside windowsill.

My initial impression of French food didn't change for a long while. For breakfast we had hard, dry bread and hot chocolate made with water. No porridge, no toast, no dripping, no butter, no Marmite, no honey, no jam. Just bread. Some children were allowed to go up to high cupboards at the end of the dining room, where they were given butter or jam that their parents had provided. Then there was the medicine trolley, which was wheeled between the trestle tables as medicines were dispensed to certain girls. They didn't look particularly ill. I longed to have jam and some medicine.

The nun in white who'd plonked me in the bath on my first night at the convent was a sister, Soeur Gertrude, and her role was to look after the domestic needs of the youngest children, which included serving us food, supervising washing and shoe cleaning, and bathing any cuts and bruises. Food became a big thing for me. I didn't like it, or I didn't like *French* food, and although I ate the bread and drank the hot chocolate for breakfast, I dreaded lunch and dinner times. When the other girls were polishing their plates clean of gravy with bread, and queuing for pudding, I sat disconsolately in front of a cooling, congealing mess of meat. Offal was what I hated most: the smell of kidneys caught in my throat, and the very appearance of tripe made me feel sick. At St Catherine's there was no meat, but at Mattaincourt there seemed to be only meat. The dining room emptied, except for me; my pudding was put out of reach on a shelf, a reward for eating my meat. Soeur Gertrude tried to encourage me — *mais c'est bon, juste un tout petit morceau, Suzanne*. But no matter how hard I tried (possibly I didn't try so very hard), the lump of meat stuck in my mouth, getting drier and woollier the more I chewed it. If there were no other nuns in the dining room, Soeur Gertrude let me spit it out into her handkerchief so I could eat my pudding and then be released to the yard to join the other children. But we had to keep it a secret.

Perhaps Soeur Gertrude told my mother how little I ate, but for whatever reason Joyce felt that what I needed was milk, and the school didn't provide enough of it. So she found a solution. Every evening, as it was getting dark, she hurried down from the main school at break time, and we'd go for a walk, through the high metal gates and along the one street of the village. The village of Almondsbury near St Catherine's School was small, but Mattaincourt, where we now lived, was more of a hamlet. The street was muddy and lined with dung heaps; streams of dung-stained yellow water ran along ditches on either side of it. At a particular house we would jump over the stream and squelch through mud to knock at a side door. Inside it was gloomy, and there was a strong smell of cheese and animals. My mother brought out a wine bottle from her coat pocket. Warm, creamy milk was poured from a big metal jug, through a funncl and into the bottle; coins exchanged hands, and I had milk to drink. I knew that we had no spare money — certainly not enough for jam or honey. What I didn't know was that the money for my school fees and food was taken directly from her salary, and if we were to escape the convent life at all while we were in France she'd have to save every franc she could. There was no question of our returning to England for a holiday.

Once again, I was the youngest in the school, and was put in a group of eight other girls. I became an object of curiosity for them. They had never seen an English girl before, with her teddy bear and doll dressed in pretty clothes. They didn't grab the doll like Christine had, but just wanted to look at it. All the same, at the end of each day, Joyce would find a tearful 'Suza' (the name the French children gave me) sitting forlornly in our room with Jill and Ted, waiting for a bedtime story.

The lessons at Maison Notre Dame were not too different from those at St Catherine's. We did sums, reading, grammar, and spelling (French, of course), needlework, and drawing, but the classes went on for much longer. We had a break in the morning, then an hour at lunch and more lessons in the afternoon. The afternoon break was from 4.00 to 4.30 (when my mother and I would go to fetch the milk), and then more lessons until 6.00. After school we would clean our shoes and be allowed to play until dinner at 6.30. After dinner we went into the chapel for prayers, then off to bed.

My two French phrases — *je m'appelle Suzanne* and *j'ai six ans* — remained inadequate as a means of communication, so the French girls began to try out some English, and would call out, 'Goodnight, Suza, sleep well,' when I passed through the dormitory on my way to bed. But, according to Joyce (I don't remember this) after two months a change took place. I absolutely refused to try to speak French, so the entire junior school developed a new sign language.

In an article for an educational journal, Joyce wrote: 'The most fantastic contortions of faces and bodies replaced speech. The idea became so popular that all the children began to use signs to each other and not just when they were trying to make Susan understand. With the French genius for gesture and wild exaggeration the thing became a most delightful game: they understood one another perfectly and even practised on the patient nuns.'

I became happier and began to understand a lot more, but still refused to speak in any language other than English. Whether this was fear of making mistakes or stubbornness, I'm not sure: it was probably stubbornness, because once we were back in England, by which time I was bilingual, I refused to practise my French — I insisted I would speak French only to French people who didn't understand English — and I didn't know any such people in England, and so, sadly, I gradually forgot my second language.

As winter approached it got very cold. I was used to being cold at St Catherine's, with its minimal heating and ill-fitting windows and doors, but here somehow it felt colder. Perhaps we had to sit still for longer periods, and didn't run around as much as we did at St Catherine's. Joyce wrote to Leonard asking for help. She didn't have enough money to buy any clothes, so I was permanently cold, and still ate as little food as I could get away with.

After my stepfather's death in 2008, I found some of my

mother's diaries for the 1950s. The entries for November and December 1952 reveal just how fed up she was with our life in Mattaincourt, although she kept this from me, undoubtedly finding my own unhappiness and homesickness an added burden. There are sums at the end of each week, noting how many francs she had spent on milk, tea, soap, biscuits, stamps, coffee, and bus fares to Mirecourt and, once or twice, to Nancy, the nearest big town. She fell ill, and her illness continued for a couple of weeks: Saturday 8 November — *Wrote to Erica* (Eric's wife, from Switzerland); *Angry at lack of heating.* Some parcels arrived from Leonard on the tenth; on the fourteenth I was ill, and then it began to snow. On the twenty-first she wrote: *Snow melted. Worked all day. Reunion at night. Feel utterly worn out and indignant.* On the twenty-fourth she felt *very depressed. Letter and books from L. Books for S from J.M.* (Jo Merchant, my teacher at St Catherine's). On Tuesday 2 December — *Felt gloomy. Tried to write article* (the magazine article referred to earlier). A week later, though, things were looking up. *Had letter from Erica! Sent off article. Wine for lunch.* And the next day I do remember, very clearly. Joyce has written in her diary: *Parcel from Leonard of winter outfit for Susan.*

The big brown paper parcel was addressed to me. Scottish stamps covered the top right corner. It felt squishy. It was so exciting! I tore open the brown paper — not only was there a warm yellow jumper nestled in crinkly tissue, but there was also a pair of brown corduroy 'trews' and a straw-coloured windcheater. And, better still, a big brown jar of pills! At last I would be handed my *'médicaments'* from the medicine trolley at breakfast. The pills were satisfyingly large, and didn't taste too bad (they were vitamin pills). My daddy hadn't forgotten me!

Christmas was coming. One December evening, after prayers, we put our shoes by the big chimney in the dining room. I understood that a special saint, St Nicolas (who didn't travel as far as England), would, later that night, once we were all in bed, visit Mattaincourt on a donkey. If we'd been good, there would be treats in our shoes in the morning, on his special day, December sixth. There were no naughty children at this school, because in the morning each child's shoes were stuffed with sweets and gingerbread.

Just before Christmas we left Mattaincourt for the first time since September. Now, at the station in Mirecourt where we'd arrived that windy and wet night three months before, things were no longer strange and confusing. I could understand what people were saying and could read some of the signs. We were going to Geneva, where we'd see Eric from St Catherine's and his wife, Erica. Eric had taught me my French phrases, and no sooner had he met us off the train than he was asking me to show him how well I could speak French now. But because he and Erica knew English, there was no need for me to try French, so I did my French shrug and said, in English, that I didn't know any French. The adults exchanged looks. I could tell I wasn't going to be able to get away with this for much longer.

After the quiet seclusion of Mattaincourt, Geneva was like a firework display — colour, lights, rushing traffic, busy crowds of shoppers with bulging bags, delicious smells of hot chocolate drifting from cafés. I was so excited I could barely speak — even in English. Eric pointed out the mountain peaks glittering in the snow over the other side of the lake. This was where we'd be going in a couple of days. In the meantime we were to meet his parents and his sister and her boyfriend, and have a special Christmas Eve meal. Overcome by the journey, the delicious food, presents I'd unwrapped from Eric and Erica and from Eric's parents, Monsieur and Madame Louis — in Switzerland, Christmas was celebrated in the evening of Christmas Eve — I lay under a warm down duvet with my doll and teddy, and felt contentment fill me to the brim.

We took a train up into the mountains — my mother, me, Eric, Erica, and Eric's sister and her boyfriend, and then a bus to the village of Samoëns in the French Alps. We stayed in a chalet close to the ski slopes. This was nothing like a chalet you would find there today. The floors were bare; there were crude wooden shutters to keep out the snow, and there was one stove in the main room. It was so cold that we dragged the beds from the bedrooms into this room. Here we would cook, eat, and sleep. There was an outside lavatory next to a shed where the skis and toboggans were kept. The outdoor pump was frozen, so we brought in buckets full of snow to melt by the stove for water for washing and cooking. Our first night there, after warm soup and bread for supper and hot chocolate made from fresh milk from the farm next door, I learned what the exchange of looks between the adults at the station meant. I was told that from tomorrow on, if I wanted anything to eat, I'd have to ask for it in French; other times I could speak in English, but at mealtimes it was French or starvation.

My days were spent on the practice slopes careening down the hills on an old wooden toboggan, narrowly missing skiers. When there was a crash and we all ended up in the powdery snow, I quickly learned how to apologise in French. I'd drag the heavy toboggan back up the slope to be rewarded by another exhilarating whoosh down the slope again. I'd be left there for an hour or two at a time, and didn't mind at all. There were other children to play with, on whom I used my *je suis anglaise*, and they seemed to understand; you don't need much language to toboggan. I got hungry, though, and while I refused to ask for anything in French at lunchtime on my first day in the mountains (and got nothing), by the evening I was so hungry, I relented and mumbled my requests for *pommes de terre*, or *un bout de pain s'il vous plait*. At night I lay under my duvet glowing with warmth and tiredness, while the adults huddled around the stove, talking and drinking schnapps and coffee. By the time we left Samoëns, I was speaking French. And another thing — I'd hardly thought about my father, although of course I'd written to him and drawn some pictures for him: the frozen pump outside the chalet with its roof held down by stones, myself on a toboggan, the mountain peaks above.

Only when I was old enough to put myself in her shoes did I understand that our first term at Mattaincourt had been a very testing time for my mother: she needed to establish an independent life for herself, and yet provide me with a home and an education. She could have left me with her mother at Deal, but I suspect that for her this would have felt like a defeat; and no matter how difficult I was, I'm sure she'd rather have had me with her than living apart. It was as if she had to prove to herself she could do it. My tears and grumpiness and my refusal to speak French (she knew I could if only I'd make the effort) must have been hard to bear. In those first few months I went on and on about England and how I missed my friends at St Catherine's, and how it wasn't fair — I wanted to go and live with my daddy in Scotland, and why couldn't we go and see Grandma at Christmas, or Auntie Gwen and Ally? At times, this must have driven her mad.

Our first day back at Mattaincourt after the holiday in Switzerland began well. I was full of beans, able to communicate in French at last, and very pleased with the presents I'd been given at Christmas: a red-leather pencil case with a zip and, inside, coloured pencils, a proper pen with a nib, two pencils, a sharpener, and a little square ruler marked in centimetres. Each item had a leather loop to keep it in place. Then there were some story books in French (not as exciting) and some dolls' clothes from Grandma in England. At our first lesson we had to say what was our best present. I was so proud of my pencil case that, rather than describe it (I hadn't let on to my teacher or classmates that I was now speaking French), I ran out of the classroom, up the polished stairs to the top floor, and through the long dormitory to the room that my mother and I shared. I grabbed the pencil case from where I'd left it on my bed and sped back. But I wasn't looking where I was going, and tripped and fell onto the corner of one of the iron bedsteads. I had bashed my leg and, looking down, I saw a hole in it—a hole which slowly filled with dark blood that spilled over the ragged edge of skin and made a pool on the floorboards. I tried to get up and walk, but the blood came faster and faster, and it frightened me. So I yelled and yelled until Soeur Gertrude arrived.

The next thing I remember I was lying on my bed, with my mother kneeling at my side. The nuns gave me something to drink, and I fell asleep. I was woken by a sharp pain. I opened my eyes and looked straight into the eyes of a man I had never seen before. Surrounding my bed were nuns—not just Soeur Gertrude, but some others I didn't know—with unsmiling faces framed by white coifs. And I'd forgotten all my French. I didn't understand a word they were saying to me. I shouted for my mummy. Soeur Gertrude looked unhappy, and shook her head. I clung to her; the man was poking something into my leg, so I began to kick. He looked very cross, and barked a command to the nuns. The nuns held me down so that I couldn't move. At last my leg was bandaged, and they went away—all except Soeur Gertrude, who soothed me and gave me another drink, and I fell asleep.

The doctor came each day to give me a tetanus injection, so not only did I have a stiff leg, as the wound was just above my knee, I also had a stiff arm. The other girls made a fuss of me and called me *un petit soldat*, and we played nurses. Finally the bandage came off and the metal clips were pulled out, but the leg was still sore. I remember vividly kneeling in front of a cupboard in the classroom, leaning back on my heels and feeling the wound burst. I looked down at my bare leg: yellow pus mixed with bright-red blood slid down my knee. It soon healed but when, after a bout of tonsillitis, the doctor told Joyce I should have my tonsils removed, I was terrified and greatly relieved when she refused to have the operation done. We'll wait until we get home to England, she told me.

The French ways of doing things became natural to me. I no longer slept in my mother's bedroom, but in a small dormitory. It was as if I had decided I would start to be happier now. Maybe this was because I had lost my inhibitions about speaking in French, maybe I just got fed up with moaning, or maybe I just began to eat properly.

The dormitory was a pretty room. We had white painted wooden beds and duvets, and the polished wooden floor gleamed. I remember the sweet smell of beeswax. A coloured wooden crucifix hung on the wall — it showed Jesus with nails in his hands, blood dripping down his arms, and a crown of thorns on his head. He looked very sad. I was woken one night by the sound of sobbing. I peeped over the duvet and could see in the faint light that came from the open door one of the children, kneeling in her nightdress, crying and praying in front of the crucifix. She hid her face in her hands, her shoulders shaking with her sobs. She was praying to Jesus to let her go home. I felt sorry for her because I was sure that the wooden figure of Jesus wouldn't be able to do a thing about it. How could he?

There was going to be a coronation in England, and it was going to happen the day before my seventh birthday. All the children in England would get presents — mugs and golden coins. But in France we weren't even going to have the day off, like we did for some saints' days. The other girls told me that France was a republic and in the olden days they'd chopped off the queen's head with a guillotine because when she was told the poor people didn't have any bread to eat, she'd said, let them eat cake. I wondered if Queen Elizabeth II would say such a stupid thing. On the day of the coronation, after lessons, I was taken up to the main school by Mère Marie Geneviève. For a surprise, she said. We went into the big kitchen where all the food for the whole school was prepared, and there on a huge table was a huge cake. *La Reine Elizabeth II et Suzanne* was written in pink icing all the way round it, and seven candles flickered on its top. I blew out the candles and was given a sugar lump dipped in brandy to suck. Mère Marie Geneviève cut up pieces of the cake, and we carried it back to the junior annexe in a basket with a white cloth on top. All the children had some that night, and they all sang to me and to Queen Elizabeth.

Not long after this double celebration, it was time to go back to England. As I ran to keep up with a porter wheeling a pile of suitcases to Customs at Calais, I told him all about how my grandma would meet us at Dover. He admired my teddy. So I told him how Ted was looking forward to getting back to England because he still hadn't learned any French. The cases were taken away and, as there was plenty of time before we sailed, we walked along the docks. The sun shone; the water sparkled. I felt at home in France, but happy to be going home to England.

The ship drew away from the dock, and I waved goodbye to France. As I turned away from the deck rails to begin exploring the decks, I made a terrible discovery. I'd lost Ted. My mother tried to reassure me — I must have dropped him, he'd turn up. An announcement was made over a loudspeaker in English and in French, and at any other time that would have thrilled me, but nobody found the missing teddy. I didn't want any of the picnic lunch we'd brought; I didn't want to look out for the first glimpse of the white cliffs of Dover.

I kept close to my mother as we jostled through the crowd to get off the boat. Grandma and Auntie Millie met us; but instead of hugs and smiles from me, they got tears. Nothing they said made me feel any better.

The next day, Grandma took me to a toy shop, and we looked at all the bears they had — big fluffy ones, little smooth-haired ones, ones that squeaked when you squeezed their tummies, ones with button eyes, ones with embroidered noses — but there was not a single one exactly like Ted. So we went for one that didn't look at all like my old teddy bear, and took it back to meet Jill. Grandma knitted him a jumper and trousers by the fire that night, and while I sat staring at the dancing flames and blue sparks, dangling the new bear by his leg, Grandma told me what was happening to Ted. A fisherman on the dockside at Calais had found him lying face down in a puddle. He'd almost stepped on him, then realised it was a toy bear and picked him up and took him home for his little girl. She'd washed him, and was now drying him by her fire. While New Ted and Jill and I listened to the sea pounding on the English shore, Old Ted and his new owner could hear that same sea crashing against the rocks of France.

# CHAPTER 5

As I recalled those first few years after Leonard left me and my mother for his new life with Monica, I thought a lot about the nature of memory. Laura's questions and the evidence she had presented me with — the photographs and the letters that had been swiftly put away — left me feeling as if maybe I had been making things up. I kept having to tell myself not to be stupid. Of course I hadn't experienced life in Scotland, or a long journey by sea to Australia, but nevertheless my confidence in my version of events was shaken. I searched my memory rigorously and reassured myself I was right.

This wasn't the first time I'd made such positive efforts to remember, although my earlier efforts sprung from a very different motive. From the day Leonard kissed me goodbye and the train drew away from the station, I consciously remembered how things had been in the immediate past; I don't doubt that someone else would remember events and places differently, but for me the images of the past that lived in my head were as vivid as technicolour film. With each change in circumstances (leaving Birmingham to go to St Catherine's, leaving England for France, leaving France to return to England and seeing my grandmother and cousins again), I recalled the people that I had left behind, the houses, the landscapes, the smells, and the tastes. Remembering became a habit, a means of creating continuity perhaps, giving myself a sense of control, so that even at the age of six or seven, I would in effect create memories.

However, my recollections of the second period I spent at St Catherine's are not as sharp as those I kept recalling when I was in France. I was returning to a familiar school routine. For Joyce, the year in France had provided a hiatus, a chance to recover from the emotional exhaustion of working with difficult and needy children, and from her divorce. Now she needed to build a new life. She also felt that perhaps it was time I went to an ordinary school. But once again the questions of earning money and finding somewhere for us to live were the first things to sort out. St Catherine's would provide a base for her to explore the future, and a place where I was happy and where I received, if not a conventional education, an interesting one.

There was no question of my sharing a bedroom with my mother. I went straight into the junior girls' dormitory. I could now hold my own against the other children, and Joyce's role in my life became more peripheral. As for my father, although I hadn't given up all hope of ever seeing him again, I was more realistic about that possibility, and the 'one day' became not a matter of weeks, or months, but of years. When I was old enough. Old enough for what, I now wonder, but at the time accepted his promises of *one day when you're old enough* ...

The lives of the older children became more interesting to me, and I was useful to them. My status as the child of one of the staff was, in their eyes, a plus. If I were caught, they said, I wouldn't get into real trouble. The senior girls' dormitory was on the other side of a landing from ours, and there was often talk amongst the girls of the Patchway Boys, lads who, I understood, came out from Bristol at night, to climb up into the girls' dormitory for 'it'. 'It' was something mysterious, but it made the girls giggle and get into huddles and tell us younger ones to bugger off. I never saw a Patchway Boy.

'It', though, wasn't just to do with the Patchway Boys. 'It' concerned the boys at school, too. I was recruited to act as a messenger between the senior boys' and girls' dormitories. After dark I slipped along the corridors and stairs from one side of the building to the other as stealthily and as invisibly as the White Lady, with tightly folded wads of paper in my pyjama pocket that I would deliver triumphantly — only to be told to wait, if it was the girls, for them to write an answer, while they giggled and conferred. The boys didn't confer. In fact, they were embarrassed by my hanging around at the door of the dormitory, waiting to see if there was an answer, and I'd often be told to get the hell out of it. On one occasion I had to dive under a boy's bed when a teacher was heard approaching the dormitory. I lay there in the dust, my heart thumping loudly in my ears while the teacher's brown brogues stopped just inches away from my head as he did his rounds. I had my instructions: if any teacher or the matron caught me slinking along the corridors, I had to say I was going to find my mum. That excuse wouldn't hold water if I were discovered under a boy's bed. However, I wasn't discovered, and my role as go-between was exciting. Nothing really bad would happen to me if I were caught. I could read well by this time, and I wonder why I didn't stop to read the love letters that I carried so close to my heart.

The steamy atmosphere of the senior girls' dormitory slunk like fog across the landing to us juniors, infecting us with a burning curiosity. Why shouldn't we try 'it'? A group of us, boys and girls, gathered around a bed, a girl lay on her back, her skirt pulled up around her chest, her legs spread wide. A boy lay on top of the girl. He, too, didn't have his pants on. Nothing happened. His penis, which we understood had to somehow get inside the girl, remained floppy. She shifted on the bed and thrust her hips upwards in an effort to cooperate. When one of the boys bent over the couple to take the limp penis in his own hand and manipulate it into place, I was quite suddenly overcome with a desire to have a wee. I dashed down the short flight of stairs along to the lavatory; but when I got there, very strangely, I couldn't do it. I returned to the dormitory to find that the experiment was over. Sex for the under-tens didn't seem to work.

After a year back at school, my mother found another job. This was in Exeter. I stayed on at St Catherine's, and she moved into 'digs' in Exeter, where I'd sometimes go to see her for the weekend. I'd be put on the train (in the charge of the guard) in Bristol, and Mum would meet me in Exeter. I didn't like going there much, though, because I didn't like the place she was living in. She had a small back bedroom, where I'd sleep in a single bed with her. Downstairs the gas fire was permanently on, even in the summer, and the landlord sat in front of it all day and all night. He'd lost a leg in the war, and one trouser leg was tied in a knot below where his knee should have been. He shook a lot and spilled his food, so the trousers were stained and spotted with grease. Also, the absent leg gave him terrible gyp. 'You can't see 'un,' he'd say, 'but I can feel 'un, and 'e's giving me gyp.' We had to eat with the landlord and his wife: spam sandwiches or overcooked scrambled eggs and strong brown tea. Occasionally we'd go out for tea in Exeter, but as Joyce was saving every penny she could to buy a place of her own, this was a rare treat.

Finally, after a second year for me back at St Catherine's, my mother managed to buy a house, and I moved down to Exeter to join her. For the first time since I was four years old, we had a house of our own.

What excitement to see all the things that had been put

into store all those years before: my doll's house, my green and yellow wooden boxes, the table that used to stand in the back room in Birmingham. With the delivery of the items from storage came a flood of memories: Leonard feeding me a boiled egg at that table, our trip to Gamages to buy the garden swing that my mother now erected in our garden in Exeter; standing at the fold-down enamel table of the kitchen cabinet, helping my mother make pastry, and baking my own shapes in the gas oven in Birmingham.

Our Exeter house was a two-bedroomed cottage, but I didn't have a room of my own because I had to share with my mother again. The rest of the house was full of tenants. One had a bedsitting room in the big bedroom, and downstairs there was a flat that two nurses lived in.

At that time, 1955, it was very difficult for single women to get a mortgage, and it was only with the help of her solicitor who set up a private mortgage for her that Joyce was able to buy the house. It became hers on April the fifteenth. She kept the handout from the estate agent, and under the description of the accommodation she has done some sums: Susan £24, Bank £20, NSC £7. She had £51 as a deposit! The price of the house was £2,650.

The rediscovery of old toys and pieces of furniture from the house in Birmingham must have prompted me to ask, yet again, if Daddy would be coming to see us. He wouldn't, my mother said. She explained that she and my father were now divorced, which meant that they were no longer married and would never live together again. In fact, he was married to someone else; someone who she used to know, who used to be a friend of both hers and my father's, and whose name was Monica. In my heart I knew that my dream of my parents getting back together was just that, an impossible dream, but the word 'divorce' was so very final, and if he had another wife now, he wouldn't want to be with us again. 'Divorce' clouded my excitement of living in a 'proper' house again, rather than a school.

At Easter we went to Deal to see Grandma and then, when the summer term began, rather than return to St Catherine's, I got the train to Exeter. For the first time in my life I was at a day school and I had a home I walked back to every day at 4.15. Now, instead of being in a class of six or eight, I was in a class of forty. However, although this might have seemed a dream come true — apart from the lack of Leonard in my life — I missed the chaos of St Catherine's. During the summer I was happy to go back down to Cornwall, to the campsite at Menabilly where I could play with my old friends. I made new friends at Heavitree Junior School, and I made sure I did just the same things as them: we danced the maypole, learned by heart poems such as 'It's a warm wind, the west wind', and did lots of intelligence tests.

At Christmas I went up to St Catherine's again, just to visit. Since we had returned from France I had regularly made train journeys on my own — from Bristol to London, from London to Deal, and from Bristol to Exeter, always with the guard keeping an eye on me and making sure I got off at the right stop. My mother had got a Christmas tree for our first Christmas at our new house, and she unearthed the old decorations that along with all our other worldly goods had been in store. The cat at St Catherine's had kittens, and I brought one down on the train with me, in a cat basket. A kitten all of my own, in a house all of my own. I called the kitten Purdy (after the matron), and the first thing he did once released from the basket was scramble to the top of the tree, which brought the whole thing crashing to the floor; glass balls shattered, and the fairy got a nasty bump on her plastic head.

Purdy knew all about St Catherine's, but I didn't tell any of my new friends about my previous life. If I didn't actually forget things such as swearing, stealing fruit and sweets, experimenting with sex, and speaking French, I certainly never mentioned them.

Joyce, too, made new friends. And some of these were male friends. One of the teachers from St Catherine's sometimes came to stay, and I liked him, but then he stopped coming, and there were others, but none who seemed to pose any threat to the cosy unit that my mother and I made. I liked other people living in the house – I was used to communal living, so long as they didn't threaten the mother–daughter unit that in my eyes was a fortress. I knew that now my parents were divorced, my mother might decide to marry someone else, but I didn't care to examine that possibility.

The man who stayed and carried on staying was Mick, who taught accountancy at the college where Joyce taught English. By this time we had only two tenants – the nurses in the downstairs flat – and I had my own bedroom. I was about to sit my 11+ exam. Soon after moving to Exeter, Joyce had bought a motor scooter, a Vespa. Mick was single, several years younger than her, and he, too, had a motor scooter, a Lambretta. Mick wasn't, by any stretch of the imagination, mechanically minded, which makes the circumstances of him and Joyce meeting rather unlikely. The encounter took place in the college car park. Apparently she asked him for some kind of technical help, and they got chatting. I suspect she'd had her eye on him for a while, because if advice on fixing her scooter was what she really wanted, she chose the wrong man.

Mick became a regular visitor to our house, staying for tea, going out for scooter rides with Joyce to the seaside and then to a pub afterwards. Although I was taken along, too, on the back of the Lambretta, I felt I was being sidelined. Every Saturday morning, he brought gifts to woo us both. My mother got flowers and chocolates while I gradually accumulated a complete set of Jennings stories and a shelf full of Angela Brazil. It was a shrewd move on his part. I looked forward to my next book and the bag of liquorice that came with it.

*Susan, Joyce, and Purdy at the front door of The Cottage, March 1956*

I was suspicious of their relationship from the start, and as it became closer, I became more resistant to it. I was rude and ungracious. One night I heard them arguing in the room below my bedroom. It was summer, and all the windows were open, the scent of wisteria floating through my room. I had moved my bed so that I could put my pillow on the windowsill, and look up at the stars. To begin with, it was just them talking loudly, and then they started to shout. Or Joyce did. I stiffened, every nerve alive to what was happening in the room below, feeling the flashes and sparks as they flew across the room and out of the window and into my space. He was making my mother sad and angry. How dare he? I sped down the stairs, crashed into the room, and yelled at him to get out of my house and to leave my mother alone. The poor man was horrified at this outburst, and my mother was angry with me. I simmered with hatred and jealousy. I realised that if she married Mick, there would be no chance at all of Leonard leaving his new wife and returning to take his rightful place in our lives. And, even worse, she could have another baby: Mick's baby.

Then they got married. They didn't tell me — I was sent to stay with Grandma and Auntie Millie in Deal, and when I came home, Mick had moved in permanently. My mother explained that they had got married, but didn't offer any explanation as to why I hadn't been invited to the wedding. Years later, I asked why I'd been sent away to stay with Grandma. She didn't want me to feel hurt, she said; she thought it would be easier for me. This, I think, was partly to do with her desire to shield me from what she knew I'd find difficult, but it was also how things were done then: perhaps children attending their mother's second marriage was considered in the same way as their attending funerals — it wasn't done. The effect, though, was to make me feel the impotence of having no control over what happened in my life.

The thing that bothered me most as the autumn term approached was what would be my name at the new school? I couldn't bear the idea of having to give up my name — my father's name — and have Mick's name, but Joyce had changed her name from Joyce Jolley to Joyce Mitchell, so perhaps it was automatic. I didn't dare ask.

I was the only girl from my class of forty who got a place at the grammar school, so I knew none of the other new girls. We gathered in the main hall, and the name of each girl was called out and the class she would be in. 'Susan Jolley — 1M' was announced, and I breathed again.

I settled into my new school and into a routine of family life with Mick. I made new friends and joined the Woodcraft Folk (rather like the Girl Guides, but for boys and girls, and socialist in its outlook — no promises to honour God, Queen, and Country, but we'd sing 'The Red Flag' as we hiked over the moors). My life was expanding well beyond the reach of my home. I still wrote regularly to Leonard, and he maintained a perfunctory and irregular correspondence with me.

One day, and I remember this clearly, two envelopes addressed in his handwriting arrived: one for me and one for my mother. His news was that he was leaving Scotland to live in Australia. He didn't mention his wife, or any other children, but that barely mattered. If he was on the other side of the world, despite all his promises of seeing me again once I was 'old enough', I knew it wouldn't happen. I took his letter up to my room and read it over and over. It was short, as all his letters to me were. He would be travelling by ship and it would take several weeks. My heart sank. I would never ever see him again. He might as well be dead. People just didn't go to Australia for a holiday. We hadn't even been to Scotland when he lived there. When someone emigrated to the other side of the world it was for good. Several weeks later I had a postcard and a silk scarf sent from Port Said. He told me the ship had sailed through the Suez Canal, and I looked it up on a map in my Pears Cyclopaedia, remembering vaguely the news of the Suez Crisis when I was in my last year at junior school. I was worried he might be caught up in a war. He wrote again once he had arrived in Perth, so I had his address.

By the time I was thirteen I had accepted Mick as a permanent feature in my life, and although I never became close to him, we got on well enough. He was very patient and didn't interfere. Leonard still occupied a central place in my imagination. He remained firmly fixed in my mind as a monumental figure, embracing all the characteristics that I felt those closer to home lacked. He would understand me. He wouldn't criticise my bad behaviour. He'd love me unquestioningly. I felt these things strongly, despite the plentiful evidence that he did not care about me. Joyce understood me very well, and she certainly loved me, but she was there and he wasn't, so she got the flak.

The moment that pushed Leonard crashing from his pedestal, momentarily at least, came when I was revising for school exams. Joyce and Mick were out. I was bored by revision, and lay on my bed listening to Radio Luxembourg and flicking through my *Honey* magazine. There was a recipe for a face mask. No more spots! It required egg white and eau de cologne. Easy. Eggs in the fridge and eau de cologne on Joyce's dressing table. I smeared the grey goo on my face as instructed, concentrating on the greasy areas — nose, chin, and forehead, and avoiding the fine skin around the eyes. My skin tightened until it felt as if it were a canvas, stretched over a frame, sized and ready for paint. I stared at the reflection of my eyes, the only bit of my face that could move. They were a nice colour, I thought, a dark blue with flecks of brown, but sad-looking. I raised my eyebrows to try to achieve a more cheerful look, but the mask was so tight it made my eyes water. I then began to make faces at myself in the mirror — frowning, grimacing, grinning — and the more I moved, the more cracks and wrinkles appeared, and my face turned into the face of an old woman, like Dorian Gray in reverse.

I undressed, and turned on the taps for a bath. I surveyed my body in the full-length mirror of a wardrobe that was kept in the bathroom. I gazed at this ugly, wrinkled face on top of a smooth young body. Long, brown legs — apart from a thick, white scar above the left knee, a flat belly, and satisfyingly round breasts. It was a pity about the brown nipples because I understood they should be pink and pert, but otherwise there wasn't too much wrong with my body. I washed away the mask from my face, fingered the polished surface of skin, poured some of Joyce's bubble bath under the gushing taps, and decided to look for something interesting to try on while the hot water coughed and splattered into the bath. My mother kept old clothes she couldn't quite bear to part with in a trunk in the corner of the bathroom. I hadn't played at dressing up for years.

I rummaged, pulling out garments and holding them up against me, posing, one hip tilted at an alluring angle. I sniffed the mustiness of old silk and mothballs. I threw the clothes into the air and watched them flutter to the floor. There was a white camisole in fine cotton lawn, neat pintucks under the bust, and delicate lace sewn around the neck and armholes. It fitted perfectly. I pulled on a white cotton petticoat, in tiers like a Spanish dancer's skirt, each tier edged in broderie anglaise. Humming a vaguely Spanish-sounding tune, I did a twirl, bent low to pick up old stockings and vests, flicking them like ribbons, clicking my fingers, and then sank into a deep curtsey to delve further into the trunk for more treasure.

Beneath the clothes were folded lengths of fabric, plastic bags of balls of wool, and old knitting patterns, and at the very bottom of the trunk was a box tied in yellowing tape. I hadn't noticed it before when I used to play at dressing up. The box held a sketchbook, with still-life compositions of jugs, apples, wine bottles, and glasses and landscapes that I didn't recognise. There were several drawings of a baby's head. Was it mine? Joyce had begun to go to art classes, and brought home paintings she'd done in oils, but this was old stuff—she must have done it years before. There was also a small red diary for 1946, the year of my birth. I flicked through the pages and yes, there it was, 3 June — Susan born 1.10pm. A Monday. On that Monday had Joyce looked at her new baby and fallen in love with her, like mothers are supposed to? No revelations of deep feelings or anything else of interest appeared in the diary — just appointments with initials, or initials' birthdays. The bath was full, so I turned off the taps. The only other things in the box were some envelopes held together by a crumbling rubber band. I knew I shouldn't read someone else's letters, but … these were old and had been shoved in the bottom of a box. I recognised Leonard's spidery handwriting. What harm could come from looking at this stuff? It was ancient history. I slipped a letter from its envelope. I began to read. Two lines down I saw my name.

*I think it would be best if you told Susan I was dead.*
What?

I read the sentence again to make sure I hadn't imagined it. No, he said he thought it would be a good idea if I thought he was dead.

If I thought he was dead I'd not ask to see him again; there would be no question about it. He would no longer be bothered by my letters and he could pretend I was dead, too.

I folded the letter, slid it into its envelope, and returned the sketchbook and diary to the box. I carefully tied the tape and put everything back as neatly as I could. I unhooked the camisole, let the petticoat slip to my ankles, and stepped out of it and into the bath. The bubbles had lost their glamour. I sank my head beneath the surface of the water and tried to forget what I'd read. He couldn't have meant it, could he?

It was about this time that I became convinced that my paternal grandfather was alive and thinking about me. I didn't tell my mother I'd been prying in her things, and so she never knew I'd read that letter from Leonard. I was ashamed of both

*Joyce's elder sister Elsie with Joyce, 1920s*

myself for reading the letter and my father for writing it. But I did talk about Grandpa Jolley. I went on and on about him. Joyce kept telling me that he must have died by now because he'd be very old. I repeated, he's thinking about me, I know he is. She didn't tell me about the promise she'd made to Leonard not to contact any member of his family. It must have been hard to withstand my nagging because I could be very obstinate, particularly when I was convinced I was right. As it turns out, he was still alive at that time, and he was thinking about me. Because I'd written him a letter.

Or, as I was later to find out, he thought I had.

My other grandparent, Grandma Hancock, and little Auntie Millie were both very old now, and they left their house in Deal to move in with my mother's younger sister, Gladys, in

Yorkshire. So there were no more holidays in Kent, but we went up to Halifax for Christmas, and sometimes I'd go there on my own for holidays. Joyce's other sister, Elsie, who was just eleven months older than her, had lived in London, where she and her husband ran a hardware shop; but Elsie had died when her youngest child was just four, and her husband was left with four children to look after — three older boys and the youngest, a little girl. I developed a crush on one of my London cousins. John was very good looking and had oodles of charm, and always had time for me. We wrote to each other — innocent letters. I'm sure he had no idea how I felt about him. Then one day — I must have been about sixteen, and had become very keen on the theatre — I wrote to say I'd be coming to London to see a play, and could we meet for tea?

After a week, he still hadn't replied to my letter. I wrote again. Hadn't he received my letter? No reply. So I wrote again. How could he do this to me? Didn't he care about me any more? No reply.

It was over a year since we'd been up to Yorkshire to see Grandma, and when I asked why we no longer went there, Joyce explained what she understood had happened. James Taylor Junior had taken over from his father in 1953, when my mother and I were living in France. To begin with, things went on much as before, and new restrictions on what the Brethren were or were not permitted to do did not have any great impact on us. But then the edicts issued by 'Big Jim', as he was known, became increasingly draconian. Joyce's younger sister, Gladys, had written to her to tell us that Auntie Millie had died, and although she understood that Joyce and I would like to see Grandma, this was not possible. When looking through my mother's papers after my stepfather died, I found the letter my mother had told me about. Gladys wrote:

We walk on a separate path, more separate than ever before, and as desiring to be true and faithful to the truth of the fellowship and faithful to the Lord, we have to maintain our household as walking in the truth of this ...

This 'banning' of us from seeing members of the family was the latest of many decrees, but one that affected us harshly. Brethren should no longer associate with 'worldlies' in any way: not even a cup of tea could be drunk at the same table, even if this were in a café. For Brethren to drink or eat with 'worldlies', or to sleep under the same roof as such sinners as us, would be to risk spiritual contamination. Joyce and I were such people — evil, contaminated by worldliness.

So that was why John hadn't replied to my letters, and why Joyce was unable to visit her mother and I never saw my grandmother again. Grandma, I learned later, had begun to suffer from dementia, and although she asked when we would come and see her, she had no real understanding of Jim Taylor Junior's pronouncements about the dangerous and evil nature of her middle daughter and her granddaughter. When Grandma died a few years later, I was so angry and upset I told my mother I was going to hitchhike to Yorkshire, and make them see that I wasn't the devil incarnate, but an ordinary girl.

You go if you must, she said, but I don't think it's a good idea, you'll only be hurt. So I said, let's both go, on the train. She refused — although she still loved her younger sister and had been fond of her brother-in-law, she wouldn't force herself on them.

My mother had a very effective way of dealing with me: she would put forward an argument as to why she thought one line of action was better than the other (usually the one I proposed), but would say that it was up to me. Thus, when

I announced that I wanted to leave school after 'O' levels, she didn't throw her hands up in horror, but asked what I thought I'd do with my collection of 'O' levels. I wasn't unhappy at school, was I? No, I wasn't unhappy, and I liked studying, but I wanted to be free. I wasn't sure what I wanted to be free for, exactly, or free of, other than the restraints put on me at school. I was given all the freedom I wanted at home — she didn't like me hitchhiking but didn't stop me, my friends were welcome, and often the house was full of her older, mature 'A' level students and others from overseas, whom she always made welcome. There were rules, but they were always negotiable — rather how things had been at St Catherine's. I didn't leave school at sixteen; I did the conventional thing and applied for university. And I didn't have the courage to make the journey to see my Brethren relations. I was too afraid of being rejected once again by the people who used to love me.

I went to Bristol University in 1964, and for the first term was in digs in a council house on a big estate on the outskirts of the city. It was while I was here that I wrote to Leonard complaining that he couldn't be bothered to congratulate me on my exam results and my getting a place at Bristol. The letter I received in return was signed by his wife, Elizabeth, and from then on it was she who wrote to me. Leonard gave up all pretence of having any interest in me and my studies. I showed my mother Elizabeth's letter, and asked her about these other children who were mentioned in it. She said she knew nothing about them — how many there were, their names, or whether they were girls or boys. She said how hurt she'd been to discover that Leonard had left her for Elizabeth (who had been called Monica at the time), but seemed unwilling to go into any further details about her ex-husband's second marriage, so I left it. My own life was far more interesting to me — being a student, and enjoying new friendships, sex, and rock and roll.

Three years later, in July 1967, Gordon and I married. Now, nearly six months into my marriage, and after weeks of going over past events in my head, I was about to go down to Exeter for Christmas where I would begin to pick up the first threads of the web of lies and evasions that had been woven around my life.

# CHAPTER 6

There were old friends to see, parties to go to, and my parents' house was full. My mother and I had a brief conversation about my visit to Laura and her husband Stan, and how they'd seemed and what the house and garden were like, but our first opportunity to talk alone came on Boxing Day.

We'd had lunch in a pub, and afterwards went for a walk along the beach at Budleigh Salterton. Clouds scudded across a pale, wintry sky, gulls battled against the wind, and waves sucked at the steep, pebbly shore. Gordon and Mick walked ahead while my mother and I followed behind.

She bent over to pick up a pebble, and held it in her hand and smoothed it with her fingers. 'What has Laura told you about your father's family?' She absent-mindedly slipped the stone into her coat pocket.

'What do you mean? Grandpa Jolley and where they grew up and that kind of stuff?'

'No, I was thinking about your own generation.'

Perhaps she knew about this other Susan. 'Well, I know he's got children — I showed you the letter Elizabeth wrote me when I first started at Bristol. She said Leonard wasn't interested in his children, and yet was proud of me and so on. When I wrote back I asked about their children, but she didn't tell me anything more. I suppose I should have addressed my letters to her, not Leonard. Bit childish, really, particularly as after that letter, when I was first at university, he never wrote. It was always her, and she said he sent his love.'

I didn't like talking about Elizabeth with my mother — it felt disloyal. But then she'd brought the subject up, and here was my opportunity to find out about the other Susan. I felt apprehensive, and it was my turn to look down at the stony beach and select a pebble. 'You remember when we went to see Laura, well, something a bit odd happened. There was this photo on her bureau, and she thought it was of me, because Leonard had sent it and on the back somebody had written 'Susan'. The girl in the photo was about my age, but she definitely wasn't me. You know yourself, don't you, in photos?' I bent to pick up another pebble and glanced up at my mother who was frowning, looking into the distance. I rushed on with what I had to say. 'And then there was another one, another photo of the same girl with two younger children, but that wasn't me either. I suppose she was Elizabeth's from an earlier marriage or something, and we just happened to have the same name ...' I trailed off. It sounded such an unlikely coincidence.

My mother put her hand on my arm. 'No, Sue, she's his and Elizabeth's, and her name's Sally, not Susan. She's your half-sister. And you're right — she is about your age. Well, five weeks older, in fact.'

I stared at her, astonished. 'My half-sister? But Laura said her name was Susan, not Sally. It was written on the back of the photo. And when I asked you after Elizabeth first wrote to me — you must remember — you said you didn't know anything about their children.'

I looked ahead: Gordon and Mick were almost at the end of the beach, where a river spilled into the sea and red cliffs rose above it.

'I don't understand ...' Once again I'd been kept in the dark.

I hurled one pebble into the grey waves and then the other. 'Why didn't you tell me? Did you know about her all along?' Either the cold wind or tears stung my eyes.

My mother suggested we walk up the beach and sit on a bench and wait for the men to come back. We sat side by side, she huddled into her sheepskin coat while I hunched my shoulders and fixed my eyes on the horizon. Why the hell did everyone treat me like a child? Why hadn't Laura said anything more about the girl in the photograph? What were they keeping from me now? Why all this mystery? Why couldn't they just spit it out — just tell the truth for once?

'It's a tangled web,' Joyce said quietly.

I didn't answer. She went on to tell me that, yes, she had known about the child, Sally, for years. In fact, she'd known Sally as a baby. All three of them — herself, Monica, or rather, Elizabeth as she was now known, and Leonard — were friends, and Elizabeth had nursed Leonard when he was in hospital during the war, and that when my parents moved to Birmingham, Elizabeth had got in touch again as this was where she was now working and living. I knew all that — she'd told me before, as well as how Monica Knight had changed her name to Elizabeth Jolley shortly after Leonard had left us. But she hadn't told me about Sally — a girl my own age. Why not? Did Mick know about this Sally, too? And what about Grandma? Had she known? Had Joyce's sisters, their husbands? Did everyone know except me?

As the sky darkened, my mother tried to explain what had happened. 'When Elizabeth (who was single) told me she was pregnant, of course I felt sympathetic. But I was rather relieved, too, because I thought it must mean that she wasn't in love with your father. I'd had my suspicions, you see. She was always coming round to our flat, and seemed smitten by him. So I was relieved when she told me that the father was a doctor she'd met at the hospital. However, he was dying of TB.' She continued so quietly I could barely hear her above the noise of wind and waves. 'She told me that she could quite easily have got an abortion because she was a nurse and they all knew how to get rid of unwanted pregnancies, but she would have the baby, despite the difficulties of being a single mother.'

She paused, as if ordering her thoughts – almost talking to herself. 'I admired her for that. I thought it was a brave decision. Anyway, shortly after that we had to move out of our flat to Chadwick Avenue, and Leonard told me it was because our landlady didn't want a baby in the flat. He arranged it all. I was so ... so gullible.'

I was getting lost. 'What was wrong with moving to a house from a flat? Didn't it make sense? More space and so on?'

'Yes, but the thing was that I believed every word he said – when he said he loved me, when he said the landlady wanted us out. In fact she was quite fond of me and would never have insisted that we left just because I was having a baby. But I didn't question her – just felt indignant. Monica, or Elizabeth as I suppose I must now call her, had her baby five weeks before you were born. She came to stay in our house while I was in the nursing home, and was there when I came back with you. She stayed for several weeks.'

'And you didn't suspect anything?'

She shook her head.

'So you thought the baby's father was a doctor who was dying and that your old landlady was being unfair chucking you out. And it didn't occur to you that the baby might be Leonard's? Do you think they imagined some kind of ménage à trois in the house? Cinq, rather?'

'I don't know what they imagined. And, no, I never suspected that Sally and you were half-sisters. I couldn't see any similarities between Sally and him. But I suppose I wasn't looking for them.'

'Why didn't you tell me this before, if you've known for the past twenty-one years?' I could hear the childish whine in my voice and mumbled, 'Sorry, go on.' I tried to think what it must have felt like for her at the time, and how it felt for her now to have to tell me this story. I turned my eyes from the horizon to look at her. She tucked her arm through mine. I should have been giving her comfort, but all I could do was try not to cry.

'Not long after Monica got a job as a housekeeper to a doctor, and as I was at home with you, I offered to look after Sally, too, so she came to our house once a week. Two of you! No easy task, that. Then that arrangement stopped, and as time went on I saw less and less of her — and your father would change the subject if ever I asked about Monica, so I stopped asking.'

'I've explained it all to Laura, in a letter,' she went on, 'and I think she's finding it very hard to come to terms with. She couldn't believe Leonard could behave like that — not telling anyone the truth.'

My face must have shown my feelings — I couldn't really take it in. But neither could I understand why she'd made that ridiculous promise not to contact members of his family.

'I've been thinking a great deal about how and what to tell you, but I wanted you to have the facts as far as I know them before you saw Laura again.'

'How did you find out that Sally was Leonard's, and not the dying doctor's? Did he write and say: by the way, I was having sex with our friend Monica as well as you, and what jolly bad luck, you both got pregnant.'

'Susan.'

I took a breath and said more gently, 'How did you find out? Did he tell you? Or did she?'

'Neither of them told me.'

Joyce had continued to believe that Sally was the child of the dead doctor for years. She learned the truth of the situation some time after she and Mick were married, when I was about eleven years old. Some very old friends of both hers and Leonard's, Louie and Les Wheeler, came to stay. They felt that it wasn't right to keep Joyce ignorant of the truth, which they had known for a long while, and that it compromised their friendship with her and Mick. Leonard had confided in Les, and it was he who had the unpleasant, and at that time necessary, task of acting as a witness to Leonard's and Elizabeth's adultery by staying at a hotel with them (not, presumably, in the same room).

'It does explain your father's dilemma. He was torn. And he always loved you, I know he did. It wasn't just Elizabeth, although I have no doubt he was deeply attracted to her. He had another child to think of, too.'

*Why are you so bloody charitable?*, I thought, but didn't voice it.

'We'll talk about it all again later, Sue. You'll want to think things through.'

*The bastard*, I thought, of Leonard. Then, *That bitch*, of Elizabeth. It was somehow easier to think in crude swear words than try to untangle all the adults' motivations, and my own feelings were so confused as to be beyond anything more subtle than expletives.

I wasn't able to take in all this information in one sitting, and spent the next few days going back over it, asking my mother more questions, mulling it over and talking to Gordon about it. But right now, on the beach at Budleigh, Mick and Gordon were making their way back towards us. Joyce and I had been sitting down too long, and I shivered.

As we trudged back to the car, I looked out over the angry grey sea and thought about my sister. Almost a twin sister — quite different from the other children Leonard had fathered. What was she like? If the photo of 'Susan' on Laura's bureau was in fact of Sally, she looked like me, but would the similarities begin and end with appearances? Would we share tastes in things like books and films? Fancy the same kind of men? Suit the same style of clothes? Care about these things? She had other siblings; *we* had other siblings. There were at least two, because of the photo of the three children on the beach that Laura had shown me, and hastily put away when I'd said I was an only child. Joyce didn't know their names and ages, but Laura would. All I knew now was that on the other side of the world, in Australia, I had a half-sister of my own age, and some younger siblings. I imagined them spending Christmas together. It must be hot in Perth; perhaps they had barbecues at the beach, and while we crunched over the pebbles and leaned into the stinging, salt-laden wind, they were running in and out of the surf, with the sun on their skin.

When I next saw Laura, just a week or two after this Boxing Day walk, she told me that I had a half-brother called Richard, who was born just after my seventh birthday, when I was still living in France, and a half-sister called Ruth, born in 1955. They'd be fourteen and twelve now. Sally was now twenty-one, like me, but she now preferred to be called by her proper name, Sarah. Laura also told me how she and my grandfather received the news of Richard's birth. The family (as they thought, Joyce, Leonard and me, Susan) was living in Scotland. The wording on Leonard's brief letter to his family was ambiguous. A boy had been safely delivered, a brother for 'S'. Mother and baby were doing well. Naturally they assumed S was Susan, and the mother Joyce.

The burning anger I felt at the way Leonard and Elizabeth had behaved towards my mother (and me — all those promises!) was tempered by an intense curiosity about my half-siblings, particularly Sarah. But the chances of actually meeting them face-to-face were remote, as remote as our physical separation on either side of the world. And even if I were to write and introduce myself to Sarah, it was more than likely that she would never get to read my letter. If I had only just learned about Sarah, it was most unlikely that her parents would have told her about me, and any letter in my handwriting would undoubtedly have been removed from the letterbox before Sarah got her hands on it.

Two years passed — I finished my teacher's training course, and Gordon graduated, and then I became pregnant. I was working as a teacher in a boys' public school, and when German measles hit one of the classes I was teaching, I rang my mother who said, no, I'd never had it as far as she was aware, so I left the school immediately. My next job was as a clerical assistant working in the organic geochemistry unit at the university, where the scientists were analysing moon dust brought back by Neil Armstrong and Buzz Aldrin on Apollo 11. Of course, I'd watched the landing on the moon, and like everyone who saw it on television been astounded at the sight of a helmeted figure bouncing over the surface of that white sphere up in the sky. On clear nights, when I felt the baby moving inside me I'd look up at the moon, remembering how, when I was at St Catherine's, I would think of my father as I gazed at it floating above the yew trees, and I wondered if for my baby's generation the moon would lose its mystery, now that scientists had seen and touched dust from its surface, now that bits of that shining disc were held in a locked room in the prosaic basement of the university chemistry block.

It was a long labour, and when our daughter Rebecca was born she was unable to breathe and was whipped off to intensive care in the children's hospital, several miles away, where she stayed while investigations went on. I didn't believe in divine intervention and yet I prayed to all the gods I could think of, even saying yes to the nurse who asked if the 'worst' was to happen, would I like my baby baptised. I didn't want her hanging around in limbo or wherever the innocent souls go. All that Catholic and Brethren teaching had left me with deep anxieties and no certainties.

In 1970, when Rebecca was born, mothers stayed in hospital for ten days after the birth; and in my case, as my husband was a junior doctor, I had the dubious privilege of a room of my own. My baby was miles away and being tube-fed, so at four-hourly intervals, when other mothers fed their babies, an orderly wheeled into my room a breast pump covered in yellow gingham. I plugged myself into it — it was no substitute for a baby. In the room next to me, separated by only a thin partition, was a young girl who was having her baby adopted. I never saw her, but heard her crying and talking to her baby, and her parents arguing the case for adoption with her. After ten days in the special-care baby unit, my baby was returned to me and I returned the breast pump to the ward orderly. I went home with my baby to our flat in Clifton. Gordon remarked that he didn't know how on earth my father had managed to go through the whole birth thing twice in just five weeks.

I was besotted with my baby, and a friend took some beautiful photos of her. I sent one to Leonard. A present came from Australia for the baby, along with a gushing letter from Elizabeth. Daddy thought the baby was beautiful, and was very proud to be a grandfather. I was so pleased to learn that he felt this way, although it would have been nice if he'd written to me himself. Mick was charmed by Rebecca, but that wasn't the same thing to me as having her 'real' grandfather love her.

We then moved to Manchester, and within a year I was

expecting another baby. It was much further to travel to see Joyce and Mick, and I missed my Bristol friends. During this time I had seen Laura once or twice, and soon after we moved to the north I met Harry's daughter, Margaret, who had moved with her family back to England from Australia. They, too, ended up in Manchester. Margaret had seen me once or twice when I was a baby (she is ten years older than me), and, like the rest of the family, she assumed that her Auntie Joyce, Uncle Leonard, and cousin Susan were living in Australia. She and her husband and young family lived in Canberra, and never had reason to travel as far as Perth. In any case, she had never really known her father's brother, and as no effort was made on his side, she had no motivation to communicate with him. When her father, Harry, told her what he had discovered, his meeting 'the wrong wife' on his arrival in Perth, she was as keen as Laura to find out what had really happened. As soon as she came back to the UK, she got in touch and we met.

Elizabeth wrote to Laura regularly now. Laura didn't tell me everything that Elizabeth wrote, and as far as I'm aware she never confronted Elizabeth about photographs of Sarah having my name on the back, or letters arriving from Joyce and me from Scotland and Australia when we were living in France or England. Nor, I believe, did Laura confront Leonard over it. It might be that now they were communicating again after such a long time, any accusations of deception could throw him back into silence. The deception had happened with all its consequences, and so what might be gained from going over it all again? And yet whenever I saw Laura, she seemed unable to forget what she viewed as her younger brother's perfidy.

Elizabeth wrote to Laura to say that Sarah and her husband Brian were moving to England, to Cambridge. Laura invited them to visit her for the weekend, and, as it happened, Gordon and I were in London for the same weekend, visiting his parents. We had arranged to go and pick up a chair that had belonged to my grandparents from Laura and Stan, and so it seemed that Sarah and I met by chance, but Gordon thought not — he thought Laura had manipulated the encounter.

Sarah had been told about me just before she came to England, and as I learned much later, had been shattered not only to learn that her parents were not married when she was born, but that her father had been married to someone else and they had a child her own age. She has told me that it wasn't only these facts that she found so difficult to come to terms with, but the extent to which things were hidden and all the deceptions that were required to keep them hidden. By this time I was well over the shock that I'd felt on the beach at Budleigh Salterton, and longed to meet my half-sister, this person with whom I shared so much.

When I first saw Sarah at Laura's, I'd sought my father in her face, but it wasn't there. Not my memory of him, anyway. What I did see in her was myself, or a version of myself. The photograph on Laura's bureau hadn't lied. It could have been of me. But Sarah was slimmer, her fingers longer, her hair somehow straighter. Her face wasn't like mine at all, but her gestures, the way she held her head, her way of walking, things that I wouldn't have thought to look for, let alone see, were oddly familiar. It was like catching a glimpse of yourself in a shop window — you know it's you because you recognise something that is essentially of yourself. Gordon found the similarities unnerving. And yet it was just what Laura had said to me when I first met her — that what reminded her so strongly of Leonard was the way I held my head and used my hands.

During our brief visit to Laura, we invited Sarah and Brian to come and stay with us for a weekend. The fact that Margaret and I lived so close to one another (within walking distance) meant that we could share entertaining my half-sister and her husband: they would stay with us, but we'd have a meal together at Margaret's on the Saturday evening. My impatience to get to know Sarah didn't stop me feeling increasingly nervous as the date for their visit approached. Suppose she didn't like me? Or my home, or my beautiful child, or my husband? I cleaned and polished, tidied away toys, planned the weekend menu. Margaret rang to tell me that apparently Brian was particular about what he ate. He liked only plain food. My menu was thrown in the bin. I was hopeless at plain food — steak and kidney pie? Apple crumble and cream? I liked French and Italian and Indian food. *A roast*, I thought — *nobody would consider a roast elaborate or fussy or foreign*. As it turned out, my food was all right, and I shouldn't have spent so much time worrying about it.

Sarah and Brian arrived at our house — I suppose they must have come by train, but I don't recall meeting them at the station. What I do remember is how I couldn't stop looking at her, checking out my previous impressions of sisterly similarities. We were in the sitting room, and I was thinking about what Laura had said about my father and how like him I was, how my hands were so like his. I looked down at my hands and then across the room to where Sarah sat on a dark-blue sofa, her hands folded in her lap. There was so much I was desperate to discover, but now, faced with the reality of my half-sister right in front of me, I didn't know how to begin. We talked about our jobs — she, like Leonard, was a librarian. I, like Joyce, was a teacher, and then we moved on to our husbands' careers. Gordon was a doctor and her husband, Brian, was a student at Cambridge. At this stage they were childless, so there could be no exchange of pregnancy or baby anecdotes. Also, since becoming a mother myself, my horizons had shifted, my brain seemed to have dulled, and my preoccupations were focussed on domestic minutiae: I rarely finished a book, and my only intellectual activity was to do the *Guardian* crossword every day with a friend from over the road.

I wonder if Sarah felt equally inadequate to deal with this odd situation. I felt I couldn't tackle the Susan/Sarah identity question straight away. To ask her if she had opened presents sent to Susan was too crass a question. And I didn't know how to refer to Leonard — if I said 'our father' it sounded as if I were invoking God. In my head he was still 'Daddy', but that sounded even worse. Also, what could I ask her about him that wouldn't sound intrusive, or as if I were complaining that she had taken my place in his life?

And yet I longed to know what kind of father he was, whether he had taken any greater interest in her than he ever did in me; what sort of holidays they'd been on together, whether he'd helped her with her homework, whether they could talk things over, discuss politics or books, friends and films. What were his politics? At one stage he had flirted with joining the Communist Party; he had been a conscientious objector during the war and lived in a pacifist commune; he and Joyce had gone on anti-fascist marches in the East End. I knew all that because my mother had told me about it. I had always felt pleased to have parents who were radical and unconventional — I romanticised the notion of living in a commune; I went on marches protesting against nuclear weapons; I demonstrated outside the American embassy in Grosvenor Square in London against the Vietnam War. I, too, was a pacifist. Mick had medals from fighting in the war; he had taken part and been injured in the Normandy landings, but I didn't admire him like I did my father. I had idealised the one to the detriment of the other, not recognising the complexity of the issues. Sarah would be able to answer some of my questions, both about my father's politics as well as what he was like as a father. But on that first occasion of our meeting, I found I just couldn't ask.

Our weekend together was in October, and by this time Rebecca was eighteen months old and I was expecting another baby. On the Saturday morning, we went for a walk with Rebecca in her pushchair to a nearby park. I find it easier to talk with someone when I'm doing something else at the same time, like walking or cooking or driving a car. It was during this walk to the park that the question of toys came up. One of Becca's favourite possessions was a toy cooker Gordon had made for her that was a replica of the one in our kitchen. Despite current feminist arguments (hotly discussed in the early 1970s) about sexual stereotyping being reinforced by the toys we gave our children, there was no doubt that my daughter just wasn't interested in cars; she liked tea sets and baby dolls.

She had a special doll she called Demma that went everywhere with her, rather like my doll Jill, and a teddy, the bear bought for me by my grandmother after I lost Old Ted in France. He sat safely in her cot all day. Many of the toys I'd had as a small child in Birmingham had been put with our furniture into store until Joyce and I moved to our house in Exeter six years later, by which time I had outgrown most of them. Now, though, they were played with again, by Rebecca. I had been particularly fond of two little dolls: one was a small, black, bean dolly (a 'mammie' doll), the other made from soft cotton rope, rather like a corn dolly, with plaited legs and arms and an embroidered face. Leonard had brought them back for me from America when I was three. I described the dolls to Sarah.

I've got the same ones, Sarah said, a black boy doll and the rope doll. A boy doll? No, mine was a girl doll, in a patterned dress and a pinny. It wasn't just the dolls that came from

America. There were clothes, too. I asked Sarah if she'd been given a dress with a white sailor collar. She had been given a dress, but hers was in checked red-and-white material with a bodice that laced up the front. And patent-leather shoes with ankle straps? No, she hadn't been given any shoes. My dress was the one kept at Grandma's in a box at the top of her wardrobe, along with the shoes, waiting for me to grow into them. I had understood that both the dress and the shoes were a gift from my father, but as Sarah didn't have the shoes, I think they must have been a gift from someone else. Leonard never saw me in my new dress because I was over five before I wore it, and he had long since disappeared from my life. I wondered if he thought of me when he saw his other little girl dressed in her American frock. Of course, I didn't voice this thought. I merely asked if she'd had to wait to grow into it, and she had.

I was childishly hurt by these revelations. I'd always thought that my father had chosen things specially for me, not for me *and* someone else — the other me, the other 'S'. Sarah probably felt as I did, but neither of us said so.

And then there was the parcel of clothes that Leonard had sent me when I was living in France. Was Sarah given a corduroy windcheater and a yellow jumper? No, but she remembered these clothes — and the trews — because she had tried them on. She and her mother had gone to a shop and she tried on the clothes, which were paid for and taken home. But then her mother told her the clothes weren't for her but for 'another little girl', and they were packed up and sent away. She also remembered buying chocolate that was sent to 'another little girl', and that it wasn't the sort of chocolate she liked, so she didn't mind so much. I thought about the tuck parcels of chocolate and Edinburgh rock sent to St Catherine's, and how exciting it was to tear off the paper and see what was inside, the sense of power it gave me when I could choose who would be given a piece of a Five Boys chocolate bar or a stick of rock, and how once, when such a parcel came when I was ill and in the 'san', I hid the sweets in my bed and the chocolate melted. Surely Sarah must have wondered who this other little girl was who was bought treats by her mother. I assume that after Elizabeth had bought the chocolate or the clothes, she packed them up and Leonard wrote the address on the parcel and the notes that accompanied these gifts, as Joyce had written in her diary on 10 December 1952: *Parcel from Leonard of winter outfit for Susan.*

On the Saturday afternoon we went for a walk in the Peak District. As we climbed a hill that rose above Kinder reservoir, we resumed our conversation about the past. I recalled that Leonard used to send me money for my birthday every year, but that although I wrote to him, he never answered. I also told her what Joyce had told me: that she and her mother had stayed in our house when we were both tiny babies, but my mother didn't know at that time that Sarah was Leonard's child. Sarah told me later that at the time of this conversation she could make no sense of this information so did not ask any questions.

That evening, we went over to see our cousin Margaret and her husband for dinner. I had always wanted a family around me, and to have a newly discovered cousin (and her husband and three daughters) and a sister, and to be doing normal family things like sharing a meal was a treat. I hadn't seen any of my mother's family for years.

Both Sarah and I had a great deal to think about. After she and Brian had gone back to Cambridge, I wondered how she had felt about the weekend, and mused over the duplication of presents. Did we, for example, each have a copy of Walter de la Mare's *Peacock Pie*, inscribed to Susan/Sally (delete as appropriate) Christmas 1953? (Mine sent by post from

Scotland). How did our father feel when he wrapped the gifts, wrote the cards? How had he felt, the man with his two women and two babies? I couldn't imagine, so pushed the thought away. I was looking forward to the birth of my second child in just a few months. Lucy was born in February 1972.

I celebrated my twenty-seventh birthday in June 1973, and three days later received a letter from Leonard. Not a birthday card — he'd long since stopped sending me those, and I believe that in any case it was Elizabeth who had organised the delivery of his paternal obligations for him. I had heard, via my cousin Margaret, that my father was in England, and staying not far away from us, over in Sheffield, at the university. I wondered whether I should drive over there with the children and say, *Hi, it's me.* But I decided against that. After the reluctance he'd shown to meet me ever since I was four, to just turn up would risk having the door slammed in my face. And there were practical problems — I was doing a job-share at this point, and although theoretically I had two-and-a-half days free a week, the job-share also involved a child-share arrangement. So, when I wasn't working I was looking after my colleague's child as well as my own. Even if I managed to sort out the child-care and the use of the car, I could end up having lost any chance of seeing him again. And so I wrote to the address Margaret gave me and asked, yet again, if either he might like to come over to visit us, or if that wasn't practicable, I might travel over to Sheffield to see him. For weeks now I had been waiting for the post with as much urgency as if I were in love with a man playing hard to get. He had to write. He couldn't ignore me this time.

At last he responded. But it wasn't the response I was hoping for. He had just returned from Europe, and had to have an operation on his foot (he suffered from appalling arthritis), and as soon as he was fit enough to travel he would return to Australia.

> I do not think it would be a good idea for you to try to visit me here. For one thing I may be gone. I want to get away as soon as possible. For another I am in a rather depressed state at the moment and have to adjust to an unpleasant medium term prospect and an uncertain long term prognosis. With luck things will not be too bad but some period of reaction is inevitable.
>
> I am anxious that you and your children should have every possible happiness. Whether our meeting would add to that happiness I do not know. I have just learned what breaking old physical scars can mean. Emotional scars may perhaps contain just as much a threat if disturbed. In any case circumstances have taken the decision out of our hands.
>
> I do hope you will all be as happy as it is possible to be in a rather imperfect world.
>
> With very much real, if distant, love,
> Daddy

I felt powerless and cross with myself. At twenty-seven I was no more able to deal with his rejection than I had been at seven. *When you're old enough*, he used to write. Would I ever be old enough? Or would he?

Dear Susan,

I am sorry to have been long in answering your letter. I had just returned from Europe when I received it and almost at once I was rushed into hospital with an infected bone of the foot. As you probably know bone infections are not easy to treat - do not always respond to treatment and the last three weeks have not been pleasant. I am seeing the surgeon again as soon as can be arranged — I came out of hospital on Sunday — and if he approves I shall be returning to Australia almost at once. It will be necessary to have further surgery in Australia but whether immediately or after some delay to make sure the original infection is quiescent I do not yet know

It is quite impossible for me to get to Salford. I do not think it would be a good idea for you to try to visit me here. For one thing I may be gone. I want to get away as soon as possible. For another I am in a rather depressed state at the moment and have to adjust to an unpleasant medium term prospect and an uncertain long term prognosis. With luck things will not be too bad but some period of reaction is inevitable.

I am anxious that you and your children should have every possible happiness. Whether our meeting would add to that happiness I do not know. I have just learned what breaking old physical scars can mean. Emotional scars may perhaps contain just as much a threat if disturbed. In any case circumstances have taken the decision out of our hands

I do hope you will all be as happy as it is possible to be in a rather imperfect world. With very much real of distant love

Daddy.

Do not imagine that I am in any danger of departing this life! All that threatens is moderately prolonged hospitalisation. Most unpleasant but not fatal and worse things happen to many

*Letter from Leonard to Susan, 5 June 1973*

# CHAPTER 7

For the six years we lived in Manchester, I never felt quite at home. Whenever we returned from a weekend away, whether to a city or the countryside, my heart would sink as we turned off the main road, down a road of bungalows and into the small estate where we lived. Although we had made some good friends and day-to-day life for me was fine, I felt as if I were treading water, waiting for real life to begin again. We had parties, did lots of things with the children, but, like so many women, I suffered from the malaise that fuelled the women's movement: I was bored by suburban life; my role as mother and housewife lacked status, particularly in comparison with Gordon, who was making his way in hospital medicine, acquiring further qualifications, doing research, and working all hours. I joined The Housewives' Register and we invited speakers and discussed books. One of our members was an American academic who opened my eyes to what was happening, out there, in the world where things happened. A book she introduced us to was Marilyn French's *The Women's Room*. It made so much sense to me.

I shared child care with a group of neighbours (all women, of course): each mother would have all the kids from the Close at their own house for one morning a week, which gave us three mornings a week child-free. When Lucy was one I went back to work, initially doing a job-and-child share with a neighbour. It worked well, but I didn't like my job very much (teaching English in a secondary modern school for boys). The one highlight of my time there, for the boys anyway, was when I asked Ozzy Osbourne, who was a friend of a friend, to come and talk to my class. My popularity rating soared, briefly.

One dull Sunday afternoon when Gordon happened to be at home (as a junior doctor, he worked a regular week plus alternate nights and weekends, and so his being at home was a luxury), we had been for a walk in the park, had eaten our lunch, and were enjoying our indolence. The sitting-room floor was littered with the Sunday paper and toys, clothes were drying on the fireguard, our dirty dishes were still on the table, and dregs of wine lay in our glasses (a Sunday treat). The doorbell rang. You go, I said. Gordon was deep into the Sunday supplements, and I was sitting with Lucy on my lap with a story book. Rebecca, now almost five years old, ran to the door, no doubt eager for something more interesting to happen. Gordon reluctantly followed her. Then I heard my mother's voice. But was it her? She was asking if Susan lived here. I leapt to my feet.

The voice belonged to my mother's sister, Gladys, my Exclusive Brethren aunt. She and her husband, my Uncle Jack, stood at the door, Jack holding her arm. She wore a long grey coat, and her hair, now fading to a mousy shade of grey, was tied back in a knot. She was unmistakably Brethren-like in both her clothing and her demeanour. Just seeing her there took me back years to visits to Deal, then later to their house in Halifax for Christmas holidays. It was like a time warp. I had changed so much and she so little, apart from the dulling of her hair.

'We've left,' she said. 'We've left the Jims.'

I stared in amazement. Did she mean she'd left the Brethren? After all this time? Who were the Jims anyway?

'It's lovely to see you,' I said. 'Come in.' I kissed her awkwardly. I made a stab at clearing up the mess while Gordon went off to the kitchen to make a pot of tea. But Gladys wasn't here to admire my housewifely skills, or be shocked by the lack of them. We talked and talked as the winter afternoon turned to night, Gordon taking over giving the children tea and putting them to bed. I fired questions at them, excited to have them back in my life, but feeling all the same like an inquisitor. The only news I had had of my Brethren relations in the previous fourteen years was that first of all Auntie Millie had died, and then Grandma. However, the lack of communication from them hadn't stopped me writing to them. I'd invited them to our wedding, I'd sent them cards whenever I moved flat or house, and I'd written to tell them about both babies. No replies, no congratulations on the life milestones passed. But I was used to that — my cousin John hadn't replied to my letters, and often enough my father hadn't either.

Their story came out gradually. The Jims were the group of Exclusive Brethren who followed the teachings of James Taylor Junior. Gladys and Jack had left only a couple of weeks before. Their younger son, James, was 'a bit of a rebel' — like his Auntie Joyce, my mother (and who wouldn't be, I thought, with all the restrictions that were placed on their lives). His rebelliousness was manifested in his attending school discos and having friends from school. One of the Brethren reported that he had been seen smoking in town with other kids, and he missed meetings. At that time you had to attend daily and several times on Sundays. Such innocuous actions! But in the eyes of the Brethren elders and their spying acolytes, this was wicked, sinful behaviour: James was associating with worldlies; through his sinful actions he would contaminate the family, indeed, the entire community with his wickedness. The family was 'shut up', which meant that they were banned from attending meetings and thus excluded from the love and protection of the fellowship. For weeks the elders came to talk to James, to try to get him to confess and show remorse, but he wouldn't. He couldn't see anything wrong, and anyway, he hadn't been out smoking with the lads. They were making it all up. His elder brother and parents were not allowed to attend meetings. James had to eat separately from the rest of the family. My aunt and uncle, too, were visited, cajoled, and bullied (they didn't use such emotive language, but it was clear that this was what had happened), and told that their wayward son would have to move out. It was sinful to sleep under the same roof as a 'worldly'.

James, who was in his late teens, still lived at home. He moved out and into a flat with a friend of his who had left the Jims. It was possible that he would never see his brother Graham or his parents again. This is no exaggeration — this kind of thing happened to many families, who even now, forty years on, have still had no contact with the members of their family who remained within the sect. Gladys and Jack were disconsolate, and James's brother furious with the religious men who controlled their lives. Graham had become more and more fed up with the increasingly ridiculous rules that were imposed by the leadership: rules that governed not only what one should believe in terms of doctrine, but ranged from an emphasis on the tiniest details of everyday life to fundamental issues that would affect the lives of the entire community. There were rules about what one might wear and what was forbidden: for example, long hair had always been worn by women, and was usually tied back, but suddenly it had to be worn loose, and at the same time men were forbidden to wear ties; and what to drink — oddly you had to have whisky in the house. You couldn't join any kind of club or association (trades unions were out, for example);

then pets were banned, and so on. Life became a minefield. Large families were encouraged. I discovered that two of my cousins had five or more children each — and they went on to have more; women were no longer to go out to work, children were not to enter higher education. Each new directive was 'backed up' by biblical texts taken out of context and manipulated to suit the ends of the leadership.

Graham presented his parents with an ultimatum: if they didn't give up this nonsense he would leave, too. After agonising for days, they came to their decision. Jack told how he'd gone to the factory gates and when James came out, he went up to him and said, come home lad, please come home, we've made a big mistake. We're leaving the Jims.

I can only imagine the emotions that they felt, but hearing the story brought tears to my eyes. I had last seen James when he was about two years old and I joined them for a holiday in a caravan at Lytham St Annes, a holiday spent shrimping and building sandcastles from the muddy sand and playing French cricket. I was very happy looking after the little boys, bossing them about. Life had seemed so innocent then.

For my aunt and uncle, the ramifications of taking the decision to leave were huge. They would lose their religious and social milieus in one day: the doors of the Meeting Room would be closed to them; they would be shunned in the street; people they had considered their closest friends and allies would turn their backs. There would be no more mutual help at times of crisis. The relatives who stayed with the Jims would have nothing further to do with them. Ever.

I didn't understand all this immediately, and they didn't try to explain it. The main thing was that they were now free to associate with us. As they lived just across the Pennines from me, one of the first things Gladys wanted to do was to come and see me and meet my husband and children. I would see my two Yorkshire cousins again and, most importantly, Gladys would be able to contact Joyce.

I phoned my mother that night to tell her this news. Although ten years before she had insisted to me that they would come to their senses in the end, by this time she had given up all hope of seeing her sister again. We agreed how sad it was that it had taken something so painful for them to see the wrongness of the Exclusive Brethren position. Once again, a long and unnecessary silence was broken. Joyce and Mick met regularly with Gladys and Jack, and although they were still involved in the Brethren, this was with a more open and tolerant group. Even if the members of this new group had any objection to them consorting with worldlies, no argument or biblical quote would have kept Gladys from trying to make up for the years of silence and rejection.

In 1977 Joyce was sixty-four years old and still working full-time, but thinking about retirement. We had moved from Manchester back to Bristol, and the children were now five and seven years old — they were at school, and I worked part-time as a secretary, and had set up a darkroom in our basement and had begun to get some work as a photographer. The centre of Bristol was much more to my taste than suburban Manchester. The children were able to spend holidays with their grandparents in Exeter, and everything seemed to be going well. Sarah and I had continued to write to each other, and there was the occasional telephone call. I told her about how I had hoped to see Leonard when he was in Sheffield, but at that point we hadn't met again as we were both busy and lived on opposite sides of the country. I was pleased to know that I had a half-sister, but all that stuff from the past seemed to matter less and less, and I didn't feel the need to dig any further. And then something happened that upset my equilibrium: a phone call from Mick to say that my mother was very ill, in hospital.

She lay on a hospital bed, her face ashen but for a spreading purple bruise on her cheek. Her hair, grey and wispy, stuck out untidily; her hands, swollen with arthritis, lay motionless on the white cellular blanket; a drip was attached to her arm, and its tube snaked across the pillow to a plastic bag suspended above the metal frame of the bed; another tube slid from under the blanket to a second plastic bag suspended under the bed, filling with urine. Her eyes were closed. She looked naked without her glasses. Her face, normally so animated, was flat and expressionless, and her shape under the blanket only a faint outline. Mick and I sat on either side of the bed, not looking at one another, both of us concentrating on the inert presence between us, willing her to show signs of life. She wasn't dead, but was deeply unconscious, in a coma. She had had a bad cold, he told me, and was sleeping in my old bedroom so as not to disturb him with her snuffling and coughing. But he had been disturbed, in the early hours of that morning. It was still dark, just before dawn. She must have switched on the landing light, he thought, which had woken him, and then he heard a loud crash.

He'd come upon Joyce lying at the bottom of the steep narrow staircase of the cottage, squashed behind the door that separated the stairs from the dining room. And now she lay straightened out under the hospital blanket. The doctors didn't know if she had fainted before falling, or had tripped and fallen and then lost consciousness. Nothing was broken. They were doing tests. In the meantime, there wasn't anything else to do but wait. When we talked, it was of practicalities: who would be picking the girls up from school, what he and I should eat for supper, what arrangements I had made about work. Neither the past nor the future was mentioned. We hovered in an uncertain present.

The next day Joyce had made progress. She was now semi-conscious. Tests showed that she was probably suffering from encephalitis. Once again Mick and I sat at her bedside. Her eyelids flickered, and her eyes opened. We each bent over her, but she didn't seem to notice us. She was somewhere else. She began to talk, and to begin with it was difficult to discern her words, but then they became clearer. Too clear. I wished she'd just be quiet again, because what she was saying, the substance of her spoken thoughts, centred not on the faithful and loving husband at her bedside, but on her earlier love, Leonard. She was back in the flat where they had lived in Birmingham before either Sally or I was born: she gestured towards the light coming in through the high window of the side-ward, but what she could see was sunlight streaming through the tall windows of the flat, warming her face; then she was apparently out walking in the hills with Leonard; there are drifts of bluebells, she murmured. Look at the bluebells, Leonard, blue drifts under the trees.

I hardly dared look at Mick. I didn't want to imagine how he was feeling. He'd no doubt find a rational explanation — the deeper layers of memory rising to the surface, perhaps. It's possible that he was sufficiently sure of her feelings for him not to be hurt by the sweet smile on her face when she recalled the man who had abandoned her and her child. It's likely that he was so glad that she was 'on the mend' that he was able to ignore the ramblings of a sick woman.

Mick and I didn't talk about it. We concentrated on her improvement. Soon she was out of hospital and back at work, but she had changed: she became more reliant on Mick, less confident of her abilities as a teacher. She decided to retire from full-time work, but would continue with her evening classes.

# CHAPTER 8

As soon as he could, in 1980, Mick also retired, and he and Joyce were able to spend time doing the things they enjoyed: Joyce took her painting more seriously, going on courses and exhibiting in local exhibitions, and they both liked going away with friends for 'leisure learning weekends'. Mick 'played' seriously with his investments — an area of his life that Joyce and I didn't begin to understand, but in which he was very successful. Laura and her husband, Stanley, also retired and moved from London to Devon, as did a very old friend of Joyce and Leonard's, Lesley Lam.

*Joyce and Mick at The Cottage, 1980s*

Lesley and her husband, Basil, both professional musicians, had first met Leonard and through him Joyce, when he joined the Quaker commune where they were also living, during the war. They were childless. I had spent very happy times at the Lams', who at one time lived in a vast, rambling house with an airy music room. Lesley played the piano and the viola, Basil the harpsichord. I liked its high tinkling sound, and when people came to the house to play, I'd sit at the back of the music room and watch and listen, entranced by the sound they made together.

*Lesley and Basil Lam, 1948*

They also had a horse called Mark and a dog called Wog (and were unaware, I'm sure, of any hint of political incorrectness in his naming). Above Mark's stable was Basil's workshop where he made harpsichords and built me a wonderful farm, complete with harpsichord string fences, cow sheds, and green-painted spongy trees. The smell of wood and glue and his pipe (did all men smoke pipes at that time?) was deeply comforting. He made me a swing and hung it from a chestnut tree in the garden, and I could swing so high I felt I was flying. Basil liked speed and adventure. He drove motorbikes and fast cars, and nothing matched the thrill of speeding down Devon lanes when they came to stay with us, and then up onto the moors.

By the time I was married, Basil had sped off with a much younger woman than Lesley, a music student. Lesley moved from London to Devon and gave up her music to work as a caretaker in a village school. After a year or two she began to travel around the world, finding work in order to fund the next stage of her journey. She travelled through Sudan while civil war raged around her, and brought me back a shell from the Indian Ocean, postcards from Egypt, and beads from Cyprus.

The old people — Joyce, Mick, Lesley, when she returned from her travels, Laura and Stan — met regularly for pub lunches and walks across the moors. Later they abandoned the walks, but visited historic houses, and still kept up the pub lunches and endless talk — about books and films and politics, plus gossip, reminiscences of the past. Much later I discovered that Leonard had found Stanley insufferable, but I liked him, and he and Mick got on well. Unlike the conscientious objector Leonard, Stan had fought in the war (in the air force; he was 'mentioned in dispatches') and for Mick, too, the war had been an enormously important experience. I saw them all regularly, and the children continued to have holidays with Joyce and Mick. For the time being, things went well. Joyce wasn't quite the person she had been, and I sensed our roles had shifted: I felt the need to look after her, to keep things from her in order not to upset her (or Mick). Or that was my justification for keeping quiet, particularly when it came to the subject of my father. Ironically, I failed to appreciate that this was precisely her treatment of me in this same regard — an approach I had resented as patronising. By now the past felt very distant to me, and I ignored it. Since her semi-conscious ramblings in the hospital, my mother had hardly ever mentioned Leonard. I continued to receive letters from Elizabeth (but none from Leonard, although she always said he sent his love — I now wonder if that were true; I think Elizabeth protected him from me, and avoided talking to him about me). Hers were mainly rather banal letters that told me how happy I was and what a wonderful husband I had, and what lovely children. They used to annoy me: she knew nothing about Gordon or the girls. And, of course, I could have just stopped writing, but, for reasons I still don't understand, I persisted in writing to Australia, addressing the letters to Leonard as well as to Elizabeth. And my letters were equally tedious — merely chatty accounts about my work, the children, and holidays. Like most parents of teenagers, there were occasional problems, but nothing as difficult as some of my friends had to deal with. Like most marriages, ours had had its seesaw moments, but we were still together. I had a job that I loved — as an exhibition organiser, I had good friends, and had become interested in photography, both as a curator and as a practitioner.

It was my thirty-ninth birthday and Laura had, as was her habit, sent me a book token. I'd planned to have a drink with my friends after work, and, as Gordon was on call at the hospital, we'd save going out to celebrate until the weekend. During my lunch break I wandered off to the nearby bookshop to spend my book token; I'd spend the evening curled up on the sofa with a new book and a glass of wine. I skimmed the fiction shelves, waiting to see what might jump out at me. Henry James? Possibly, but a bit too much like work. Ruth Prawer Jhabvala? I liked her books. Then a name did jump out at me. Elizabeth Jolley. Could it be *my* Elizabeth Jolley? Elizabeth was a prolific writer of letters, but of novels, too? Of novels published by Penguin and on the shelves of a Bristol bookshop? Intrigued, I pulled out the book and turned to the back. The photograph of the author looked just like Sarah. Sarah hadn't at any point mentioned that her mother was a writer.

I turned to the biographical notes to check that it really was Elizabeth. *In 1959 she moved to Australia with her husband and three children.* Reading those bland, matter-of-fact words had the most bizarre effect on me. I felt physically sick, as if I'd been kicked in the stomach, and yet while my body was experiencing such a strong reaction, my mind was saying, this is a ridiculous, irrational way to respond. Of course, the notes on the back of the book were correct: that's what she had done, moved to Australia with her husband and three children. But I felt invisible, my existence denied. It took a huge effort of will to pull myself together, literally to steady myself and walk to the till clutching the book. I walked back down Park Street as if I were sleepwalking, but by the time I was back in the office, I felt okay. After work I had a birthday drink with my friends and then drove home to make tea and make sure the girls did their homework before bed. I behaved as if nothing out of the ordinary had happened, and anyone with any sense would insist that nothing out of the ordinary had.

However, it didn't feel like that. Once the girls were in bed, I collapsed again, and such misery as I hadn't experienced in years overwhelmed me. There was no one I could talk to about it. Gordon was at work (and would probably say I was overreacting); I couldn't go crying to my mum; friends would have thought I had flipped. So, instead, I wrote a letter to Leonard and let him know a whole lot of things that had been tucked away safely in a dark corner of my mind for years and years. I let it out, my angry words cascading over an airmail letter. Why the secrecy, why had he ignored me so consistently, so determinedly? And rather than screw the letter into a ball and toss it into the wastepaper basket, I carefully addressed it, and before I had time to change my mind, nipped out and up to the postbox.

I then began the book. Elizabeth wrote well, her prose was spare, and her dry, quirky sense of humour appealed to me — so different from the letters she had been writing to me for the last twenty years. I don't remember which of her books it was; since then I have read most of them as they were published in the UK, but I do remember that I felt oddly displaced by one of the characters having my middle name — Miriam. In later books I would sense that I shared something ghostly with the characters or situations she created. It was as if I were looking into a shattered mirror that reflected fragments of my mother's life and troubling glimpses of my own past, views of Birmingham I remembered but as in a dream. To me, a lot of it seemed to be a way of justifying her own and Leonard's behaviour. But this was all in the future. All that struck me as I read that first book was the use of an unusual name, my name, for a character — hardly a character at all — a scrawny baby.

As I drove to work the following morning, I began to feel foolish about my outburst, and thankful that nobody had witnessed it. I told Gordon that his stepmother-in-law was a writer and, intrigued, he read the book that I'd bought. It wasn't his kind of thing, he said, although, like me, he was amazed at the discrepancy in style between the letters to me and the fictional writing.

Naturally I didn't forget about my overwrought letter to Leonard, but weeks went by and I didn't hear from him. I reminded myself that letters took a long time to cross the world — and surely he wouldn't ignore my pleas for an explanation or an apology. It wasn't really anything to do with the biographical notes on the cover of the Penguin. It was what those words had triggered in me. At last a letter arrived — two: a scrap of paper from Leonard and a longer letter from Elizabeth. Leonard hadn't written to me since he had refused to see me more than ten years before, when he was in Sheffield and I in Manchester. I have kept both of these letters. This time he wrote:

> I am very sorry you were distressed by what I would have thought an unimportant publisher's bit of publicity. I do not care for this silly personal publicity but publishers seem to think it necessary. It was not done, I think, say forty years ago.
>
> I cannot see what good can come from going over what happened forty years ago. Indeed I do not think it right to accuse or to justify. It could only hurt. I had always thought that your life was happy and successful. Indeed I am sure it is, and trust that it will continue so.
>
> The heart must keep its own sorrows, and its joys.
>
> With much love,
>
> L

The past is indeed a most strange country and as for the future in the natural course of events there cannot be too much of it for me.

What was I to make of this? He clearly felt he had to reply, or Elizabeth had told him he should, but it didn't make me feel better, although I was glad I'd sent that letter and not ignored the hurt I'd felt. He was annoyed with me and had no intention of explaining his behaviour.

Elizabeth took a different approach. Her letter was long, and full of sympathy and understanding:

Dear Susan,

Your letter came today. I can't tell you enough how sorry I am that the biographical detail in the little novel upset you so dreadfully. It is somehow worse that it is in one of my books arriving in England. I wish that it were not so. I do hope you will be able to feel better and to go on happily in your happy life. I hope the photography will be a tremendous success and that you will enjoy the south of France [where we would be going on holiday].

I can understand that you feel hurt and critical and that you want to write your 'litany of complaints'. Please do write them. I always answer letters and have never felt that our letter writing was purely superficial.

She went on to say that she knew that I had seen Sarah, and knew that Ruth (my other half-sister) had written to me (*and longs to claim you as a sister*). Reading this made me feel dreadful — guilty for making a fuss, and unhappy that I felt our letter writing was superficial. To me, this seemed the most honest letter I had ever received from her. She continued:

I am so deeply sorry that you have been so upset. If Leonard was unable to tell his family about his divorce it is not really for us to be critical. We cannot possibly understand what it was about his upbringing that made this so difficult for him ...

It wasn't about the divorce, as they both knew — it was about the lying and the secrecy.

... I do not try to excuse our behaviour, as you say in your letter, marriages break up so why all the secrecy. It is not so simple, it is the leaving of a person and a child and it is the being with another person and a child, there is really nothing I can say except that obviously simply by my own life with your father I have hurt you and still hurt you. I wanted to protect him from a reawakening of the pain but had to read your letter to him.

She said then that perhaps it was Leonard's shyness and reserve that had stopped him speaking to his parents (in fact, his mother had died before he left Joyce) and his brother and sister about what was going on in his life.

I had to accept this although wrote to explain to Harry before he came to Australia.

At the time I just didn't believe this last sentence because of what Laura had said to me back in the autumn of 1967, when Gordon and I met her and Stanley for the first time. Laura was quite clear that Harry turned up in Perth expecting to see Joyce, not Elizabeth, who was a complete surprise to him. His daughter, Margaret, whom he went on to see immediately after his visit to Leonard and his family in Perth, also remembers his surprise. However, as his decision to go to Australia was a sudden one, taken and acted on in a matter of a week or two, and he travelled via the United States, it is probable that Elizabeth did indeed write to tell him of his brother's change of circumstance, but he didn't receive the letter until he got back to England.

Elizabeth ended her letter to me with these words:

To see a child hurt is the worst thing and this is what we have seen today in your letter. I wish for you not to feel hurt but rather for you to go forward in your own happy life.

A second letter arrived from Elizabeth the following day:

Daddy feels his letter is not adequate. We feel that we are
inadequate and we want you to know that. It is your tears
we think of so much.

Her letter was honest and heartfelt. She referred to Ibsen's
*The Wild Duck* and how the character Gregers (spelt Greggers
by Elizabeth) *a rather humourless loveless 'hunting dog'* draws
out the truth. *Perhaps the truth by itself is not enough,* she
wrote. I agreed; I knew the truth, or thought I did. It was an
explanation I was looking for.

When I next saw Laura on her own I asked her about their
childhood, trying to discover what it was about Leonard's
upbringing that might have been such a problem. Joyce
had already told me something of my father's family
background — that my grandfather, Henry, was a self-taught
man and deeply religious. Laura said, yes, that was true, but I
should understand just how ill-educated his family had been
and how driven he was. His father (my great-grandfather)
had been illiterate and had worked as a gardener in the rather
grander houses around Diss on the Norfolk–Suffolk border.
He had five children who all attended the local elementary
school in Diss, and while the youngest, Henry, left Norfolk for
London to find work and new horizons, his elder sister, Alice,
worked her way up from being a teacher's assistant to being a
teacher at the school in Diss.

Henry had been very ambitious for Laura and her brothers
and had encouraged them to study and to improve themselves,
not just by working hard at school, but at home, too, through
Bible study and wider reading. Sunday lunchtimes, for example,
would be spent discussing the issues raised in that morning's

Dear Susan,

Your letter came today. I can't tell you enough how sorry I am that the biographical detail in the little novel upset you so dreadfully. It is some how worse that it is in one of my books arriving in England. I wish that it were not so. I do hope you will be able to feel better and to go on happily in your happy life. I hope the photography will be a tremendous success and that you will enjoy the South of France.

I can understand that you feel hurt and critical and that you want to write your "litany of complaints". Please do write them. I always answer letters and I have never felt that our letter writing was purely superficial. I knew you had seen Sarah and I know that Ruth has written to you. (She longs to claim you as a sister.) I am so deeply sorry that you have been so upset. If Leonard was unable to tell his family about his divorce it is not really for us to be critical. We cannot possibly understand what it was about his upbringing that made this so difficult for him. I simply accepted that he could not speak about it. The situation as it was then all those years ago was an intolerable one and he faced the pain in the only way he could. If I seem to excuse him it is only that I love him very dearly and have loved him for a very long time. He is getting old and

*Letter from Elizabeth to Susan, 1 July 1985*

sermon. Her parents were poor, although not as poor as some of their neighbours in Bow, and had made considerable sacrifices to allow their children to continue their education. They all got grants and scholarships, but these didn't cover living expenses. As the youngest, Leonard — in Laura's view — was spoiled, particularly by their mother, who he could get to do anything for him (which is what he managed to achieve with Joyce and Elizabeth, it would seem). This, according to Laura, was partly because he was a sickly child (which might have been the first manifestations of the arthritis he suffered from later in life) and was often too sick to go to school. Not only did he spend a great deal of time reading and dreaming, he was free to wander through the park, fascinated by birds and flowers.

I asked Laura about what happened later, after he'd left home, and how her parents felt about his pacifism and socialism, and to my surprise she told me they supported him in his views. She added, significantly, given Elizabeth's take on his refusal to tell his family he was leaving Joyce, that they would have been disappointed at the break-up of the marriage, but would have understood. They would not condemn. She also said that her parents were both very fond of Joyce, and her father would have wanted to carry on seeing us.

None of this offered me an explanation of *why* he found it difficult to tell his father about his abandoning Joyce and me. Unless he was so used to being the golden boy that he couldn't bear to admit he'd failed at something.

Later that year, Harry died. He had been living in Manchester with Margaret, but he was buried next to his wife Lilian in the churchyard at Cockfosters. As Sarah and I would both be attending the funeral, we arranged to meet for lunch in London before the service. This was the first time we'd met since she and Brian had visited us in Manchester. After the service there was tea at the vicarage, and then Sarah and I left to travel back into central London together before catching our separate trains home. It was on this journey that I told Sarah about the letters from Australia supposedly written by me and Joyce — perhaps it was because we'd been in a rare family situation, or perhaps it was because it had been Harry's visit to her parents in Perth that had led to our meeting here at this time. It just seemed right that I should say something, so I did. It must have come as a shock to her, but there was no time to discuss it, and in any case all I had was Laura's word that these letters existed — I had not seen them for myself.

I didn't see Sarah again until a few years later, when I was visiting friends in East Anglia and went to see her and Brian and meet their little daughter for the first time.

Following my emotional outburst on my birthday there was one further letter from Elizabeth that referred to it, when she told me that she'd forgotten that Miriam was my second name when she chose it for the baby in her book, and that nothing personal was intended. After that the correspondence between Elizabeth and me resumed its usual sporadic nature of news exchange. I got on with my life: the children were growing up, and I was now teaching at the art college in Bristol and doing some freelance work. I hadn't given up on Leonard, and I was aware that we had what's called unfinished business or, at least, that I had. I suspect he rarely, if ever, thought about it. After all, he too had a life to get on with — and not a very pleasant one physically. He was in pain much of the time and bedridden. Laura told me that Elizabeth nursed him devotedly while simultaneously pursuing her writing and teaching career (she taught creative writing). She was rapidly gaining an international reputation.

While Elizabeth's star was ascending, Joyce's was falling. One Saturday evening in early December 1988, Mick rang. It was unusually late for either him or my mother to call, and we had friends to dinner. I was immediately anxious that something was wrong. For some weeks, whenever I had suggested we go and visit them, he'd put us off: Joyce wasn't feeling up to it. I was always very wary of laying claim to my mother, and didn't want to upset him by insisting on going down uninvited. It would imply that he wasn't looking after her properly. He was, in fact, very caring. And although I'd been concerned about her health, she'd been fairly upbeat whenever I spoke to her on the telephone. Her arthritis was worse, so she found it difficult to do her pottery and she'd had a violent allergic reaction to a bee sting back in the summer. But no, she hadn't had another fall; she was behaving peculiarly, he said. She was talking nonsense, and had begun to do the crossword, but instead of filling it in properly, she'd started writing back to front, mirror-writing. The hubbub of boozy chatter from the dining room jarred. Can I speak to her, I asked Mick. No, she was in bed now, but maybe we could come down the following morning. He suggested Gordon might have an idea of what was going on. Gordon was a gynaecologist, and I was fairly sure wouldn't have much idea about people's brains, but Mick clearly wanted some kind of medical assurance. Gordon suggested Mick ring the GP, and if he got nowhere with him, to take her directly to the hospital.

Once again, I sat by my mother's bed, in a single room close to the nurses' desk. She looked lost, her eyes darting about the room as if things had just flitted by and she'd missed them. A nurse wheeled in a tea trolley. She placed a cup of tea and a biscuit on the little over-the-bed table, and Joyce looked horrified. Come on, drink it up before it gets cold, I encouraged. There's nothing worse than a tepid cup of tea, or so you say. I tried to joke, but was utterly thrown by this change in my mother. It was worse than when she was coming out of that coma. She was like a different person — a timid, frightened, childlike person. She held her hand out towards the cup of tea. I smiled encouragement, but she immediately withdrew her hand as if she'd had an electric shock. I can't, she whispered, they won't let me. Who won't let you? Them. Where's Gordon, she said, he's the boss of this hospital, isn't he?

'No, Mum,' I said. 'You're in the hospital in Exeter. He doesn't even work here.'

We had no idea what was going on in her mind. It was as if all the normal pathways were crossed; she seemed to have changed personality. She started talking about the Americans, saying they were taking her money and her valuable paintings. She didn't have any valuable paintings. Or much money to take. And why the Americans? Nonsense, you see, Mick said.

The consultant was carrying out tests. She hadn't had a stroke, nor was there anything wrong with her heart. All in good working order.

The next day, she told me that they were making a film in her house, which was why she had to come and stay in this hospital; Elsie was at home, though, she said. Her sister Elsie had died years before. I went to Marks and Spencer, and bought her two soft pretty nightdresses and a new dressing gown. Still there was no diagnosis.

I had to go back to work, and although Rebecca was now in Australia, working as a sailing instructor in Sydney, as part of her gap year, Lucy was still at home and had just started her 'A' levels. I telephoned Rebecca. I missed her terribly and needed to speak to her, to reassure myself that she was all right. I also had to tell her that her grandma was ill. I thought if she sent a card to the hospital it would somehow help to pin Joyce down to reality as the rest of us understood it. I wanted to gather my family around me, but it was impossible.

Christmas was approaching, and we had arranged to go to Australia to see Rebecca and Gordon's brother and family, who she was living with. I had also written to Leonard and Elizabeth to say I should like to meet them. We had been to Australia several times before, once for three months when the children were still at primary school, and each time I had asked to see Leonard, and each time there was a reason why this was impossible. I wasn't going to be fobbed off with excuses this time.

My last-but-one visit to see my mother in hospital was so upsetting I was tempted to cancel all the arrangements and stay at home. I had walked into the ward with my bunch of flowers and couldn't see her straight away. Then I did: she was sitting by her bed, knickers around her ankles, a dirty off-white nylon nightdress hitched up to her waist, and a sickly pink dressing gown draped over her shoulders. What had happened to the soft, warm nightclothes I'd brought in for her? Why hadn't someone come to either help her to the loo or neaten her up? Was this the way our hospitals treated old people? She looked so vulnerable that I felt I couldn't possibly leave her here. They weren't doing anything for her — just more and more blood tests. That's what I said to the poor overworked nurse who I pounced on. She was apologetic, and said something about staff shortages, and that all the old peoples' clothes were taken to the laundry and if they didn't know which was theirs they were put in something decent.

Mick was distraught, and he sought comfort in medical terms and looked up all the information he could. A diagnosis was slowly being formed — of systemic lupus erythematosus, and the treatment would be steroids. Getting the correct dosage of the drugs she needed was a delicate and complicated matter.

My last visit was less distressing. Joyce was decently dressed and was trying to read. She could read aloud, but didn't seem to comprehend what she was reading. It will improve, we were told. She seemed to understand that Rebecca was in Australia, and said that, yes, we should go and see her. But it was with a heavy heart and strong misgivings that I boarded the plane for the long flight out. We would have a week in Bali before going on to Sydney for Christmas with Gordon's family. And this time I was determined to call in on my father, even though he was many thousands of miles away on the far side of the country. It was forty years since he had lifted me up in his arms and promised we'd see each other soon. It was time for me to take the initiative.

# CHAPTER 9

For me, the new year of 1989 began in a remote farmhouse near Wilsons Promontory in Victoria, where Gordon and I were staying with friends. We listened to the radio and toasted each new declaration of Australia's new year — first in Sydney and Melbourne, followed by Adelaide, and finally in Perth. England's new year wouldn't happen for hours yet, by which time we'd be down at the beach, lying on hot white sand and diving through surf as cold and bubbly as champagne.

Rebecca and Lucy had opted to stay in the city and party the night away with their cousin and her friends. I had spoken to Joyce on the phone just before we left Sydney, and it was a relief to hear her anxieties about our leaving Rebecca and Lucy behind in Sydney while we went down to the coast. Surely this meant she was connecting again with things that existed in external reality, the world as most of us experienced it. I reassured her that we were only away for a few days, and would return to Sydney to pick up Lucy and then travel on to Melbourne. I told her that Gordon would return to England, and Lucy and I would spend a few days in Perth, where we'd be staying with some Irish friends, Walter and Colleen. I didn't say that Lucy and I were going to go over to have lunch with my father and Elizabeth the day after we arrived in Perth, and then the following day we would go with them and my half-sister Ruth and her little boys for a day trip to Wooroloo, their place in the country.

That was the plan, anyway.

I telephoned Elizabeth from Melbourne to confirm the details. 'Daddy's not been well,' she warned me, 'I'm not sure he'll be up to it.' I cringed at the use of 'Daddy', but she had never referred to him as Leonard to me. It was always 'Daddy'.

My heart sank; this was an excuse. He'd told me to keep away from him before, when I wrote to ask if I might see him when he was in England: *I do not think it would be a good idea for you to try to visit me here.* I was twenty-seven when he wrote me that letter; now I was forty-three, and I wasn't going to be put off this time by any excuses. 'We have our tickets for Perth,' I said to Elizabeth, 'and our friends are expecting us, so I'll phone as soon as I get there. I really want to see him, even if it's only for a short visit. And Lucy is so looking forward to meeting her grandfather,' I threw in as extra emotional ammunition.

Two days later, Lucy and I were in Perth, at our friends' house. But Lucy was ill, struck down by a violent sickness: she was so sick she couldn't even keep down sips of water. 'I think I'll phone and cancel,' I said to Colleen. 'Nonsense,' she replied. 'You've come all this way. Lucy will be okay with me.' Lucy also wanted me to go, but I wasn't convinced by her show of bravery. She looked dreadful: her face was shiny with sweat, pale under the suntan, with dark circles under feverish bright eyes. 'Go on, Mum, I'll be fine. Honest.' I phoned Elizabeth to say I would be coming but Lucy wouldn't, as she was ill. I immediately regretted it: Lucy needed me. Colleen promised to phone me at the Jolleys' if she judged Lucy had got any worse.

So I stood alone in the shade of a deep verandah while exotic birds cawed high in the branches of the trees surrounding my father's house. As I hesitated before ringing at the door, not only was I wishing Lucy were with me, but I began to doubt for the first time the reasonableness of my request. What right did I have to disturb a sick old man and his elderly wife? I glanced behind me where, beyond the leafy front garden, a wide suburban street burned brightly in the midday sun. All was quiet and tidy; there were no passers-by. I wiped my hands on my skirt and took a breath. *There are things that need to be said*, I told myself, *explanations owed to me, before he dies*. I rang the doorbell.

I waited; I pushed my fingers through my hair and pressed my lips together, wondering what I looked like, wondering what he might be expecting. What connection did I have with the child he had kissed goodbye all those years ago?

No one came. Wasn't anyone in? Perhaps he was telling Elizabeth, 'Don't let her in. I won't see her.' A flush of guilt swept over me. I should have told Joyce I would be doing this. I'd been tempted when we spoke on the phone and she sounded herself again, but then I'd rationalised that it would have caused more upset than either she or Mick could deal with, so I kept quiet. Now I felt that it showed more cowardice on my part than selflessness. Hadn't Leonard used those same arguments to justify not telling his own family that he was leaving Joyce and me? I thought, *I'm more like him than I like to admit*. I was about to press the bell again when the door opened.

The face of the woman who stood before me was familiar from the covers of paperbacks: a long nose, glasses, short wispy hair, greying, and despite the Australian sun her skin was pale. She was slighter than I had imagined, though, and bird-like. She wore a long skirt and a shapeless blouse, a folksy kind of style. By this time she was a highly respected writer in Australia, and was well known in the UK and the

United States. She had won many prizes, and the previous year had won the prestigious Australian literary prize, the Miles Franklin Award. Not only was I looking at my father's wife for the first time (if you don't count the times I saw her when I was a baby), but I was looking at a literary celebrity. An article I had read about her described her as being a sweet-faced grandmother (it continued: *who writes about eroticism, pedophilia and obsession*). She was, of course, a grandmother, and she looked her age; also, her build suggested frailty. But to me she appeared sharp — watchful and wary. She smiled, and her smile was welcoming, and yet her eyes were guarded. She took my hand in hers: mine, hot and sweaty; hers, dry and cool. There was a faint scent of something familiar — Pears soap, perhaps?

'Susan. Do come in. Your father's still in bed, but I'll get him up for lunch.' Her voice was high-pitched, and there was a brisk efficiency about her — I remembered that she'd trained as a nurse. We stood in a hallway, dark after the brilliant light outside. The sound of music playing — Bach, I guessed — came from a room to my right, the door half open. Elizabeth glanced at the door. She turned towards another door, on my left, and gestured me through. 'Sit down. I'll get you a cold drink.'

I went through. I didn't sit, but stood in the centre of the room, taking it in. This was where my half–brother's and sisters' lives had been played out, where the family sat and talked, where visitors were entertained. It was nothing to do with me, and yet, strangely, I immediately felt at home in this room. What was it that was so familiar? The light was cool and tinged with green from the trees outside, like the light in a beech wood in England in the spring. Perhaps it had an essence of Englishness about it. Bookshelves lined the walls, a faded Indian rug lay over the floor, and a picture hung above the mantelpiece. Always fascinated by the pictures people choose to put on their walls, I took a closer look. It was an old print of a wrecked ship on the Goodwin Sands, the treacherous quicksands off the coast of Kent where Grandma had lived and my mother had grown up. Perhaps Joyce had given the print to Leonard, or they'd bought it together when we three went to stay with Grandma before he left us. I realised that it was the combination of these things — the books, the rug, the atmosphere — that made the room seem so familiar. It could have been a room in my mother's house.

Voices came from the room across the hall. She must be telling him, it's Susan — she's waiting in the other room. Perhaps he'd refuse to see me, even now that I was just a few yards away. I told myself not to be ridiculous and to distract my attention from what might or might not be being said, I turned to read the titles of the books. They were systematically arranged, which was what I would have expected — he'd been a librarian, after all. I noticed a row of Virginia Woolf titles. I pulled one out, *The Voyage Out*, and thought how appropriate a title to bring with you to the other side of the world. It was a Hogarth Press edition of 1933, and on the flyleaf was my mother's handwriting: *L.J. Jolley, 25.12.37, JEH*, the initials of her maiden name: Joyce Ellen Hancock. I hastily pushed it back into place. I didn't want Elizabeth to catch me going through their library.

I perched myself on the edge of an armchair and was fiddling in my handbag, looking for a lipstick, when Elizabeth came back into the room. She put a glass of water on the coffee table and said that Leonard would see me now, and afterwards she'd get him up and dressed. I stood up, swallowed, and, wiping my hands again on my skirt, followed her, nauseous with nerves, as if I were going in for an oral exam that would determine my future. He was my father, an old man, crippled by arthritis, to be sympathised with, not feared. I was no longer a child, I was much younger and stronger than him, I was in control now, wasn't I? Not at all. My feelings were in control of me — a backlog of longing and resentment, a potent mix of emotions that threatened to spill over in tears. I prepared my face to smile.

Elizabeth opened the door; I followed. He was in bed, propped up on pillows. Music filled the air. And then, abrupt silence. He must have switched a remote and turned the music off. He looked up at me, briefly, then away, his gaze following Elizabeth as she moved to the far side of the bed, and gently laid her hand on his shoulder. I looked down on my father, and he turned his head back to face me. It was strange to look down on him like this, because in my imagination he had towered over me. Now I saw the reality — an old man, lying on a bed, his thin frame propped up on pillows and, despite the heat, a red tartan travelling rug pulled up over his knees. His hands rested on his lap. The long fingers were twisted and claw-like, blue veins standing out from the thin, mottled skin. Although I'd known he would be frail and wasted, the reality of the man leaning back on the pillows was a shock. He must have said something — hello, maybe. I don't remember any words, just the dizzying sensation of looking down on his face, a streak of straight, dark hair pulled across the high forehead, hollow cheeks, and bony nose, lips curved like my own. But it was his eyes that held me, that I found so disturbing. Looking into his eyes was like looking into my own eyes. It was too much. I looked away, through the window to the bright, ordinary day outside.

This all happened in a few seconds — the music, the silence, the glance at the sick old man, then out of the window, and finally turning back to him. But it seemed to take much longer. I bent down to kiss him on the cheek, not sure if this was what I should be doing, but it felt right to me. Afterwards I thought, how ironic, a reversal of roles: the parent lifting up the child to kiss her goodbye; the daughter bending over the father to kiss him hello.

He asked how I was, said he was sorry to learn that Lucy was ill, and apologised for still being in bed at midday. It looked as if they'd be in for a spell of unrelenting heat. He had his fan — it whirred in the background — but couldn't be doing with air-conditioning. Too dry. The situation felt surreal. I had imagined that I would recognise his voice, that hearing him again would bring forth a childhood memory, say, of my sitting on his lap, listening to him reading me stories; but I didn't recognise it. The memory of his voice was lost to me. We were like two strangers meeting for the first time, exchanging remarks about health and the weather.

Elizabeth said she would get Leonard up and dressed, if I wouldn't mind waiting a bit longer in the sitting room. This time, I sat down and tried to sort out my thoughts. I had to do something other than talk about the weather. This was my father, whose absence I had felt for forty years. There had been times, of course, when I hadn't thought about him at all, but he was always somewhere behind my conscious thoughts, lurking ghostlike. That was it — his absence had haunted me. I had come here in the hope of exorcising this ghost by getting answers to questions: why the deception, the lies, and the broken promises — the house in Scotland, how he'd see me 'soon', then 'when you are old enough', and then not at all? I wanted him to say sorry. I wanted to see that he meant it; that he did love me, as he said in those few letters I had received from him. *With very much real, if distant, love.* My mouth felt dry. I drank down the glass of water and hoped there would be wine with the lunch; I could do with a drink.

On the plane from Melbourne to Perth I had rehearsed scenarios where I subtly introduced the questions for which

I was seeking the answers. But those scenarios were like a dream that fades as you wake. You retain the feeling of the dream, but the detail, just how you achieved that sense of control and articulateness, is obscured by the reality of the day. My mind now, as I waited in that familiar-feeling front room, was blocked. Again, I felt as if I were about to take an exam, and although I'd revised and knew all the facts and the arguments, they'd slipped from my grasp; it was like trying to catch smoke. I had to pull myself together.

Okay, I could say how pleased I'd been to meet Sarah and then somehow bring up the way in which we'd discovered that Leonard had brought us identical presents from his trip to the States. From there we'd move on to — what? A pity about all the presents my grandfather sent to Australia for me. By the way, what happened to them? Did you tell Sarah, or Sally as she was then, that they were for her? Did you put them in the bin or, perhaps more charitably, take them to a charity shop? Why did you lie? Don't you realise you were denying me my identity, denying me my family? And who began all this? Was it you, Leonard? Or you, Elizabeth?

A minute later, Elizabeth poked her head around the door and asked me to come through to the dining room.

The table was set for four. I was hoping to meet my half-brother, Richard, who still lived with his parents, and assumed that the fourth place was for him. But apparently not. Elizabeth had laid the table that morning before she knew Lucy would not be joining us. 'Richard's busy,' Elizabeth said. 'He'll be out all day, I'm afraid.'

'That's a pity. I should have liked to meet him,' I said, thinking he probably didn't want to meet me. Unlike Ruth, he had never made any contact with me. I had no reason to think that Ruth wouldn't want to meet me — hadn't Elizabeth written that Ruth *longs to claim you as a sister*? She must be in her mid-thirties now, and we'd exchanged a few letters. I knew that she had married an older man, Bert, and that he'd had to have heart surgery, and she'd sent me photos of her boys when they were born. I was looking forward to meeting Ruth, and disappointed that Richard absented himself.

Elizabeth showed me to my seat and dashed out again to fetch my father. Leonard shuffled in, supported by his wife. There was a toughness about her, a wiriness that suggested resilience and determination. I wondered what it was about her that had made her so sexually fascinating to him, but I couldn't see it, or didn't want to. I pushed aside the thought of Joyce and Elizabeth/Monica as competitors for my father's affections, but the thought wouldn't be banished entirely. *This is about me and them*, I told myself, *not Joyce and them*.

Leonard lowered himself into the chair opposite mine, while Elizabeth busied herself with pouring wine, asking if we got much Australian wine in the UK now. I listened to myself nattering on about wine, how I'd been asked to give a Californian vintner a crash course in French, as he was planning to visit French vineyards to learn their techniques, and how the hills around the convent where Joyce and I had lived in France were covered in vineyards, but one never saw wine from there on the supermarket shelves. There, I'd mentioned her name, and referred to the time of her and Leonard's divorce. Had I put my foot in it already?

Leonard looked at me with those sad eyes, but said very little. I wondered if this was his usual way of being with people, or just with me. I noticed he wore hearing aids — perhaps I'd been mumbling. Should I repeat myself, speak loudly and clearly? What, and say something stupid, like when Mum and I lived in France amongst those vine-covered hills, she'd fetch me milk in a wine bottle? Thank Elizabeth belatedly for sending warm clothes for me, the yellow jumper and the corduroy windcheater? I felt that I was treading on dangerous ground, that mines might explode and send Leonard back to his bed, felled by the shrapnel before I'd begun to ask the questions I wanted answers to.

I, too, fell silent. I felt somehow outmanoeuvred, although there was no obvious way in which we were in conflict. Why were we talking about wine, which held no interest for me, and I was pretty sure, no great interest for them either, when there were so many other important things to speak of? Elizabeth filled the silence by asking me questions — about Lucy's illness, what we'd done over the holidays in Sydney and about Gordon's family. She watched me closely as she talked. I felt as if I were being inspected, examined. Was she looking for traces of my mother or my father in my features and demeanour? Was the situation one which she might use in some future fiction?

'And your mother? Is she still in hospital?'

I had written from England to say that I was considering cancelling the trip to Australia because of Joyce's illness. Elizabeth had written straight back:

I am sorry your mother is so ill and I do understand your conflict about leaving the country while she is ill. There are times like that and it is hard to know what to do. I always think the positive choice is the better one.

I had found this both comforting and encouraging. She understood me. And now she had chosen to mention my mother.

'They think it's lupus erythematosus,' I said, 'and it seems to be affecting her brain.' Leonard and Elizabeth exchanged a glance. I was unable to interpret it, and wondered if I wasn't somehow betraying Joyce by mentioning the fact that her illness had mental ramifications; I wished it were a broken hip or something more physical. 'But she's getting better,' I hastily added, cross with myself for referring to these mental problems. 'It's not dementia, it's an auto-immune disease,' I said quietly, as if in defence, as if dementia would be seen as a failure on her part, a fall from being a bright, intelligent, and independent woman to a helpless, confused old lady.

'Do you remember Max? Lesley Lam's brother?' I looked over to Leonard. A flicker of interest crossed his face. *Ah*, I thought, *I've managed to get his attention.*

Elizabeth responded quickly. Perhaps she, too, was relieved that I had shifted the direction of the conversation.

'Lesley of Lesley and Basil?' Elizabeth turned to Leonard. 'I'm sure he remembers Lesley, don't you, Leo? Didn't you meet the Lams when you all lived in the commune at Charney Bassett?'

Leonard didn't reply. I later learned from a biography of Elizabeth by Brian Dibble, published in 2008, that Leonard had been infatuated with Lesley (he was engaged to Joyce at the time and was also interested in Elizabeth), but I had no idea of this as we sat around the table in Perth. I knew that Joyce went down there to visit him at weekends, and she and Lesley and Basil got on very well. But when Elizabeth said something like, 'I'm not sure if we ever met her brother, though. Was he a musician too?' she seemed to imply that she, too, had been a visitor to the commune. But it wasn't clear. Perhaps I'd got it wrong, and she'd met Lesley and Basil later.

Leonard frowned. I wasn't sure whether this was supposed to indicate that yes, he did remember Max but didn't want to or whether he was merely trying to remember the man. His taciturnity and permanent frown made it very difficult to interpret what he was thinking.

'Yes, Max was a musician,' I said. 'More involved in education than performance, I think.'

'I met Max,' Leonard said, slowly, 'but I didn't know him well. And how is Lesley? I imagine she's still in the land of the living?'

'She's well. She used to keep a horse in stables nearby, but doesn't ride any more. And her dogs have got progressively smaller — the latest is a dachsund called Dandy. We see a lot of her.'

Lesley had always treated me like the child she and Basil never had, and I was very fond of her. I filled Leonard in on Lesley's travels since her divorce from Basil, and explained that Max and his second wife had split up ages ago, and that Max had developed Alzheimer's disease. He had moved in with Lesley, and for some years she had looked after her brother until he became so ill that she could no longer care for him. 'It was hard for Lesley. He'd go out and buy hundreds of CDs on his credit card, amassing a huge debt that he didn't have the means to pay off. Then he'd go missing and get picked up by the police.' I trailed off. The reason I had mentioned Max was that Joyce had witnessed both his decline and the stress it caused Lesley. She felt great sympathy for them both, and told me she wouldn't want to suffer the loss of mind herself, or be such a burden to Mick. I didn't say any of this. I just said, 'Mum used to worry when she forgot things that she was getting senile. She used to say she'd rather be dead than lose her mind.'

No sooner had I said this about Joyce preferring to die than lose her mind than I regretted it. Would she want them to know this was how she felt? But it somehow seemed important to me for them to think of Joyce not as a victim, of illness or of old age. Did Leonard worry that he was losing his mind? I remembered how, when I had seen my mother lying helpless and confused in that hospital bed, I feared that she might be making a sudden and horrific descent into senile dementia, to a place where we could no longer reach her. The diagnosis of lupus was, in a way, a relief.

'They're treating her with steroids,' I said, 'and they sent her home for Christmas.' This, in fact, had been very much at the last minute; Mick was not expecting it, and, fearing he wouldn't be able to cope on his own, he'd asked Laura to come over and help. 'And so Laura stayed for Christmas,' I told them, 'but she's back at home now, and an agency nurse comes in twice a day.' The more I said, the more guilty I felt. I should be caring for my mother instead of betraying her by sitting down to eat and chat with the two people who had betrayed her and hurt her more than anyone else in her life. Here I was, supping with the enemy, not even looking after my sick daughter, but leaving her to be looked after by someone else.

'Has Laura mentioned that Lesley's living in Exmouth, too, quite near Laura?' I asked. 'She and Joyce and Laura see a lot of each other.' I looked towards Leonard. He and Laura corresponded, intermittently. Why did he remain so distant? So silent? I waited for a response, but he avoided my eyes, looking over to Elizabeth, ignoring me.

The news of these old friends from years back still seeing one another occasioned a worried glance from Elizabeth back to Leonard. Was it because I was talking about my mother too much? Reminding him too much of things he'd rather forget? 'How lovely,' Elizabeth said, 'that Laura was there to help Mick,' and then rapidly changed the direction of the conversation. 'Rebecca's going to study medicine, isn't she? Gordon must be very pleased about that.'

The phone rang. My pulse raced. Colleen? Elizabeth sprang up to answer it in the kitchen. 'It wasn't your friend,' she said, coming back in almost immediately. 'Nothing important.' She sat down again. 'Rebecca will be following in her father's footsteps — another doctor in the family. You must be so proud of her.'

This matter of parental pride had peppered Elizabeth's letters to me:

> Daddy is very proud of you and is pleased that you have a
> nice home and a kind husband and two clever happy little
> girls.

Much later, I learned from Dibble's biography that she had harboured a lifelong fantasy of being a doctor. There were lots of things I found out from that biography that would have been interesting and useful to know when I went to their house in 1989, but it would be another twenty years before the biography was published.

'I am,' I replied. 'But I'm not sure if she knows quite what she's letting herself in for, with the long hours on call, the endless exams, the pressures and responsibilities of the job.' I looked across at Leonard, thinking that Gordon had been almost as absent from his daughters' childhoods because of his job as my father had been from mine. I didn't say so.

'She must be bright,' Leonard said. 'She's going to Edinburgh University, isn't she?' I was pathetically pleased that he remembered which university she'd be going to. Of course, this mention of Edinburgh could have offered me a way into asking the questions that were itching to be asked, but instead of taking the bull by the horns, or grasping the nettle, or whatever metaphor that could be applied to the situation, I didn't do it. I could have said, yes, she's going to Edinburgh, lucky girl. Such a great city. But, of course, you know it well, you lived there for years. And then asked why he had felt the need to pretend to his father and brother and sister that Joyce and I had been living with him in Scotland throughout the 1950s. Didn't he find it painful to be reminded of his deceit twice every year, when Laura and Harry and Grandpa Jolley sent me birthday and Christmas presents, and wrote to Joyce as well as to him? And on top of this, to compound the situation — if what Laura had told me since our first meeting all those years before were true — by sending drawings and thank-you letters back to his family? Drawings that weren't drawn by me, and letters that weren't written by Joyce? Laura wouldn't have lied to me about this, I was sure. And yet I hadn't seen any actual evidence of such correspondence.

I didn't say a word of this; I didn't have the courage. I was, in fact, quite relieved to talk about my children and their futures rather than my mother and the past, because of the way Leonard had appeared to switch off when I mentioned her name, concentrating on his food, not meeting my eyes. He had some difficulty using a knife and fork, and so I suppose the business of eating did require concentration on his part. Elizabeth had asked about Joyce and I had answered, and Leonard had looked bored. His lack of interest was probably more to do with either her health being the subject of conversation (he had spent his life being ill), or just not wanting to be reminded of her and how he had behaved towards her. I realised afterwards that I wanted him to like me: I didn't want to upset him or annoy him, which all this stuff about Joyce's illness seemed to be doing. And which any reference to the past was almost bound to do. I couldn't ask awkward questions and expect him to like me for it. I wanted him to admire me, be proud of me.

I wondered if he was proud of Sarah — she had followed in his footsteps, working as an academic librarian. 'I was so pleased to meet Sarah,' I began.

Elizabeth stepped in briskly. 'She told us that you had met. I believe you lived near Margaret in Manchester at the time. Such a small world. And didn't you mention in one of your letters that you knew Angela Carter? I liked her enormously. We both attended a conference on women writers last year.'

Now Elizabeth took control of the conversation, and I let her. Each time a topic arose that could have led to some discussion of my real reasons for being there, she deftly shifted the direction we were heading in. Perhaps I didn't try hard enough. It was as if the mere fact of having got here had exhausted my resources and my will.

I so much wanted Leonard to engage with me, but he was withdrawn, and although he appeared to follow the conversation between Elizabeth and me, he made very little contribution apart from the few questions he asked about Becca's forthcoming medical education. He did seem to like the idea that he had a bright granddaughter. I wondered if I came up to scratch on that score. Despite Elizabeth's frequent remarks in letters that I was a success at everything I touched, this was far from true. My life did not include a career plan — I worked hard at projects I enjoyed, but I earned very little, and wasn't making my way up any ladders.

Perhaps a direct question, addressed to Leonard rather than Elizabeth, would at least make him look at me.

'Are you in touch with the Wheelers?' I said. 'I'd love to know how and where they are these days.' Louie and Les Wheeler were the couple who told Joyce that Sally was Leonard's child. Les Wheeler had been a close friend of Leonard's, and I had an idea that the Jolleys had stayed with the Wheelers on one of their trips to England — I couldn't remember who told me this, but at the time had wondered whether Louie and Les had found themselves compromised by loyalties to both parties and so had dropped out of touch with Joyce and Mick and me.

The Wheelers, however, proved to be a non-starter. Elizabeth got up to fetch something, and Leonard busied himself with a drink and a napkin and appeared not to have heard me.

'Les,' I said, clearly and loudly, 'Louie and Les Wheeler. I was wondering if you'd been in touch with them. I used to see a lot of their son David, but he went off and studied law, and then he got married and, I don't know, we seemed to drift away from each other. I haven't heard from them in years.'

Leonard held his wine glass in his crooked fingers and drank. He put the glass down and dabbed at his mouth with a napkin. I felt like grabbing the napkin from his twisted fingers and taking him by the shoulders so he had to look at me. Don't ignore me when I'm right in front of you. Talk to me. Make some connection. I sat mute with frustration. It was clear to me that the only one he wanted to connect with was his wife. He looked up as Elizabeth came back into the dining room with a tray.

I could feel tears pressing against the back of my eyes, and was glad to have the diversion of clearing the table to give me the time to collect myself. Elizabeth said she was thinking of getting a dishwasher, or had got one and what a bonus it was, or something along those lines. I had stopped listening. I wonder now if Leonard was just pretending to be deaf when he didn't respond to me. I also had the impression that whenever Elizabeth was obliged to leave me alone with Leonard — when she took plates away or brought in the next course — it was for as short a time as possible. During lunch I had become more and more frustrated, and yet at the same time unable to act. Was it Elizabeth freezing me out, or Leonard? Perhaps she was only doing what he wanted her to do. I was powerless in front of this couple. I was relieved when at last the meal was over. Leonard needed a sleep after lunch. I needed to escape.

I left with promises to see them the next day, when we were going to visit Ruth. Once again, I leaned down to kiss my father's cheek. The door of the dining room closed quietly behind me, and I followed Elizabeth down the dim hallway to the front door. The light outside was so bright it was as if I was entering another world. I pushed my sunglasses onto my nose. I didn't want to be seen with tears in my eyes.

Elizabeth stood at the front door, watching me as I walked away. I could have turned back, asked her questions without Leonard being there listening and yet infuriatingly silent. But, of course, I didn't. I was angry with myself, for my inability to confront them, aware that even if I tried, I'd not be able to stop tears gathering in my eyes. I'd never been any good at face-to-face confrontation. I was fine on paper and in my imagination — I could be as clear-headed and articulate as anyone, as cool as you like. As I walked back up the road, still empty of passers-by, I tried to gather my thoughts, but they were tattered and flying all over the place. Would the occasion have been any different if Richard had been there? I half looked out for him, wondering if perhaps he was waiting somewhere around the corner, out of sight, waiting for the coast to be clear so that he could go home. Perhaps he didn't want to see me because he'd heard awful things about me. But maybe he was just shy. I understood from what Laura told me that he had a troubled childhood and a difficult time at school, or rather not at school, since he refused to go. He had no qualifications and no career plans, as far as I could gather, and didn't seem to keep the jobs he had for long. But Ruth was a different matter altogether. Elizabeth assured me she was looking forward to meeting me and Lucy.

Colleen was waiting for me just up the road. She had read many of Elizabeth's books, and was intrigued by my relationship with this famous Australian author. 'How did it go?' she asked. It was only once I was in Colleen's car that I began to shake. 'Awful,' I said, 'I ballsed it up.' I had failed to ask the questions that I had thought I would ask. Now I was exhausted and cross with myself.

'You're seeing them again,' Colleen said. 'You've got time.'

But did I have the courage?

My main concern, though, was Lucy. Colleen said that Walter had dropped by and was asking a colleague of his to call in to have a look at her, if that was okay with me. Back at Colleen's house, seeing Lucy still pale and sweating, still unable to drink even a sip of water, put the frustrations of the afternoon into perspective. The doctor came and gave Lucy an anti-emetic injection. He was pretty sure it wasn't anything serious, and she began to improve amazingly quickly.

It was now evening. Dinner was prepared, Colleen's boys were in bed, and Lucy was sleeping properly. Walter was still at work.

'Tell me all about today. I can't wait,' Colleen said.

I'd just begun when the phone rang. It was Elizabeth. Her first question was about Lucy. 'How is she? Has she stopped vomiting? Dehydration, that's the main problem. She mustn't get dehydrated.'

I told her about the doctor's treatment and that she was lots better, her temperature had begun to drop, and she was now fast asleep.

'Children never cease to be a worry,' Elizabeth went on, 'even when they're grown up.' I thought she was probably thinking about Richard, who must have been in his mid-thirties. Had he been interested to know what I was like, I wondered.

I asked if Ruth was expecting us the next day, and her answer was vague.

'It depends on how your father is feeling in the morning. He doesn't say much, but he was so touched to see you.' She paused. Was he? I wondered if this was really the case. She hurried on, 'He gets tired, and he's not quite over the virus he had, and then the excitement of today has exhausted him. I think we'd better have another talk in the morning, when we see what sort of night he's had.'

There was nothing I could say in response to that, other than to thank her for welcoming me, and hope that he had a good night.

Elizabeth hadn't finished. 'I'm sorry, Susan, I did think while you were here that you didn't have the chance to say things you might have wanted to say. You must say whatever is in your mind, don't feel you can't. I'll phone again in the morning, when we see how Daddy is. And Lucy, too.' I felt a flush of gratitude — she did understand why I was there, after all. I went to bed relieved that Lucy was getting better and that the frustrations of today's experience would not be repeated.

The following day, Lucy was a lot better, but Leonard was still exhausted, and perhaps, Elizabeth suggested, we would all benefit from a day to recoup. I asked if Lucy and I should go and see Ruth on our own, but that suggestion was rejected. It wasn't convenient for Ruth after all. I didn't believe this entirely, but felt I was in no position either to argue or to go behind Elizabeth's back and contact Ruth — which in itself would have required some detective work, as I didn't have her address or her phone number. It was clear that when Ruth and I met, Elizabeth intended to be there, too. I found that I, too, was tired out, and we spent an easy, relaxing day with Colleen and her little boys, at home and then in the park in the afternoon. Elizabeth rang again that evening to see how we all were and to make arrangements for the following day. It appeared that we would not be meeting Ruth or going to the place in the country. Leonard wasn't up to it. But Lucy and I should go over to their house for lunch again. When I asked if this time Richard would be there, she said that she was afraid he had something on. I had thought Ruth would want to meet me and Lucy, but now wondered whether my half-siblings didn't want to see me, or their parents didn't want us to meet.

This time, with Lucy at my side, I didn't quake on the front verandah, nor flinch at the sight of my father's face. I'd replaced the face I remembered from forty years before with this old man's face. This was the way I would remember him from now on. Lucy was intrigued. She'd read some of Elizabeth's books, had had long conversations with her great-aunt Laura, and was close to her grandmother Joyce, and so, although she knew much of my story, it was at a remove. To her, it was interesting more than emotionally draining.

Before lunch we sat again in the front room, Lucy and I on a sofa facing Leonard, who sat upright in a chair, the tartan blanket over his knees. As on the previous occasion, Elizabeth was busy with drinks and preparations for lunch, coming in and out of the room, making sure we had whatever we wanted. He seemed distant, though, and only perked up when he asked Lucy about her school and her plans. She had just begun her 'A' level courses, doing English and History and French. He asked her a few questions about which books she'd be studying, and then resumed his silence.

We had lunch, we talked of this and that — very little of any consequence. Lucy has always been very sociable and interested in people, so she responded well to Elizabeth asking her about her life and her plans. I was almost as quiet as my father. On several occasions I thought, *Go on, say those things you wanted to say — you'll never get another chance*. And, after all, Elizabeth had invited me to do so on the phone. But when I tried to form the right sentences, when it came to it, the words stuck in my throat. My father sat opposite me, head thrust forward, frowning at his plate, to all appearances resenting my presence. How could I ask this sick old man to explain his behaviour of forty years ago? How could I accuse him of lies and deception while I sat at his table and was entertained by his wife? And was it all him, or was Elizabeth also responsible? Had she instigated any of the deception, or merely colluded in it? I glanced over at her. She was smiling, and chatting to Lucy. *Did you send the photos to Laura that made out that Sally was me?* I thought. *Or did Leonard? Did you plot your complicated web of lies together, or did one little deception lead to another, and once begun, you both got so entangled you had to carry on pretending?*

I just couldn't do it. And despite her saying on the phone that she understood there were things I wanted to say, Elizabeth made no attempt to encourage me to enter that territory. She kept the conversation going, kept it light and dry. Stupidly, I played along: I was very English, very polite and restrained. I now wonder if I might behave differently if the situation were to be repeated today, and honestly don't know if I would have the courage to tackle their united front. I kissed them both goodbye, and as we left the room where Leonard sat once again, wrapped in his tartan blanket, he looked up and gave an unexpectedly sweet smile.

The first thing Lucy remarked upon, after we had said our goodbyes and were walking up the street to where Colleen was waiting for us again in her car, was how like my mother's house it had felt. 'It even looked just like The Cottage — same sort of furniture and paintings. And all the books.'

'I suppose their tastes were formed at about the same time.'

'Yes, but you know it even smelled the same — a sort of old books and wicker furniture smell.'

She was absolutely right about that. I hadn't noticed the smell, but now I thought about it, it was part of that atmosphere.

'And what did you think of your grandfather?'

'Well, he looked familiar, too. I would have turned round if I passed him in the street because he looked so familiar. And his hands, I know they're all gnarled with arthritis, but I could see where my hands came from.'

So Lucy had seen her own hands in his, and I had seen my eyes.

'And Elizabeth? Was she what you expected?'

'Not really. I thought she'd be more witty, like her books. She sort of guided the conversation, I thought, and seemed a bit nervous.'

I squeezed Lucy's shoulder. I was glad she had come with me, and interested to have my own impressions confirmed by her more objective view. I realised that throughout these two lunches, the one person who was in everyone's mind, but rarely on anyone's lips other than mine, and then only briefly, was Joyce: the ghost at the feast.

The following day we were flying home. I had to go back to work, and Lucy had to go back to school. As we headed towards Singapore, I wondered whether this was it, the unsatisfying end to the story. I had messed it up. I told myself that perhaps I'd go back one day, have a second chance to do it properly, ask those simple but impossibly difficult questions. *Why did you lie? How could you plan so much deceit, for all those years?* And the most difficult question of all, *How much of it was you, Leonard, and how much your wife? Who was the instigator and who the perpetrator?* At the very basic childlike level, I wanted to ask, *Do you accept me now? Do you love me?* But I guessed I would never see my father again.

# CHAPTER 10

I returned to England disappointed with myself and reluctant to think about those few days in Perth. True, I'd met my father at last, but what had been achieved, other than the actual meeting? Those years of deception and denial had not even been discussed, let alone probed. The opportunity had been wasted, and nothing had been resolved. I would not normally use the word 'closure' but, I suppose, closure is probably what I was seeking and what I had failed to achieve.

I threw myself into work, and didn't have the time to go down to Exeter to see my mother. We did, however, talk on the phone. Her health was greatly improved, and she was keen to learn all about our trip and how Rebecca was getting on so far from home. I wanted to tell her about Leonard, but somehow the right moment never came up — she was getting deaf, and telephone conversations were frustrating. I would need to talk to her face to face. I had always had a close relationship with Joyce, and in the past we had talked at length about my father, and her relationship with him. But since her illness, the dynamics of our relationship had shifted: throughout my childhood she had tried to protect me from the harshness of Leonard's behaviour towards me, making excuses for him, telling me that he loved me (and consequently maintaining his position on a pedestal), and now I felt I should protect her. How could I tell her what had happened without causing hurt? What could I actually say? How would she take it?

After several telephone conversations when I didn't broach the subject, I decided that, however awkward or tricky it might prove, I should tell her, and that I would find the way. So when they came to visit a few weeks later, I thought this would be the moment, when Joyce had the time to absorb the information, think about it, and ask me whatever she felt she needed to know. Having seen how uncomfortable Mick had been at her hospital bedside when she slipped in and out of consciousness and talked only of Leonard, I was apprehensive about how he would respond — not so much to my news, but to Joyce's reaction to it. Although she wasn't suffering from the mental disturbances she'd had when she had been admitted to hospital before Christmas, she was still not quite the person she had been, and one of the things that seemed to have broken down was a kind of social filter. She had always been very sensitive to people's feelings, but now she tended to speak her mind.

On the Sunday afternoon we went for a walk through the village. It was cold, but dry and sunny. Joyce leaned on Mick's arm and walked slowly. Some friends, John and Jenny, had asked us to call in on them. They knew that I had been to see my father, and I had discussed with them how to approach telling my mother that I'd seen him. We sat in front of the fire and drank tea, and they and Joyce and Mick caught up. After a while, I said I'd go on home and start preparing dinner; Joyce and Mick would amble back later.

That evening, I had a phone call from Jenny. 'I thought I should tell you,' she said, 'not long after you left this afternoon, your mum said to us, "Of course, Sue could have seen her father when she was in Australia, but I don't think she could bear to."' Apparently, Mick looked embarrassed and suggested it was time he and Joyce got going, too.

'Nothing more was said?' I asked.

'No, but I thought I should let you know.'

'Do you think Mick guessed I'd been to see my father?'

'I don't think so, no. It was more he just didn't seem to want your mum to talk about it.'

I was thrown. Why had Joyce said this to them and not asked me? Was she expecting Jenny to say, of course, it would be too difficult for Sue. I was in a quandary. I interpreted my mother's words as meaning, *This is what I want to believe*. No right moment to tell her would now appear, and so I left it.

I felt I'd been weak: I hadn't confided in Joyce; I hadn't asked Leonard the questions I wanted to have answers to, and now I never would. *I'll deal with it all later*, I kept telling myself. I need time for things to settle. In February 1989, I had a letter from Elizabeth:

> You must ask any questions which come to your mind. I did think while you were here that you did not have the time or the chance to say things you might have wanted to say. Sometimes things 'come over' one later on. As you could see Leonard is frail and he finds it very hard to hold a pen and to write.

She went on to talk about the weather they were having and then returned to Leonard:

> He was very pleased to see you, being shy and reserved he does not express things which other people might by outward gesture but I want you to know that he loves you and is proud of you.

It was kind of Elizabeth to write me this letter, and showed the same understanding as when she'd telephoned me at

Colleen's after my first visit to them. But was it true, what she said, or was it wishful thinking? I'm sure she genuinely wanted me to be happy, and I suspect that by telling me that my father loved me and was proud of me, she thought this would make me happy. I wanted to believe it, but his taciturn behaviour while I was actually with him did nothing to imply this was the case. Although I knew it was physically almost impossible for him to put pen to paper, and I recognised Elizabeth's thoughtfulness, I should have liked just a few words from him. He'd written a few words on a Christmas card to me just weeks before. He could hold a pen — just about. My suspicion was that the pleasure she thought he'd felt at my visit was maybe something she wanted to be true, like my happiness.

I thought about my encounter with Leonard a lot. I wrote to him and Elizabeth, as I always had (and didn't keep copies of my letters, so have to guess what I said from her responses). He didn't write to me again. I haven't kept all of Elizabeth's letters, but in one from March 1990, in response to a letter from me in which I had tried to articulate my feelings about my childhood, she wrote:

> You must not let yourself have feelings of being rejected, I mean when you were a little girl. I am afraid Leonard found himself in a situation with too many responsibilities which he could not manage. This is not an offering of excuses just a statement which I make now but could not have made then. We were very pleased you were able to come and visit last year. Lucy is a sweet girl and Rebecca sent us a nice letter. I do hope they will both be very happy. Leonard is very reserved and it is not easy to know how much he is pleased about something, but I do know he was pleased you came. He is not able to write, he can't manage

a knife and fork either but a spoon is all right! I can still get him into the car and he enjoys going out. I will write more often so that you know how he is.

Once again, she was insisting on both his pleasure in meeting me the previous year and his inability to hold a pen, and therefore communicate directly with me.

He got worse. And in December 1990 she had to have a gynaecological operation, and Leonard went into a nursing home nearby while she recuperated. In February 1991, she wrote about the Gulf War:

I do wish this awful war had never occurred. There is so much suffering from it for people who just happen to live there.

Leonard was still in the nursing home; she was told she could no longer nurse him at home, and so she fetched him back to the house every afternoon and wheeled him back in his wheelchair for him to sleep at the nursing home after their evening meal together: *He is allowed to have his wine and whisky, his books and radio.*

Elizabeth's letters to me after we had met were more frank than those that preceded our meeting. Perhaps she felt she knew me better, or could trust me. Maybe she had been dreading meeting me as much as Leonard had, and it was a relief to know that I wasn't the avenging stepdaughter I might have been. And I acknowledged that Elizabeth really did wish for my happiness.

In November 1991 I heard from my cousin Margaret that Elizabeth was in England and booked to do a reading at the Festival Hall in London. Margaret had been alerted to this by Laura, who had asked her if she and her husband planned to attend the event. I decided not to join them. If Elizabeth had wanted to see me she would have told me about it. Apparently, following the Festival Hall reading, Laura and Elizabeth spoke at length on the phone. Laura didn't mention this to me, although she said to Margaret that she was happy that Leonard was being well looked after.

Some months later, I was working on a large exhibition at Harewood House in Yorkshire. I wrote from there to tell Elizabeth and Leonard about my work and said that Margaret had told me about seeing her at the Festival Hall reading. I had this reply:

> About my visit to the South Bank last November. I would so much liked to have seen you. It was arranged in rather a rush, I think a decision to have a writer from Australia must have been rather a 'last minute' one. ... I did not want to be away for too long. I was <u>very surprised</u> to see Margaret and her husband at the Reading. I have never met them before. I never tell people that I am reading somewhere in case they feel they have to come! If I am invited again I shall certainly tell you, and you must promise not to come if you don't feel like it. I do hope life will continue well for Rebecca and Lucy, they have done so well. And I hope your own work and Gordon's will flourish. You have a good project ahead of you with Harewood. Enjoy Egypt. All love from us both, Elizabeth.

'I would so much liked to have seen you' — was it unjust of me to doubt that she would have liked to see me? In a later letter, she enclosed a photo of Leonard taken at the nursing home. His eyes were vague and his expression placid. He was becoming increasingly frail, and was showing signs of dementia. She visited him daily, reading to him or getting him to read aloud his favourite poets, Wordsworth and Rilke. *Poor Elizabeth*, I thought, *trekking down to the nursing home every day, seeing her husband deteriorate*. He had always had a bright mind and sharp wit, although a broken body. No one could question her devotion to this difficult man.

# CHAPTER 11

During the years when he was in the nursing home I continued to write to Leonard, as I always had, but had no further direct contact from him. Elizabeth wrote and kept me informed as to his state of health, which deteriorated fast. I was teaching at the art college in Bristol, and both Rebecca and Lucy were at university in Edinburgh, Becca now well into her medical training and Lucy studying history.

It was 14 February 1993, and Mick's seventy-fourth birthday. Gordon was on call — again. I drove down to Devon for the day, to have lunch with Joyce and Mick and Laura. Following her husband Stan's death several years before, Laura had moved from their retirement home in the country and now lived in a flat in Exmouth, just a few miles from Exeter. From the flat she could walk to the shops and get to adult-education classes. She was studying for an Open University degree, although at her present rate of progress she calculated that she'd be well over a hundred by the time she graduated! Unlike Leonard, whose mind was deteriorating, Laura's was as sharp as ever, her tongue as acerbic and her wit as keen. Over the years I had become close to her, and since Stan died would go and see her or Lesley Lam, or both of them, whenever I was visiting Joyce and Mick.

I parked my car by Laura's flat and we walked down the

hill to the Imperial Hotel, where we were to meet Joyce and Mick. Neither of the elderly women wanted much more than a sandwich for lunch, so we stayed in the bar rather than go to the restaurant. The bar was warm and stuffy, but comfortable with its worn furniture and dull food.

Joyce was quieter than usual, and when we came to leave I asked if she fancied a walk along the beach, but she said, 'No, you and Laura go. I think I'd rather go straight home,' and looked towards Mick, who said it was a bit breezy, and that they'd better get back and hunker down.

We stood up. Joyce looked tired, her cheeks pink from the overheated hotel bar, but her brown eyes dull.

'Are you okay, Mum?' I asked.

'I'm fine, just a bit tired.'

'What she needs is a nen.' Mick took her arm in his. A 'nen' was a 'nice early night', something we'd teased Mick about for years. My mother was a late-night person, and Mick liked to be in bed with a cup of Horlicks and Sherlock Holmes by 10.30. Often Joyce would stay downstairs, reading, listening to music, doing the crossword, or writing letters until midnight and beyond.

I gave her a hug and kissed her flushed cheek. Mick gave me a peck on my cheek and told me to drive carefully. In the past, Joyce would ask me to telephone when I got home, but now she seemed to have accepted that unless she heard otherwise, I'd have got there in one piece.

Waves slapped against the sand, and a salty wind whipped away the stale air of the hotel bar. Laura held on to my arm as we crossed the road to get down to the beach. She tugged at her wig with the other hand — it wouldn't do to have it fly away. Some time ago, despairing of the skill of hairdressers to do anything with her thin, wispy white hair, she invested in two wigs: an everyday one, nondescript grey, which was rather thicker, I think, than her real hair ever was, and a smarter wavy one, of a more glamorous design. She wore the everyday wig for the Imperial Hotel.

It was not an ideal beach-walking day; the sand was sticky underfoot, and the sun hidden behind streaks of bruise-coloured cloud. It was as well, I thought, that my mother had decided to go straight back home to a warm fire. We walked slowly and without talking, leaning into the wind. I bent towards Laura to shout in her ear, wouldn't she rather go back to the flat now? No, she said, but she should like to sit down. Over there, by that breakwater.

She lowered herself to sit on a lump of concrete, and we huddled against the damp wood. Laura hugged her knees in the way a child might, rather than a woman in her eighties. She gazed out across the sea. 'I've been thinking,' she said, 'about when I die. I've been making arrangements.'

'What sort of arrangements?' My mouth was dry. She must have discovered she had some untreatable illness and was trying to find a way to tell me. I smoothed the gritty sand with my palm, avoiding looking at her.

'Putting my affairs in order, clearing the decks. You'll find all the relevant information in the top drawer of my bureau.'

'Laura, don't say that ...' I touched her shoulder, but she shrugged me off.

'Now, don't be silly. I've no plans to die just yet. I merely want you to know where everything is.'

She looked away from me to the misty horizon. *It must be raining out at sea*, I thought, and shivered. Despite her breezy words about having no intention of dying, I felt as if the gloom of the day was seeping into my skin; I rubbed my hands on my coat. She turned her face towards me. Her eyes were brimming, but it was probably the cold wind.

'There's an envelope in the bureau, addressed to you.' She

smiled, as if she was aware of sounding melodramatic. She wasn't ill; she wasn't about to die. In fact, she looked well — the wind had whipped colour into her cheeks, and her tone was so matter-of-fact that I was able to push aside my feelings of gloomy foreboding.

'Oh, what's in it?'

'It's for you to see after ... after I'm gone.'

I raised my eyebrows. Laura had never struck me as a woman of mystery and intrigue. 'You can't say that and then tell me I'm not to have it until after you die. It's not fair.'

'It's not important. Some ... papers ... that's all. It's just that I'd like you to decide what to do with them. And some letters. The important thing is that you should know where all my papers are, so that when it comes to it, there won't be any confusion.'

I was confused already. 'What letters?'

'From Australia. From Elizabeth. Letters she's sent over the last, what? It must be about twenty-five years. Since I learned of her existence. I think something should be done with them. And you're the one to do it.'

I knew that Elizabeth and Laura corresponded, but also that, despite the fact that both Elizabeth and Leonard had made trips to England since the unravelling of what had really happened between my birth and my marriage, they had never met.

'You've kept all her letters?'

'Not all. Just some.'

'So why don't *you* do something with them?'

'I am. I'm leaving them for you.' She paused. 'Because I think you might find them interesting. And then you can decide. Time for tea, don't you think?'

'But ... why?' She appeared not to hear me. Her deafness was at times quite convenient.

I wasn't at all sure I wanted to read those letters; I might discover things I'd rather not know, things that would challenge my views of both Elizabeth and my father. I stood up and held out my hand to Laura, but she tried to push herself up on her own. Obstinate old woman, talking about dying one minute and refusing help to get off the ground the next. She relented, and held out her hand for me to pull her upright. We walked along to the next steps from the beach to the Prom. As we climbed the hill to her flat with its view of the wide sweep of estuary and the horizon beyond, I began to think, *Well, maybe it would be interesting to see what Elizabeth wrote to Laura, or even more, what Laura wrote to her* (and I wondered if Elizabeth had kept Laura's letters). By the time we reached her front door, I was decidedly curious.

We sat in front of the fire, warming our hands and drinking tea and eating cake. Behind me, tantalisingly lurking in the shadows, was her bureau. My curiosity was growing. I wanted to see the mysterious envelope that lay in that bureau, and perhaps persuade her to hand it over now.

'So, can I see the papers I'll need when you die?'

She got up stiffly and we crossed the room. She showed me where everything was kept: a copy of her will, bank statements, lists of her investments and of charities she supported, her pension book, bills arranged by date, her address book, lists of people to contact 'in the event'; she made sure I put in my diary the name and address of her solicitor and her financial adviser. All was orderly and clear. But there was no envelope with my name on it.

'I'm going to think about that other matter,' she said, reading my thoughts. That was it. The conversation was over. I left, saying I'd see her again as soon as I could, but I had a lot of work on, mostly up in Yorkshire. As I drove home I felt uneasy. I didn't want to think about death, whether Laura's or anybody else's, and the list of people to contact 'in the event' was particularly chilling. I supposed that at some point she'd want to discuss exactly how she'd like her funeral to be conducted. I thought, too, about Joyce — about how quiet she had been, absent, almost, from the conversation at lunch. Perhaps I should have gone back to Exeter when Mick and she left and had tea with them, instead of walking along the beach with Laura.

The next time Laura and I saw each other was much sooner than either of us imagined. When I'd kissed my mother goodbye and she and Mick had set off home in his battered car, I had no idea of what was coming.

Mick called me less than two weeks later to tell me that Joyce had been admitted to hospital, suffering from pneumonia. If only I had gone back to Exeter with her, spent just an hour alone with her while Mick got on with whatever he had to do — prepare the laundry for collection the next day, check on his investments in the financial pages of the Sunday newspapers — Joyce and I might have talked about the past, and the future.

My mother lay under a blanket on a narrow hospital bed in a single room, an oxygen mask over her face. She pulled it off when she saw me. Her cheeks were flushed and her eyes unhealthily bright; her body looked slight, almost childlike under the thin blanket. A dull despair descended on me — I was losing her. Mick was determinedly positive.

'We'll have you home tomorrow.' His voice sounded cheerful. But I knew from the look of acceptance on her face and her difficulty in breathing that she was dying.

The doctor came in and gestured to Mick, Gordon, and me to move away from the bed. 'All we can do now,' he said, 'is to make her as comfortable as we can. The antibiotics have had no effect, and the oxygen is to make breathing easier for her.'

My fears were confirmed. I wanted to stay until her last breath, but I felt I couldn't leave Mick to go home on his own. Of course I could have asked Gordon to take him back, but I could see that Mick didn't want this.

'She just needs a good night's sleep,' he said. 'And I think we could all do with that. We'll be back first thing in the morning, and if there's any change, they'll telephone us.'

'Do you mind if I sit with her, just for a few minutes, on my own?'

Mick and Gordon went outside, and I could hear them talking to a nurse.

Joyce lay still and quiet. She was barely conscious. On the bedside table her glasses were folded next to a glass of water. Her lips were pale. I held her hand, the skin silky and slippery, but cold.

I bent my head close to hers. 'Your hands are cold. Shall I get you another blanket?'

'No, I'm beautifully warm. Stay here with me,' she said, and she squeezed my hand.

I listened intently to her breathing. For a moment I thought she had stopped breathing altogether, and I held my own breath, but then she gulped some air, and so did I. I stroked her hand, remembered how when she left me at Grandma's to go off on a holiday, it was I who was in bed, clinging to her hand, begging her not to leave me. Even though it was painful for me to sit by my dying mother, I wouldn't beg her not to leave me now. I sat by her bedside, holding her hand for about fifteen minutes. Her breathing was easier, and she fell asleep. Mick and Gordon came in. It was time for us to go. I left her room, turning at the door for what I knew would be my last view of her, an impossibly large lump in my throat, and tears stinging my eyes.

Mick insisted that Gordon and I have their bed—he would sleep in a single bed in my old room. I lay where her head had lain that morning. The pillow smelled of her, not of a perfume or stale sweat, just the scent of her skin. I lay on my back, staring at the ceiling, willing my own easy breathing to enter her lungs, wishing I'd had the strength to insist on staying with her. I knew the moment she died, because I felt a kind of release, as if taking a big breath, then sighing it away, up into the clear night air. I looked at the bedside clock. It was midnight. Five minutes later, the telephone rang: it was the hospital to tell us what I already knew.

Her funeral took place at Exeter Crematorium. She hadn't said what she wanted, and Mick thought she'd probably want to be cremated. When I rang her sister, Gladys, to give her the details of the time and place, her first words were, 'But Sue, we bury our dead.' She tried to cover her shock and upset, but it was clear she thought if her sister were cremated, she would never be reunited with her family in the afterlife. I now worried that we were doing the wrong thing, that all those Brethren beliefs were deep inside my mother and that she wouldn't have wanted her body to be burned. I spoke to Rebecca and Lucy about it, and Lucy told me that she had talked about death with her grandmother when she, Lucy, was about twelve, and that my mother had been quite clear that she believed that when you died it didn't matter what happened to the body. It was the memory of the person living on in other people's minds that mattered. I tried to hang on to that idea.

Mick left it up to me to arrange the funeral; he came to the florist's with me, and to the undertaker's, but was incapable of making decisions. You decide, he kept saying. When I asked him what he wanted to do after the ceremony—should we book a room and a buffet in a hotel, like Laura had done for Stanley when he died?—he said, 'Whatever you think best.' I thought my mother would rather people came to the house; she'd always enjoyed entertaining, and I'd deal with the food and drink. I think he was in denial about her death: he really had believed that she'd come home from the hospital.

I read reams of poetry trying to find the right thing to be read at her funeral, but it was so difficult, as her tastes ranged so widely. To narrow the search, I decided to look at the books on her bedside table, to see what she either had been reading recently, or which favourite poets might be always at hand. On the top of the pile was a collection of Brontë poems and, marking a page, a slip of paper. The poem was 'Retirement' by Anne Brontë, and the page being marked was too fortuitous to ignore. This was the poem she should have at her funeral. In it, the poet speaks of wishing to be alone. She invokes her spirit to *stretch thy wings / And quit this joyless sod, / Bask in the sunshine of the sky*.

Gladys didn't come to the funeral — it was, anyway, a very long way for her to travel. But Laura did, and she wore her best wig. Jo, my teacher from St Catherine's, took my arm in hers as we left the chapel and gently told me, Joyce wanted to die, Sue, she told me so, but couldn't bear for you to know. I knew it wasn't rational, but I felt that by marking that page with a scrap of paper, she had told me.

Later that year, in July, Laura and I were back in the bar of the Imperial Hotel. Summer sunlight revealed scratches on the dark bar furniture and the worn threads of the fading upholstery, and once again the place was almost empty despite it being the holiday season. I was thinking about my mother, and wishing I could turn the clock back. When she died so suddenly, so much was left unsaid. I told myself that everyone feels this way when someone close to them dies; it's normal to feel guilty.

I had seen Laura a couple of times since the funeral, but always with Mick, or Mick and Lesley, and usually for a pub Sunday lunch. Gordon was rarely there, as I usually went down to Devon when he was on duty. Today Laura had said she would like to see me on my own. I was aware that I kept looking over her shoulder to the door, almost expecting Joyce to come through, leaning on Mick's arm, smiling to see us both here, waiting for her.

'The last time we came here,' I began.

'I know,' Laura said, and I realised she was thinking about it, too. 'Have you written to your father to tell him?'

'Yes. Elizabeth wrote back.' Her letter had been well meant, *I hope you are able to feel comforted remembering your mother.* I appreciated her sympathy, but it was Leonard's I wanted, even if the physical pain of writing made tears come to his eyes. 'But nothing from Leonard. Maybe because he can't. Or maybe he's losing it. His mind, I mean.'

Laura looked down at her hands, narrow and elegant, yet capable. I pictured Leonard's hands; the same long fingers, but bent and twisted by arthritis, incapable, now, of holding a pen. She turned her gaze towards the window, to the sunshine outside, as if looking into the past. 'He was so clever, so in control. But now I think Elizabeth does everything for him. She tells me she reads him my letters — I don't like the idea of that at all — and says he keeps thinking we're still children. Apparently he's waiting for me to come home from school.' She smiled ruefully. 'I don't believe a word of it. It's what she'd like to think; and she says it because she thinks that's what I'd like to hear. She fantasises.'

'I don't know — people's minds often turn to their childhoods when they're losing their short-term memory, don't they? What would be the point of telling you it if it wasn't true?'

Laura blew her nose and pushed her plate away, her sandwich unfinished. 'As I say, she fantasises. She makes up what she'd like to think is the situation.'

I said, 'Don't you believe he thinks about you, then, about your childhood? Were you close as children?'

Laura looked up. 'Close? I'm not sure that's the word. He was the baby of the family, very clever and very spoiled. Not that we had much ...'

She smiled, and I felt she was relieved for the conversation to shift direction, happier to talk about the distant past, before things went awry. I had another glass of wine, and she had a coffee, as she reminisced. She recalled the time when my mother had come into their lives. Laura was teaching in the Midlands, and Joyce and Leonard were students at University College, London. I was surprised when she said, 'I was quite jealous of her, you know. I remember coming home for a weekend, and there were all her clothes in the wardrobe of my bedroom. I felt displaced. I thought they made much too much fuss of her. They treated her like another daughter.' Which is, of course, what she became when she and Leonard married.

I glanced at my watch, and Laura noticed. 'You'd better be getting back home. The Sunday-night traffic will be awful.'

We walked along the Prom, and this time she let me hold her arm. The beach was beginning to empty of families, and the windsurfers were out, skimming over the waves, the green-grey English sea turned to shimmering gold in the evening sun.

'I won't come in,' I said when we reached her front door. 'I must get back. We're going to the pictures tonight, and then I'm off to Yorkshire at the crack of dawn.'

'Please, do — just for a moment. I have something for you.'

It was a manila foolscap envelope. 'I decided you were right. There's not much point in putting off these things. It's something I've written, some verse, and I'd like you to look at it. I'd like to have your opinion.'

I was expecting her to hand me a bunch of letters, and was flummoxed by the very idea of Laura writing poetry. 'But I don't know anything about poetry,' I blurted. She looked so flustered that I hurriedly said, 'I'd love to read it, though.'

She smiled and changed the subject. 'I'm still thinking about what to do with all those letters. I think we'll leave them where they are for now.'

Laura writing poetry? It was certainly a surprise, and the following months turned out to be a rewarding time, working with her to put together a collection of her poems. I was sorry that she hadn't told Joyce about her efforts. They had spent hours talking about books and poetry, and I think Joyce would have given good feedback. Perhaps a vestige of their old rivalry still remained; perhaps that's why Laura didn't want to reveal herself to my mother.

As for Elizabeth's letters, I wondered *why* Laura had thought of leaving them for me to read after she, Laura, would be dead. What could I do with them that would make a difference to anything? Either to her feelings of betrayal and hurt, or to my own confusion about the character and motives of my father in his treatment of me and of my mother? I was still feeling raw from Joyce's death, and this didn't seem the right moment to mess about with things that could make me feel worse, so I was glad she had reached the same conclusion as I had.

A week later, I received a letter from Elizabeth. As usual, she was full of praise for my children:

I think they are courageous and are the product of your good example and upbringing—which brings me to your mother whose death you are trying so hard (to use a phrase) 'to come to terms with'. She would not want you

to grieve but grief is right and natural and you are missing
the one person you could 'always report back to', I put that
in inverts because it is an awkward phrase. It is this person
to whom we could tell things and be comforted which we
miss so much. ... It is very nice that she was able to see you
happily married and successful in your art, and to see the
girls grow up.

This, it struck me, was generous, thoughtful, and kind.
Later, when I learned from Brian Dibble's biography about the
tumultuous relationship Elizabeth had with her own mother,
and her close relationship with her father, I wondered if, when
she wrote me this letter, she had been thinking of her father as
the one person to whom she could tell things and be comforted,
if he were the person she missed so much. If this was the case,
what a contrast it provided to my own relationship with my
distant and uncomforting father, whose protestations of 'real,
if distant, love' left me feeling only confused. Elizabeth's
understanding was a comfort to me.

# CHAPTER 12

I was back in Exeter. It was nearly six months since my mother had died, and her clothes had long since gone. Now I was clearing out some drawers bursting with stuff that she hadn't used in years. She used to chastise herself for being a hoarder, but couldn't kick the habit. This will come in handy one day, she'd say, or, waste not want not. There were remnants of fabric, balls of knitting wool, reels of cotton, embroidery silks, a couple of cracked plastic-covered tape measures (inches both sides, no centimetres), a bundle of knitting needles tied together with cream bias binding, a round wooden box that had once held Fry's Turkish Delight and now held buttons, a Strepsils tin with rusting curtain hooks, several old purses and diaries (I pounced on those — disappointingly containing nothing much other than appointments), a hairbrush with thin white hairs still clinging to it, and a cheap manicure set in cracked red leather that I had given my mother when I was thirteen — the kind of stuff that accumulates in some corner of most houses.

I didn't like doing this clearing out and chucking away. To me, the ephemera are more redolent of a person than anything they might wish to leave for posterity. I felt as if I was clearing my mother out as I yanked the drawer out completely to turn it upside down and get rid of the old dust.

Stuck between the base of the drawer and its back panel were three old paper photograph wallets. I tipped out the contents — no prints, just negatives, black-and-white negatives from the kind of film that would have been used in a box brownie. I held them up to the light, but they were smudged and the light was poor. I slipped them into my bag to take home to look at properly and perhaps print up.

I had a darkroom at home left over from when most of my work was photography, and which I still used from time to time. I held one of the negatives up to the light. Some people in a garden? It was impossible to see properly. It might well be that these were the negatives of some of the photos that I'd spent hours poring over when we first moved to Exeter when I was nine years old, and like everything else, they came out of store. Although she was careful with books and clothes, Joyce hadn't bothered with photographs. She had quite a collection of old family photos, but they were all stuffed into a leather bag rather than arranged neatly in albums.

I loved looking through these pictures when I was a child, pondering on my younger self, telling myself about the people and the places — perhaps the attraction of these old black-and-white photographs lay in their ability to capture the past and give it back to me: the pictures offered a sense of continuity. In that bag the only photograph of Leonard was of him in hospital. There was not a single one of him with me, or him with my mother. Sometimes, when I took pictures of my own children with their father, I'd wonder if any had ever even been taken of me with Leonard. And if they had, what had happened to them. They could be here, in these hidden wallets. Rather than try to work out what was in the pictures by squinting at the negatives, I decided to print the whole lot, see what emerged from the developing tray, and do it methodically, one by one, as the negatives came out of their wallets.

*Leonard and Joyce in a London park*

The first picture showed a group of people in a garden. I recognised the small figure of my grandmother and the two women either side of her: my mother's elder sister, Elsie, and Joyce herself. Behind them stood a man with white hair, my grandfather, who died before I was born. I'd seen others like this before. I held the next negative up to peer at it in the gloom of the red safety light. The emulsion was very thin, but I could make out the outline of a young man sitting on grass. It was Leonard — I could tell by the way he held his head. So this was why she'd shoved the wallets of negatives to the back of a drawer. Maybe she couldn't bear to look at pictures of him. I imagined her throwing the prints on a fire, or ripping them into pieces, but incapable of getting rid of the image completely. The negatives were a kind of get-out clause. I was impatient to see the pictures, but knew that given their frail condition, I had to go carefully and slowly. I exposed a test strip. Bits of the scene emerged — from white sky to black grass, his face too deep in shadow to see. Stop, bath, then fix. I selected an exposure, checked the focus, stopped down the lens, and made the exposure. Develop, stop, fix, and wash. The print drifted in circles under the slowly running tap, coming into view, then disappearing behind the first picture, the family snap in the garden.

Leonard sat on grass, his ankles crossed, hands resting on his knees. His hands weren't the twisted painful hands that I'd seen held in just the same position in his room in Perth — they were just like mine. He half-smiled at the camera, his dark, floppy hair falling over a high forehead. He appeared to be in a park, as there were deckchairs behind him and a fuzz of trees. Abandoning my methodical approach, I turned on the ordinary light, holding one negative after another up to it. They had to be there, together in the park, taking pictures of each other on a sunny summer afternoon. I found what I was looking for. Joyce, too, sat on the grass, leaning on her right hand. She gazed at the photographer from behind round glasses: her hair, parted in the centre, shone in the sunlight; her face was rounded, her full lips curled in a slight smile. She didn't look at ease having her photograph taken. A pram stood under a tree behind her, but at some distance. Could it be my pram? Might I have been there, kicking my feet in the warm summer sun?

Impatient to see what else was there, I tipped the contents of all three wallets out and picked through them rapidly. The third wallet held what I was looking for — more pictures taken in a garden, but not ones of my mother with her parents. These were pictures of a baby, of two babies. There were six negatives, splodged and scratched, three of which featured Leonard. The first one had been taken quite close up. In his arms he held a baby, his face tipped down towards her, smiling. He wore a short-sleeved shirt, and the baby was naked. She lay in his arm, her bottom in the crook of his wrist; his thumb reached her armpit. The fingers of his other hand supported the tiny head. The baby was frowning, her toes curled out. Newborn. Impatiently, I went through the process of making a print, to join the other three prints swirling in clean running water.

The next photograph showed two babies lying on a rug spread on the grass. The babies were naked. The one facing the camera looked very new — she was lying on her side, her skinny legs akimbo, her bellybutton still protruding, her face screwed up. It was me. I could tell by the feet — they were undoubtedly my feet. I looked back to the picture of Leonard with the baby in his arms. That was me, too — no question of it. In this picture, the babies were lying head to toe, the other baby on her front, her knees drawn up under her belly, her face hidden by my kicking legs. The third picture showed him again with a baby in his arms. This time he was bare-chested, and the baby clothed. The picture was taken too far away for me to decide which child this might be. She looked bigger — could it be Sally? But then, there he was with *both* babies, one in each arm, both clothed in nightdresses. Standing awkwardly in his long shorts, he looked at neither child but at the photographer.

*Leonard with two babies, June 1946*

I left the darkroom, the tap running over the swirling photographs. I walked out into the garden. *Bloody hell*, was all I could think. *What the hell was going through his head as he held his two babies in his arms?* Later, I printed the rest of the pictures: one of Monica breastfeeding Sally, another of Joyce holding me on her knee. In these pictures, the two women look remarkably similar. Both are barelegged but wearing lace-up shoes; both have their long hair pulled up into a kind of roll, away from their foreheads. Elizabeth smiles, not at the camera but to the side. I imagine she's smiling at Leonard while Joyce clicks the shutter. In her photograph, Joyce gazes down at her

*Elizabeth with Sarah*

crumple-faced baby. And there she was again, this time standing holding me, smiling — at me or the person behind the camera: Leonard, or possibly Elizabeth?

So the three of them were there in that suburban garden together, photographing each other. Even now, when I look again at those photographs I can hardly believe that Joyce had no idea Leonard was the father of both babies.

*Joyce with Susan*

It was shortly after this, in July 1994, that Leonard died. Sarah had rung me to give me the news — they were about to fly to Australia for a holiday and so, sadly, she didn't see her father before he died, but was able to attend his funeral. Two days after his death, Elizabeth wrote to tell me about it. She was utterly devastated, and although I had been expecting it ever since I had met him — he looked so frail and sick — it was a shock. I finally had to accept that I never would have that conversation with him, although I'd known it in my heart ever since I'd kissed him goodbye on that hot January afternoon in Perth in 1989. I remembered the unexpectedly sweet smile he gave as we left the house. Elizabeth wrote a second letter to say Leonard had left me some money in his will.

Perversely, I was initially affronted by this gift of money. My reaction was to feel about it as I had about the cheques that I had received over the years, that it was blood money. But then, I reflected, it was thoughtful of him, and a kind gesture. I wondered when he had made this will. Was it after we had met, or before? I guessed before. I wished he had thought to leave me some personal memento rather than money. I wanted an object I could hold or look at — something he had cared about, that he thought I might care about. The more I thought about it, the more it mattered to me, and after a week or two of thinking, not wanting to make demands, but becoming increasingly sure that this was a request I should make, I wrote to Elizabeth to say how grateful I was for the money, but to ask her for a memento. She sent me a parcel — his watch, six volumes of eighteenth-century poets that my mother had bound for him (she had spoken to me about how he had bid for this collection at an auction and how she'd gone to a bookbinding class to learn how to bind the six volumes), and a set of Virginia Woolf novels, including *The Voyage Out,* all given to Leonard by Joyce.

The money went into the general pot, but the books I treasure. Every now and then I open one of the *Collection of Poems in Six Volumes. By Several Hands,* which had belonged to a B.A. Herbert, and was printed in the year MDCCLXV. Not all the 'hands' reveal their identity or the identity of those to whom the verses are dedicated (there are lots of initials and dots and dashes). Poems dedicated to key figures of the time, such as Pope and Walpole and the Duke of Marlborough, are next to those dedicated to such as *To The Memory of an agreeable LADY, Bury'd in Marriage to a Person undeserving her.* Alongside these are Gray's 'An Elegy Written in a Country Church Yard' and poems by William Shenstone, but mostly the poets are either anonymous or their names would be familiar only to someone who had studied the period — a wealth of verse, bristling with classical references, satiric comment, and romantic longing for the bucolic pleasures of the ancient world. Some made me laugh — 'An Ode to a Gentleman, on his pitching a Tent in his Garden' — and then there are topical snippets, such as the 'Prologue spoken by Mr. Garrick, at the Opening of the Theatre in Drury Lane in 1747' by Samuel Johnson, as well as Johnson's 'London, a Poem In Imitation of the Third Satire of Juvenal'. This is a period I've studied and taught, focussing on its art, architecture, and garden design, rather than the literature.

If only I'd known Leonard had these books when I sat at lunch with him, I should have liked to talk about our shared interest, walked in imagination through the gardens of Stowe or Stourhead. But this didn't happen. So when I occasionally look at the books, I indulge myself by imagining a time when my parents were together. I imagine Leonard's excitement when he discovered the books, the tension in the auction room when the bidding began. I imagine him bringing them home and Joyce offering to bind them for him, enrolling at a class so that she could learn how to do it properly. The binding looks amateurish and has probably lowered their monetary value as antiquarian books, but it was something they did together, and I think Elizabeth recognised their symbolic value to me.

In late August, Mick brought Laura up to stay with us for a weekend. It was very hot. After lunch on the Sunday, while Mick sat outside in the shade reading the paper, I showed Laura the photographs I had printed. She was very saddened by her brother's death, and regretted that they hadn't met once since he had left for Australia in 1959 (although they had corresponded, she told me). But neither his death nor her sadness stopped her feelings of outrage at his behaviour all those years before. 'How could he?' she murmured. 'Poor Joyce.' And then stabbing her finger at Elizabeth nursing her baby on her knee, 'And how could *she* have the audacity to sit there enjoying your mother's hospitality?'

There was no answer I could find to these questions. So I asked her if she recognised the park where the photographs of Joyce and Leonard sitting on the grass had been taken. Might it be Victoria Park in Hackney? And did she think that might be my pram in the background?

'Wetherell Road, where we lived, was right next to Victoria Park, so yes, it could be there.' She peered at the pictures closely. 'But then it could be any London park. However, I think this was well before you were born. This is how I remember them when they were students.' She handed the photos back to me. 'I've got a few old snaps that have got rather scratched. I don't suppose you could do me some nice prints of those, could you?'

'Of course. It would be useful if you could find the negs, but if you've only got prints, I can make copies.'

'If it's not too much trouble.'

Laura rarely asked me to do anything for her, so I was happy to have a go.

'Thinking of photos,' I said, 'you don't happen to have the ones that were supposed to be of me when I was a child?'

She frowned. 'I can't remember seeing them for years. Dear me, I keep intending to sort things out ... But I'll have a look. It really is time I got my spare room cleared. There's no space for anybody to sleep in it. It's still full of boxes from when I moved to the flat. I must do some proper sorting out.'

The autumn was a hectic time for me, juggling part-time teaching in Bristol and research for a big historical exhibition at Harewood House in Yorkshire that would run throughout the following year. I was glad to be so busy; it meant I didn't dwell on my mother's death. I got on with life, which is what everyone says you should do. I spent hours in the city archives in Leeds and more hours at Harewood House, trawling for information through old ledgers, books of letters, housekeepers' accounts, servants' pay slips, diaries, drawings, architects' plans, and latterly (historically speaking) photographs and Super 8 films, trying to put together the story of the house during the previous two hundred years. Then I would dash home to prepare work for college.

One afternoon I was at my desk at Harewood House, making my way through a box of someone else's family snaps, trying to identify who was who and looking for clues as to where the scenes captured on film might be. At Harewood? Sandringham? Barbados (where the family had a home)? I thought, *This is daft. Here I am, following clues to other people's pasts, when all the time the clues to my own are lying in boxes in Laura's spare room, waiting for me to make sense of them, and I've done nothing about it.* I pushed aside my box of photographs and quickly wrote a letter to Laura to ask if she'd begun her sorting out and if in the process she'd come across any of the letters, drawings, and photos that she had told me about when we first met in 1967. I had been too backward in asking for the evidence that she had assured me existed.

A letter was waiting for me when I got home. Laura hadn't found any photographs or drawings, but, she wrote:

> I see no reason why you should not read the letters from Australia and in your place I would want to know (as far as is possible) what really happened. I believe in bringing all the skeletons out and giving them a good shake ...
>
> If you let me know when you are coming to Exeter I will dig out the letters ... I have written out a timetable of events and have endeavoured to be factual.

She enclosed this 'timetable' — four closely written pages torn from a pad.

It wasn't so much a timetable as an account of how Laura understood the past. I knew the first bits — how Leonard and Joyce met, how Leonard and Elizabeth met and so on, and read through it quickly. Laura had told me that she had never really understood why Joyce made that promise to keep quiet about Leonard leaving her. Here she reiterated her views, pointing out again how painful the effect of this promise was to herself, her father, and her brother:

> Leonard 'made' Joyce promise not to tell his parents or friends. This promise she kept faithfully (I should not have. A promise extracted under emotional stress which in order to spare one person causes pain to several others is not to me binding but to Joyce a promise was a promise).
>
> You visited your Grandparents twice, once as a tiny baby and once as a small child — which I remember clearly.
>
> After Leonard and Elizabeth went to Edinburgh letters and jam continued to arrive. These letters were signed with an indecipherable scrawl.

(I puzzled over the jam: jam making was something both my mother and grandmother did every year — as I do now — and I assumed that she used to send some to her father-in-law, and Elizabeth continued to do so in her name). I assumed that the scrawled signature was supposed to be Joyce's. At least my grandfather registered it as such. Sending jam, writing letters in Joyce's name — what on earth was going on? I read on, hoping to find an explanation:

Your grandmother died in 1949.
I said the letters were not in Joyce's handwriting but this comment was brushed aside.

Did Laura regret her lack of action, I wondered. If she had insisted that she was right and pushed her point of view, might things have turned out differently? She was no shrinking violet, and the Laura I now knew would not have been fobbed off by her father's and her brother's dismissal of a very reasonable observation. I sensed that she was angry with her younger self for not arguing more forcibly.

Leonard wrote very infrequently and his letters were very stilted. He did not write any lies but he wrote (say) 'S ... is doing well at school'. S ... was naturally translated as Susan.
After Richard's birth he wrote 'Mother and baby are doing well', not 'Joyce and baby ...'. I remember this clearly as from L it sounded so awkward.
So for many years we thought that you and your mother were in Australia and we did not know that E. and Sarah existed.
Your grandfather sent you a Christmas present every year which I believe you never received. Thank you drawings and letters came in reply.

How much of this Leonard knew I have no idea and now I'll never know but he was at fault even if he only stood back and did not enquire. Elizabeth was probably living a novel rather than writing one!!!

P.S. It is only potentialities we inherit from our parents.

The P.S. was typical of Laura — a wry comment that told me that, although she had criticised both of my parents (Joyce for making a silly promise and Leonard for lying, or at least concealing the truth), she didn't want me to feel that I would turn out to be either gullible or deceitful.

I thought about those presents, and the letters and drawings that my grandfather had received in thanks. I thought about the letters that weren't in my mother's handwriting. Had Leonard written them? I desperately hoped that he hadn't. The more I thought about it, the more I doubted that he would have gone to such lengths to try to disguise his handwriting. His writing was like nobody else's I had ever seen — very difficult to disguise and virtually impossible to replicate. Was Elizabeth, then, the writer of these letters? And if she was, did she do it off her own bat, or was she somehow forced to do it? The questions that had plagued me when I visited Elizabeth and Leonard in Australia were no closer to being answered. What would Elizabeth have to gain from pretending to be my mother?

Another thought lodged in my mind. Who drew the pictures? Sally? After all, Grandpa Jolley was her grandfather as much as he was mine. Perhaps, when she opened a present with a label that said, *To Susan*, she thought her grandfather was just a muddled old man who'd got her name wrong, believing she was called Susan, not Sarah. I have since learned that this was not the case. Sarah assures me that she never received any parcels or letters addressed to 'Susan', so I can only assume that they were removed or destroyed as soon as they were delivered to the various houses the Jolleys lived in in Edinburgh, Glasgow, and Perth.

Faced with Laura's account, neatly written up as a kind of chart, I felt utterly dispirited. It didn't matter whether it was Leonard or Elizabeth who had perpetuated the deception; its effect had been to deprive me of a family who would have loved me. However, I wanted to see the evidence, to make my own mind up before I condemned my father for being 'at fault', although I found it hard to believe that Laura was wrong about him.

I rang Laura to say I was keen to inspect the skeletons. Would next weekend suit her?

# CHAPTER 13

I rushed down to Devon the following Sunday. After having lunch with Mick, I drove over to Exmouth to see Laura. There had been an accident, and the short journey from Exeter to Exmouth took so long that I barely had time to say hello and drink a cup of tea before it was time for me to head off home again. There was no walk along the beach gazing at the sunset, and no further talk of her eventual demise. When I left her flat, Laura handed me a small parcel wrapped in brown paper and tied with string. 'This is the earlier lot,' she said. 'There are more.' I made a remark about spies and set off, the skeletons sitting on the passenger seat next to me. It took hours to get home.

The next day I was teaching in Bristol. As soon as I got back from college, I tore open the parcel. I was still wearing my coat and had barely given the dog a hello. He sat alert, swishing his tail on the stone floor of the kitchen in joyful anticipation of the walk he usually recieved when I got home.

Two plastic folders and a Penguin book fell onto the kitchen table. The book was *Central Mischief: Elizabeth Jolley on writing, her past and herself.* The fatter of the two folders held a wad of envelopes and air letters in Elizabeth's handwriting. I tipped them out — a sea of words. I selected a letter from the top of the pile: light and insubstantial, the words in blue-black ink spilled across the page and crept up the margins, filling all the available space.

Her letters always felt so insistent, as if she were saying, 'Listen, listen, this is how it is.'

I picked one from the middle of the pile, as one would a card from a deck, and began to read. The letter was addressed to 'My dear Laura' and was dated 25 October 1970. Elizabeth wrote:

> Susan sent a nice little photograph of her little baby girl. I have sent her an Albany Rug and 2 little dresses. Leonard doesn't want to write but please don't tell her that as I couldn't bear to hurt her. He hardly ever writes a letter in any case, I write and send his love. He didn't even want to look at the photograph. I suppose he doesn't want to look back at all and I don't want to say anything of this to her so am keeping things going. She won't know anything of how he feels and I just feel that as a Grandfather he must send presents even if it is me doing the sending. He can't bear the thought of being a Grandfather ...

She couldn't bear to hurt me; he couldn't bear the thought of being a grandfather. I couldn't bear to read this. I put it aside. It wasn't intended for my eyes. She said Leonard didn't want to write to me, but I understood he wrote to his sister. Might there be a letter from him tucked in there amongst the noise of his wife's correspondence? A clue to the character of the man who remained so distant from me? I rifled through, but there was nothing as far as I could see in his distinctive spiky script. Disappointed, I pushed Elizabeth's correspondence with Laura to one side. Through the yellowing plastic of the other file I recognised my mother's handwriting on two envelopes. I wondered why Laura had included these. She hadn't said anything about Joyce writing to her.

The first letter was written on 25 October 1967, shortly after Gordon and I had made that trip to London to meet my newly discovered aunt; the second, a year later. I sat down, and the dog sighed and rested his head in my lap. As I read, I imagined my mother writing. She was on a low chair by the fire, where she always sat when she was reading or marking students' essays, a standard lamp casting light on the page, her face in shadow. The cat would try to nudge his way onto her lap and would be firmly pushed away. I could hear her voice in the words. There were crossings out and alterations. This wasn't a letter that had been drafted and refined. She put her thoughts directly onto the page. Here she told the same story that I had heard on the beach at Budleigh Salterton on Boxing Day 1967, and much of the information was familiar to me. I had, of course, seen her and Laura together on many occasions during the twenty-six years since this letter was written, but mostly these meetings happened after the two women had retired. The first time they had met since 1949 was early in 1968, a few weeks after Joyce had written this letter, and they must have talked at length at that meeting. It felt strange and uncomfortably voyeuristic to read a letter between two people I knew so well. But because of the nature of my work as a researcher and curator, I was used to reading other people's correspondence. Mentally, I put on the researcher's hat. Usually, I wore white cotton gloves for such work, and even as I put the plastic folder to one side and smoothed down the folds of my mother's letters, I thought, *I should put these in acid-free envelopes*. I might have had the researcher's instincts, but it was the daughter who took over as I read:

My dear Laura,
Since Susan phoned to tell me that you had written to her you have been in my thoughts more or less

continuously — but I've been waiting for a long enough space of time to answer your letter.

Although I have naturally got used to the thought of silence I was forced to observe for all these years, yet I feel very happy to be able to break it — because, of course, I felt very sad and frustrated in having to refrain from writing to your Father or to you. I don't think I <u>could</u> have agreed not to write to Mother if she had still been alive when Leonard and I parted. As far as Leonard is concerned it surely must be a relief to know at last — that everything is known to at least one or two persons other than Monica and himself and me.

She fills Laura in on the Leonard/Monica/Joyce friendship, Monica's pregnancy, and her baby's birth, followed five weeks later by my birth:

She (Monica) came to stay in our house while I was in the nursing home, and was there when I came back with Susan — for several weeks. Eventually she got a job as a housekeeper to a doctor, but I had the baby one day a week. Then gradually I saw less and less of her — and L wouldn't talk about her — so I didn't question him or know where she had gone. He had become very gloomy and physically distant with me, though he said that he loved me — and I believe that he did. Needless to say I — unfortunately for me — loved him deeply — and was totally under his influence. You know what a dominant personality he has. He always made me believe that he was right and I was rather silly (though perhaps he didn't intend to do this) and I utterly believed every word he said — I mean that I couldn't conceive that he would lie to me. But he was withdrawn and worried.

My imagination moved further back from the writing of this letter, all the years after the events she recounted, to the time when they actually happened — to Joyce coming home from having given birth, to find another woman and baby in her place. How must she have felt? And she'd told me when I had my first baby that she hadn't been able to breastfeed me, and there amongst the photographs taken in the suburban garden was one of Elizabeth breastfeeding her baby, a look of deep contentment on her face. No wonder my mother had got rid of the prints. She must have been so angry once she found out the true situation, utterly betrayed. And she loved my father deeply. She had told me before how she admired him, his intellect, and how small he would make her feel. 'Silly' is the word she uses here. I wondered if he made Elizabeth feel silly, too. And if he would have made me feel silly and inferior, had we known each other.

Joyce's letter covers the ground of what happened after she and I left Birmingham, and takes Laura up to the time of her marriage to Mick. She explains how she discovered that Sally was Leonard's child:

It was only after this [her marriage to Mick] — when Louie and Les Wheeler were once visiting us, that I discovered that Monica's child Sally was really Leonard's child. This partly explains his dilemma — but still leaves his conduct, and especially Monica's (or Elizabeth's) very reprehensible. And of course it is extremely awkward to try to keep some sort of contact with Susan, as Monica does, by sending presents in L's name and letters in her own (as Elizabeth of course) and yet keeping all knowledge of Susan's existence from Sally, and Sally's from Susan. I really think, however, that Susan will have to be told about Sally. She has always had a craving to have relations — and asked Elizabeth about their children. However, I haven't yet decided what to tell Susan — though she knows that I resented Elizabeth writing to her in the tone of a loving and understanding relative of some kind. Beginning letters with Sue Dearest! What hypocrisy — but I suppose that she has a strong sense of guilt and tries to appease it somehow. She was trying to prevent Susan from pursuing questions about the family, by saying that Leonard would not speak of the past and therefore would not tell his children about his child Susan.

Joyce begins to end the letter, but typically writes a couple more pages before she signs off. And even then there is a postscript:

On reading this through I feel that I probably sound very unsympathetic towards Leonard and Monica — but this isn't quite how I do feel. I know that Leonard suffered terribly because of the situation in which he put himself — or allowed himself to be put. And I think he would have suffered less if he had been able to admit or confess everything. Yet there was always the question of how Sally would feel and also how Susan would, when old enough to know. Still, he had to allow one woman and one child to suffer more than the other — and he chose [to leave me for] Monica. He said that at least I would have the consolation of knowing that I was not 'in the wrong' — but it wasn't really much consolation — and of course, not knowing the real truth until years afterwards (about Sally I mean) I could not see his dilemma, and only felt that he had rejected the (at that time) adorable and innocent Susan for another man's child, and me for a woman who had not acted morally in pursuing a relationship which it would obviously have been better to abandon. I'm sure that he wasn't really in love with her when he married me. If he was, then still he should not have married me—that would have been a really terrible thing to do—I certainly would not have forced him or persuaded him, much as I loved him.

However, they have doubtless both suffered enough—only surely now they must be glad to be free of the deception—except as regards Sally. You must decide whether you let Leonard know that you know what the truth is. He may not realise that I know the truth about Sally. I have never written to him since I found it out. Sorry to be so long-winded—but the matter is complex—and even now I cannot say that I can be dispassionate about it.

J.

My dear Laura,

Since Susan phoned to tell me that you had written to her you have been in my thoughts more or less continuously - but I've been waiting for a long enough space of time to answer your letter.

Although I have naturally got used to the thought of silence I was forced to observe for all these years, yet I feel very happy to be able to break it - because, of course, I felt very sad and frustrated in having to refrain from writing to your Father or to you. I don't think I could have agreed not to write to Mother if she had still been alive when Leonard and I parted. As far as Leonard is concerned it surely must be a relief to know at last - that everything is known to at least one or two persons other than Monica and himself and me.

However, I'll tell you what happened - as I feel I now have a right to do! Leonard met Monica (now called Elizabeth) at Pyrford where she was doing a pre-SRN nursing course after leaving School.) I knew that he liked her, & she him, but thought it was mainly that she admired the most intelligent of the patients whose tastes were similar to hers (in music) and that he liked some one to admire him who was also kind & interesting. But after he left Pyrford and got the job in B'ham he wanted to marry me, & I had no reason whatever to imagine that he had any reservations — in fact, I'm sure he hadn't them, but afterwards he was cruel enough to suggest that he felt that we had to marry — but that I was not in love with him!

However, Monica took a job in the Q. Eliz at B'ham, visited him in the library

*Letter from Joyce to Laura, 25 October 1967*

The matter certainly was complex. and I felt Joyce was far more sympathetic towards both Leonard and Elizabeth than they deserved. I also felt that she tended to blame Elizabeth, the interloper, rather than my father. I couldn't decide whether this was because she was writing to his sister, or because it felt more comfortable for her to think of Elizabeth, the younger woman, as the instigator of the situation, the seductress.

I opened the second letter that Laura had chosen to keep. It was dated 20 December 1968. It was much shorter — clearly they had met and talked several times in the previous twelve months. Just once does Joyce return to the subject of Leonard:

> I have a lovely blue and white wash basin full of Roman hyacinths just coming into bloom — but I guess you've got bulbs of all sorts, judging by last year. I often think of your father's skill with bulbs, and how lovely the garden at Wetherell Road was, on summer evenings, with the campanulas, and the mock acacia tree. I do wish I had not been forced to stop seeing him. It was a very sad mistake L made in hiding all from you. Still, it's surely better for him now.

None of it was new to me in the way of facts, or even Joyce's feelings. I knew she had been deeply in love with Leonard, and I knew from what she told me that she felt betrayed, but that once she discovered that Sally was Leonard's child it had made her understand his actions better. Reading these letters left me feeling wrung out, empty, and dried out, missing my mother as acutely as I had in the weeks following her death. I wondered if Joyce had shown Mick her letter to Laura. I thought probably not.

I felt the need to get out of the house, and decided to take the dog for a walk across the fields down by the river where the banks of the Severn have been cut away by fierce currents and the rushing tide. It was near to the time of the autumn equinox with very low and high tides, the time of big 'bores' when the river runs the wrong way, casting up trunks of trees, bits of shattered boats, petrol drums, and occasionally the bloated bodies of drowned animals. Here you can hear curlews calling, skylarks bobbing up and down as if they're on elastic, and low flying herons that patrol the ditches between the fields. It was low tide, and chocolate-brown mudflats, carved into channels and scoops by powerful tides and swirling eddies, gleamed in the setting sun. Nobody else was around — no dog-walkers, or bird-watchers, or men with guns hiding behind bushes, their sights on the wildfowl that feed on the mudflats. Nobody but me, the dog, and a thousand or more birds, feeding on the mud and then, for no obvious reason, rising in a white cloud, tinged with pink from below, to move off to another section of the river. I walked for an hour until it began to get dark, and I turned for home.

I had stopped thinking; I could only feel sadness and guilt at my lack of guts in comparison with Joyce's strength. I hadn't told her I'd seen Leonard; I'd not stayed with her until the moment she died; I hadn't done what I felt I should have done.

I walked back past the churchyard, its gloom mirroring my sadness. Even as I felt sad, I also felt an ironic detachment from the scene that could have come straight from a Brontë novel — mist slowly rising from the long grass between the tombstones, deepening shadows below the sooty branches of ancient yew trees, and soggy chrysanthemums dying on the graves (but, I smiled to myself, there would have been no glowing bright plastic flowers on the graves at Haworth).

I've never been to the plot in Exeter Crematorium where they scattered my mother's ashes; I didn't know where it was until just a year ago. In the weeks after Joyce died, an idea grew in my mind that we might take her ashes to Kent, maybe sprinkle them over the grey waters of the English Channel at Deal, or toss them into the wind off the cliffs at Dover. Mick was too upset immediately after the funeral for me to even approach him with this notion of mine, and when I finally asked what he'd like to do with the ashes, he said he'd already arranged to have them scattered in the garden of the crematorium. It was the 'usual thing'. It was too late. In any case, I don't think he would have wanted to make the trip to Kent or take part in any ritual of ash scattering. Too maudlin, perhaps, for his taste. Yet again I had been too careful, too reticent to ask what I wanted of Mick.

After dinner, I sat at my desk to look more carefully at the letters from Australia. Laura had arranged them in chronological order. The most recent was dated February 1972, the year Lucy was born. Had Leonard got used to the idea of being a grandfather by the time his second grandchild was due? I read:

Dear Laura,
Leonard wants to thank you very much for your letter. We had been thinking about you and wondering how you are getting on ...

The letter revealed nothing; mostly it was about Leonard's health — which was bad, as it always had been. I turned the pile over, so that I could read the earliest ones first. I have them in front of me now as I write, and still they astonish me.

There are three significant letters, and the first, according to the date on it, 14 October 1963, is in Elizabeth's handwriting. This is four years before Harry was greeted in Perth by 'the wrong wife', before he or Laura or my grandfather knew there was such a person as Elizabeth Jolley. The letter is short and here quoted in full:

> Dear Grandad,
> This Rug is a present from all of us. We went to Albany and saw the woollen mills and we thought of you when the winter comes on and we thought you would like a Rug. We are all well and our weather is beginning to get hot. We had a lot of Rain this last winter.
>> Love to you from us all
>> Sue
>
>> Mum and Dad are at work they would send their love if here.

A circle of red biro surrounds the 'Sue', and Laura has written at the top *Written by Elizabeth!* And below, a note: *Susan was never in Australia.*

I imagine that after Gordon and I had left her house after our first meeting, back in 1967, Laura went back to look through the shoebox of letters and photos, and dug these letters out to re-read. I had certainly shocked her with my insistence that I had never been to Australia and my denial that the girl in the photo was me.

I had known since that day in Laura's house in Buckhurst Hill that letters had been written in my name, but I hadn't seen them; now, holding the evidence in my hand rekindled my anger at the deception. As I read the letter to 'Grandad' I felt even worse that my grandfather (who, in any case, I called Grandpa, not Grandad) had no idea that the little girl who visited him in Hackney and who had climbed onto the bed in which his sick wife lay was not the writer of this letter; that the real Susan was living just a few hundred miles away and would have loved to

(written
by
Elizabeth!)

Dear Grandad,
This Rug is a present
from all of us. We went to Albany
and saw the woollen mills and we
thought of you when the winter comes
on and we thought you would like a
Rug. We are all well and our weather
is beginning to get hot. We had a lot
of Rain this last winter.
Love to you from us all
Mum and Dad are at Work (Sue) they would
send their love if here.
Susan was never in Australia.

*Letter from 'Sue' to Grandad*

see him. I remembered insisting to Joyce that Grandpa Jolley was alive and thinking of me. I had been right about that. 'I' wrote to him, so he must have been thinking about me when he read this letter. Also, I reflected, I was seventeen when 'I' supposedly wrote this letter, a great deal more sophisticated and articulate than its language suggests.

I turned to the next letter. This was written on 13 January 1964. It is addressed to Harry—Leonard and Laura's elder brother—and is about a present, a rug, presumably the one 'Sue' had sent the previous October. This letter, too, has some underlinings in red biro. I immediately glanced at the end of the letter to see if this one, too, was supposedly from me. It wasn't; it was signed Joyce and, as Laura said, the handwriting is nothing like my mother's. It is unmistakably Elizabeth's. The fictional Joyce writes:

> Leonard was upset over your letter because he is so far away and not able to do anything also he is not well himself and is hardly able to walk at times and quite frail, it is lucky his work is of the nature it is so that he is able to do it. He has written but perhaps the letter has gone astray, he finds it hard to write because he would not want to tell any one he is ill. It is very sad for him but he is very patient.
>
> I am very sorry about your Father, it is always sad when some one you love becomes old or ill but please don't blame our present for adding to his illness and confusion. When a letter comes so many thousand miles it should not bear an attitude of blame, especially if you don't know how the people are who are going to receive it. Leonard is not a letter writer but then neither are you or your wife or his sister and husband for you don't write to him. Some people write and some don't; I am exchanging letters every few days with my own family and we never feel cut off or unloved by each other.

At this last sentence I felt like ripping the thing up. At that time my mother and I had no communication with her sister or the rest of her family because they were with the 'Jims', those Exclusive Brethren who forbade them to have any contact with us. Exchanging letters every few days? Elizabeth might have been exchanging letters with her sister and parents, but not us. At that time we hadn't heard from our own family in years. I was also incensed that Harry might have thought Joyce would have referred to his wife as 'your wife' rather than by her name, Lilian (but perhaps Elizabeth didn't know the name of Harry's wife), and also that she would have referred to Laura and Stan as 'his (Leonard's) sister and husband'.

> Laura wrote to say your father had been pleased to have the present, and asked the children to write back which they were doing. They are waiting for photographs to be developed but perhaps it is better not to write or send them. What shall we do?

What should they do? Tell the bloody truth for a change. The letter closes with these words:

> Your letter is one long accusation; it is no one's fault when an old person becomes older. You should know that.

Having just read an authentic letter by Joyce, I was horrified that Harry might have thought for one minute that Joyce would have written in this manner. I had to show Gordon this travesty. He read it with increasing incredulity. 'Do you think your father knew about this?' he asked. I had no idea. I doubted it. Surely anyone in their right mind wouldn't have allowed it to be sent. Not only was it cruel and unpleasant, it was fraudulent. Elizabeth seemed to have set about creating a nasty and whining persona for my mother which could only cause great pain to the recipient of the letters. It seemed to me that this was the work of a mad woman. Perhaps she was having a nervous breakdown or something. There was even a mistake with the dating: the letter from 'Joyce' was dated 13 January 1963; but, given the content of the other letters, I think it was supposed to be dated 13 January 1964. Poor Harry, what must he have made of this diatribe from the sister-in-law he thought he knew?

The next letter was dated 17 April 1964, and was signed 'Rich' (presumably Richard); but again, although there had been some attempt to disguise the handwriting, to my eyes it looked remarkably like Elizabeth's. 'Rich' wrote to 'Aunty Laura':

> Please thank Granddad for the Christmas present. We have put it in the Bank except we bought the underwater swimming equipment you see in the photo and Sue bought the cotton to make herself the shift.

So this was the photo of the girl by the gate that Laura had had framed and had thought was of me. I remembered the picture of the children with their snorkelling gear, and would have liked to see it again, but Laura had not been able to find it. 'Rich' continues:

> It was Mum who wrote not Sue. She is away just now. School is back and we all got colds and sore throats and Ruth is pretty bad. It is pretty hot and no air today. Sue has sent a letter but was not sure if she put your address right.
>
> Please give Granddad our best love and love from all of us. Rich. Love from Ruth and Sue.

PS The cat you see is Moses I rescued him from the River when he was a kitty. There were three nearly drowned. Two I gave away. R.J.

Again, Laura has written on the letter: *I wonder who wrote this? Sally, Richard and Ruth did not know Susan existed.*

I am in no doubt that Elizabeth wrote these letters. So my question was more, what drove her to do this? Did Leonard 'make' her do it as he had 'made' Joyce promise to make no contact with his family? Surely he was not ignorant of her actions. Did she hide herself away in her room and write these letters because she felt it was the only way to protect her husband from his family — from his brother's 'one long accusation'? I should be fascinated to know what Harry wrote and what incident prompted his letter. Here Elizabeth Jolley, the future novelist, is clearly not in control either of her characters or the plot of this particular fiction; she is confused about what letters have been sent and by whom, and which ones might have gone astray.

The rest of the letters are dated after the time Harry visited Elizabeth and Leonard in Perth.

Much of what I read was upsetting, but one letter in particular made me angry. It was dated 14 January 1968 — just a few weeks after I had first met Laura, and less than six months since Laura had known of Elizabeth's existence. Elizabeth writes:

We had a letter from Susan which surprised us as she said in it she had only just heard that Leonard had a family, I can't think how she can write this because I have been writing to her and I told her some years ago we had 3 children and she seemed to take it all in. Either she has forgotten or else she is pretending! She wrote to us often when she was studying and I always wrote back and sent her presents. She just wrote to say she was 'disillusioned' but she wrote that some years ago too.

She was right that I had known that Leonard and she had a family. I'd known this since I was eighteen, when she first wrote to me to say that Leonard took no interest in any of his children. What I had only just heard and was still, in January 1968, reeling from, was the fact that the eldest was the same age as me and that her father was my father. I had learned of this only two weeks before, when Joyce told me, on the beach at Budleigh Salterton.

I couldn't take any more. I put the rest of the letters aside to read properly another time. I wrote to Laura, thanking her for giving me the letters and *Central Mischief,* and put it all aside for the time being.

However, in the weeks after I first opened Laura's package of correspondence from Australia, I kept returning to those forged letters. Each time I looked at them, the shock of my first reading returned, and I would fantasise about how I would fly to Australia, return to that bungalow tucked behind high trees, and thrust these flimsy scraps of paper in Elizabeth's face. The practicalities of such a journey would have been difficult — money, time off work, and so on. But mere practicalities didn't prevent my going to Australia. It was more a question of what such a dramatic act could possibly have achieved. Obviously, I showed the letters to Gordon (but not at that stage my children) and to one or two close friends. They urged me to do something about it. What? I'd ask. What could I do?

I could have written to Elizabeth. I could have said, look what Laura has given me. How do you explain these letters — these scraps of paper covered in scrawl, supposedly written by me, Richard, and Joyce that I am convinced were written by you, Elizabeth Jolley, to Laura, my grandfather and Harry? I could have telephoned. I imagined what I'd say, I even drafted a letter, but then thought about my own motivation: was I really seeking an explanation, or was I out for revenge? What would my mother have done had she seen that letter written in her name? What good could possibly have come from so aggressive an act? There was bound to be something in Joyce's religious upbringing that would have influenced her actions, or plain simple honesty that made her the person she was—a person who would keep a promise extracted under duress. I lacked her honesty. But was my lack of action a weakness, a desire not to rock the boat? I don't like conflict; I avoid it.

After several years, I fleshed out my fantasy of going to Australia and confronting Elizabeth with the letters. I fictionalised such a meeting and reorganised the timescale so that Leonard was still alive. I wrote it first from the main character's ('my') perspective, and then wrote the scene from her father's point of view. It was a satisfying exercise of the imagination—all the ends were neatly tied. In reality, of course, they remained loose and ever unravelling.

Some time later, when the burning fury that the forged letters aroused in me had calmed down, I read *Central Mischie*f, which I found fascinating for the insight it gave me into Elizabeth's character and her approach to writing. She's very insistent that her fiction is not autobiographical, and yet it is clear to me that in a fundamental way it reflects not just her concerns as a woman, a lover, and a mother, but deals very specifically with the details of her life—more so in the trilogy that is recognised as the most autobiographical than in others, maybe. All the same, much of her fiction that I've read (and I'm no Elizabeth Jolley scholar) deals with triangular relationships, which I can't help but see as alluding to her relationship with Leonard and Joyce.

Even in other less clearly autobiographical books — for example, *The Sugar Mother* — I was struck by the strange sense of finding aspects of my own life reflected in it. Edwin, a middle-aged academic, is married to Cecelia, a gynaecologist. They are childless. Cecelia is to go away for a year. A mother and her innocent-seeming daughter, Leila, move into Edwin's house. He falls in love with the young woman, who then becomes pregnant (or possibly she already is). Edwin is very excited about the baby — he falls for him, too, and dreads the return of his wife, who has become increasingly shrill and unattractive to him. Leila and her mother hand over the baby, and he awaits the return of Cecelia. When I finished reading it I felt depressed and displaced, and only gradually realised that this was to do with my subconscious casting of Joyce in the role of Cecelia, Elizabeth as the innocent Leila, and, most difficult of all, I saw Sarah as the longed-for and adored baby.

In the first essay in *Central Mischief,* 'What Sins to Me Unknown Dipped Me in Ink?', Elizabeth writes about why she writes. She refers to the story of Electra:

> Clytemnaestra tells Electra that a daughter can never know
> and understand the previous experience of the mother.
> ... I agree, one should not speak
> Bitterly. But when people judge someone, they ought
> To learn the facts, and then hate, if they've reason to
> And if they find no reason, then they should not hate.

Elizabeth was here possibly thinking not so much of her parents (which the context of the quotation would suggest), but of the situation vis-à-vis Leonard, Joyce, and herself, and consequently the effect of her behaviour on me and her own three children. But, as in so much of her work, this essay is allusive. As my sister, Sarah, has pointed out to me, her recollections and ideas are presented and described rather than analysed. Sarah adds that, for her, the most truthful sentence in the whole essay is 'Writing fiction is not easy for me; to write facts is almost impossible.'

My request to Laura for the letters was an effort to 'learn the facts'. I wanted to understand what could have made Leonard and Elizabeth behave as they had; I had no desire to hate or accuse. But, ultimately, those letters threw up more questions than answers. I did, however, begin to understand Elizabeth's strange romanticism about my life, her need to tell me how happy I was, her efforts to contribute to this happiness (telling me how proud Leonard was of me, and later of my children), reiterating what a success I made of everything — work, marriage, motherhood — when she had no real idea of the shape or trajectory of my life.

After reading this essay, I dug through my own stash of correspondence from Elizabeth and Leonard to remind myself what exactly she had written to me. At one point, when Rebecca was four (my age when Leonard left me and my mother), Elizabeth had asked me for a photograph of my daughter, so I sent one, and a calendar that Rebecca had made. Elizabeth wrote:

I must thank you very much for the lovely Christmas card, and then today came the picture of dear little Rebecca, what a dear face she has. Such a sweet face, it gives us pleasure to look at her, thank you for sending us the photograph and thank her for the lovely drawing and the calendar. What a good mother you must be (and Father is good of course) but it is mother, I think, who has patience to help a little girl to make the calendar.

Why did she have to write like this, I thought at the time of first receiving the letter. Why embroider? And now I think, what a load of eyewash to say that it gave 'us'—by which I was to understand both her and my father—'pleasure to look at her.' I think that, even if he did look at the photograph, it would have given Leonard nothing but pain.

On the subject of drawings and presents, in her first letter to Laura, sent on 31 August 1967, Elizabeth says: *whenever you have sent a present for Susan I have posted it to her and I think I have sent one or two letters from her to you earlier.* (Is she remembering those letters signed 'Sue' and 'Joyce'?) Laura has written on this letter: *Susan says she received <u>no</u> presents, and I had no letters.*

I wondered if Laura had ever challenged Elizabeth about this, or indeed the letters from 'Sue', 'Rich', and 'Joyce'. By passing them on to me, she was, I suppose, asking me to do something with them.

It seemed to me that it was a different person who had written those letters than the Elizabeth who had written to me just a few weeks before Laura gave them to me, sympathising with me about Joyce's death: *I don't think that the passing of time makes the loss any less but perhaps the pain is less painful after a while.*

The next letter of any interest I had from Elizabeth was two years after Leonard had died in 1994. It was not at all personal; it was typed and came from Curtin University. Addressed 'to whom it my concern', it was a request for information and records to be used by Dr Barbara Milech and Dr Brian Dibble for biographical/bibliographical research they were undertaking on Elizabeth. At the bottom of the formal request Elizabeth had scrawled, *Please ignore this if it irritates or bothers you. With love Elizabeth.*

Did she not realise what she was asking? Had she possibly forgotten all about the deception and the tangled web she and Leonard had woven?

# CHAPTER 14

I pondered for some time as to what to do about this request. Here, after all, was a way of dealing with the uncomfortable information I had about Leonard and Elizabeth. I could meet the two academics — Brian Dibble and Barbara Milech — and offer my account of the past. I could show them the fraudulent letters. I wouldn't have to confront Elizabeth directly; the academics would do it for me. But would they first of all believe me, or indeed use any hard information I might give them fairly? Or would they interpret it totally differently, and put an Elizabeth 'take' on it, like she did in her fiction?

In March 1996, shortly after receiving the letter from Curtin University, I heard from Brian Dibble directly: he would like to meet me when he came over to England next. It didn't take long for me to decide that this was not what I wanted. I wrote back to say I was sorry but that I didn't want to speak to him, giving as my reason the fact that I was still feeling raw after my mother's death and couldn't face trawling through the past with a stranger. I knew that he had also approached Laura and my cousin, Margaret, and they would tell him whatever they wished. A further reason I had for not meeting with him was that if this were an authorised biography, which was what I understood it to be, it was up to Elizabeth to reveal what had really happened. It would give her a chance to make good the damage that her and Leonard's actions had caused.

And then, in September 1996, Laura sent me her second batch of letters from Australia. These dated from the mid-1980s, and included several from my father to her, written much earlier (there had been none from him in the first batch). The package came with a book Leonard had produced back when he was a student, with a publisher friend of his and a notebook of hymns and poems written by my grandfather, which Laura told me she couldn't bring herself to read when she first found them after my grandfather's death. She wrote:

> As a result of my 'declutterisation process' I am passing it [the book] to you as you may be interested. I am also sending the last of Elizabeth's effusions*.
>
> The final end of all artefacts is the wasteheap but I am passing the decision to you.
>
> Love, Laura.
>
> * I am not sure why I am so doing. L.

As well as asking me to provide Brian Dibble and Barbara Milech with information and records, Elizabeth wrote to Laura and to my cousin Margaret. At this time, Dibble was working on two biographies — one on Elizabeth and one on Leonard. He asked Laura and Margaret for information regarding Leonard's early life. I was puzzled that anyone might wish to read a biography of my father. Surely the only aspect of his life that had any relevance to anything the reading public might find interesting was his affair and eventual marriage to the famous writer, Elizabeth. However, both Laura and Margaret agreed to help him. Laura gave me the draft of some notes she had prepared for Brian Dibble (she wasn't sure that she'd ever sent these to Brian, and I don't think they ever met, although they spoke on the phone). She wrote:

Leonard had very high standards. In one fundamentally important way he failed to conform to them. I suggest that he could never exonerate himself and his solution was to ignore all his pre-Australian life and to sever links with his family except for the occasional non-informative letter to his parents, (which was very very cruel.)

I do not make any comment on the reasons for the failure of his first marriage. I have no personal knowledge of the circumstances.

I do however strongly criticize his neglect of his parents and above all his complete neglect of Susan and his extraction of a promise from Joyce not to communicate with his parents. Joyce, I think, behaved in a foolishly honourable manner in keeping this promise.

I cannot understand how Elizabeth consented to have her biography written. Once a researcher started listing dates queries would arise and it is even more surprising that she suggested that Margaret, Susan and I should be contacted.

On another occasion, Laura said to me that she thought that it was Joyce's Exclusive Brethren upbringing that influenced her in keeping this 'ridiculous' promise. I wonder if both my father and my mother behaved as they did because of their different, but equally strict religious backgrounds; but whereas the Jolley children were encouraged to read and argue, and expected to discuss the Sunday-morning sermon over lunch, Joyce's encounters with the Bible and religion were quite different. Her childhood and teenage years were spent under the influence of a loving but very strict father, a convert to the Exclusive Brethren. Hers was not an intellectual family: in her family you did not question, you obeyed, guided by the scriptures; you read the Bible and improving stories, not novels and poetry, and frivolities such as the cinema and theatre were strictly forbidden.

Joyce told me how her father would keep her and her sisters kneeling at prayer after breakfast while her friends hung around outside the house, calling out that they'd miss the train to school (from Deal to Dover) if she didn't get a move on. She was quietly rebellious, and ultimately followed her dreams to escape the narrow confines of her family's religion and their distrust of higher education. I think that probably Laura was right, that Joyce's religious background did influence her to stick by a promise (especially as Leonard was threatening suicide), and that Leonard, having got what he wanted, couldn't face having to admit to his family that he had failed in what he perceived to be his parents' expectations of moral behaviour. 'He doesn't suffer fools gladly' was a phrase I frequently heard applied to him — by my mother, Laura, and later by Elizabeth and his biographer. Perhaps he couldn't suffer his own foolishness, and so compounded it with lies and evasions.

Laura never mentioned to Brian Dibble the existence of the forged letters. I wondered why. Would it have been a step too far for her? Was she expecting me to dish the dirt? After all, she had sent me the second batch of letters very soon after being contacted by him. By doing so she could honestly deny having any material in her possession that would be of any interest to him, and at the same time pass the responsibility of making use of them to me. Although when I told her that I had no intention of meeting with Brian Dibble and Barbara Milech, she said she understood my attitude completely. At this point, I didn't trawl through the Australian letters. I'd read enough already. I was sick of the whole thing.

I heard from Margaret, who told me that she had met Brian and Barbara, and how very nice they were. When I did meet them, years later, I could only agree with her. They were very nice. But at this time Brian didn't push me, and I decided to let things develop as they would. My hope was that Elizabeth would give them the whole story. The biography was taking a very long time to research and write. It was ultimately published in October 2008.

I still went down to Devon every few weeks (usually when Gordon was on call) to visit Laura and Mick and Lesley Lam. We would have lunch in the Imperial Hotel in Exmouth — at least two or three of us, and sometimes all four. Mick was still living in the house he and Joyce had shared, and managing to fend for himself and do some gardening, but the place was gradually becoming more dilapidated and filling with even more books.

Lesley had moved again, this time to sheltered accommodation close to Laura. Hers was a dark street. Whenever I went there I was struck by the smallness of the flat. It provided such a contrast to the huge, rambling house where she and Basil had lived in Hertfordshire, with its airy music room, stables, and barns. Tall, rangy Lesley looked out of place in her poky flat, and everything about her smelled of cigarette smoke, although she had a self-imposed rule that she would not smoke in front of visitors. Personally, I would not have minded at all; in fact, I liked the smell of tobacco, having once been a smoker myself.

Mick and I had walked Lesley back to her flat after one such Sunday lunch at the Imperial, and were having a cup of tea with her before heading back to Exeter.

The phone rang. Lesley picked up a pad she kept on the coffee table before going over to answer the 'damn phone — always going off when you don't want to be bothered with it'. 'I have to write everything down or I forget it immediately,' she added, flapping the notebook around. She couldn't find a pen. Mick took one from the top pocket of his jacket and handed it to her. He was never without a pen, and something to write on, and in the days before most of the people he knew had given up smoking, a box of matches or a lighter to light a lady's cigarette. He himself had long since stopped smoking.

Lesley sat down, telephone cradled on her shoulder, pen poised. Her caller was Brian Dibble, asking if she would meet him and Barbara. She gracefully declined, excusing herself from further conversation at this time by saying she had visitors. She didn't say who the visitors were, and merely said goodbye and hung up.

He had wanted to speak to her again about her time at Charney Bassett, the Quaker commune where she and Basil had lived and where they had first met Leonard and Joyce. 'It's so long ago,' she said. 'I don't think I have anything further to add to what I've already told him.' She shook her head at her forgetfulness. 'I'm getting a silly old woman. I'd forgotten — he wrote and said he'd telephone. He sent me this book, signed by Elizabeth,' she added, pulling a copy of *Central Mischief* from an envelope. 'I've no wish to read it. You have it if you like.'

'I've got a copy. Laura had one she didn't want.'

'Maybe Lucy or Becca would like it. I don't even get through the *National Geographic*s Mick brings for me.' She smiled at Mick and dropped the book into my bag. I noticed that Mick said nothing, and Lesley didn't offer him the book. I wondered if she didn't want to talk to Brian Dibble about Leonard in front of Mick. Did they ever talk about that part of the past that Mick had not shared with her and Joyce?

Lesley glanced around her tiny sitting room as if to prove that there wasn't room in it for so much as one slim volume. A desk was squeezed against one wall, bookshelves crammed with books, photograph albums, and tapes on another; a kitchenette opened out of the third wall, while a grandfather clock out of all proportion with the room, a barometer, and a couple of easy chairs filled the rest of the space. I sat on a dining chair by the desk.

'Sue, when I die, would you like to have that painting of Basil?' I had long admired her ex-husband's portrait.

'But Lesley,' I began, thinking *Oh no, I can't bear this talk of death. First Laura talks about it, then my mother doesn't talk about it, but goes and dies without proper warning, and now Lesley's at it.* 'You see,' she added, I'm trying to sort out all this ... stuff. Before it gets too late.'

The desire to sort stuff out was spreading amongst the old people. Mick had whipped through Joyce's clothes and bags as if he were emptying a sinking boat of unnecessary ballast, stuffing carrier bags and lugging them to charity shops. I wished he'd get on and throw out some of the books — there were literally thousands of them, bookshelves covering almost every wall of their house, but he hadn't touched her books, and kept accumulating more of his own. His appetite for reading was huge: poetry (particularly the 'war' poets), novels, history, and biography, and he was a great fan of Conan Doyle and a member of the Sherlock Holmes Society, writing articles and attending meetings.

Mick said something about that eventuality not occurring for a good long time yet.

'It's a lovely portrait,' I said.

'Then you must have it.' She leaned over and put her hand over mine, pleased, perhaps, that this was one thing she'd sorted out. 'When the time comes.'

She leaned back in her chair. 'But there is something I should like you to have now.' She stood up, cleared her throat, and disappeared into her bedroom. Mick looked bemused when Lesley returned and put on the coffee table a giftbox for Yardley's soaps. She tipped out the contents — it was her jewellery box. Lesley wasn't one for jewellery: she was an outdoorsy woman, at home with dogs and horses, even though neither of these had been part of her life for some years now, and she tended to wear tweed skirts and jackets, a brooch pinned on the lapel. She sorted through the rings with her nicotine-stained fingers. 'I don't wear any of this stuff any more. No occasion to.' She picked out a gold ring with three large amethysts in an elaborate Victorian setting. 'I'd like you to have this. It was my mother's, and I've been thinking of giving it to you for some time. Your mother offered to buy it from me for you when things were financially rather tight and I was selling things — like my viola. I wouldn't let her do that. I said I'd rather you had it as a gift from me.'

'Oh Lesley ...' I felt like crying, but grinned instead. 'It's beautiful.'

She laughed her throaty smoker's laugh. 'And useful. Amethysts protect the wearer against drunkenness.'

'In which case ...' I took the ring, and it fitted me perfectly. 'Thank you.'

I turned the ring on my finger, the light from a table lamp glinting on tiny chips of diamond either side of each of the amethysts.

The painting remained on the wall of her flat, above the desk, until she died in April 2002.

Her death came suddenly. The last time we spoke was when she, Mick, and I went out for a Sunday pub lunch. The pub was called The Digger's Rest. While Mick was standing waiting at the bar, Lesley turned to me and said, 'I've had enough, Sue. I wouldn't tell Mick that, but really I've had enough.' She told me that she'd left her solicitor with arrangements for her funeral, the music to be played and so on, and that she'd given a few personal gifts to friends; the rest would go for sale for various charities she supported. 'And, of course, you must have the painting of Basil. And this.' She took a small diamond ring from her pocket. I protested. She folded my fingers over it and patted my hand. She swiftly changed the subject as Mick came back balancing a tray of his bitter, Lesley's sherry, and my red wine.

A week later she had a stroke, was admitted to hospital in Exeter, and apparently never regained consciousness. However, when I held her hand and asked her to squeeze mine if she could hear me, she did. She squeezed hard. I said goodbye to her, she squeezed my hand again, and I left the ward with Mick. She died two days later. Another link with Joyce and Leonard was gone.

By this time, April 2002, Laura had sold her flat with the dramatic view of the estuary because she, too, had begun to feel she should do the sensible thing and move into sheltered accommodation — somewhere modern and warm and convenient, with someone on hand should she have a fall (she'd tripped and broken her collarbone, and was now nervous of going out in icy or very wet weather). Mick helped her organise the financial aspects of the move. Laura undertook the final step in her 'declutterisation process', giving hundreds of books to charity shops and the remaining correspondence from Elizabeth to me. I pushed the letters and cards into a file, still uncertain why she gave them to me and unsure of what to do with them.

Both Laura and Mick suffered various illnesses but 'soldiered on', as Mick would put it. And then, not many months after she had moved into her new flat, Laura phoned me. She had been for a regular check-up with her optician, and he or she had asked when she had last looked at herself in the mirror. Rather affronted, Laura asked if perhaps her wig was on crooked. But it wasn't that. When she looked in the mirror that was offered her, she saw that her eyes were bright yellow. 'My skin had gone yellow, too. I looked a fright,' she said.

A domiciliary visit by the consultant physician was arranged, and the next day, July fifth, she was in hospital. Mick, Gordon, and I went to visit. She really did look very yellow; but, other than feeling tired and complaining about the noise the other patients made, she said she was fine, and looking forward to getting back home. This never happened. Laura was diagnosed with pancreatic cancer, and died a few weeks later. As soon as she had been told the diagnosis and prognosis, Laura set about making sure everything was in order. She spent a long time writing figures on bits of paper, working out what money was where, and what needed to be done to make everything easier for me and Margaret when she died.

Like Leonard, Laura had never been someone to show much emotion, but she did say to me one day that if there was an afterlife and if she came across Leonard there, she'd give him a piece of her mind. She said it in a joking way, but then looked at me with such sadness and said, 'I'm still not able to forgive him completely.'

Mostly, when I visited, I was sent on errands — to buy her a new nightdress and soap, and to return to the mail-order firm a dress that she would no longer need. 'No more dresses for me,' she said. I found it so sad, but her pragmatic approach was typical of Laura, so I did whatever she asked, finally bringing in some books she particularly wanted — any detective fiction, she said, to provide an escape from the ward, and Wordsworth. She said she knew enough of the Bible and the Book of Common Prayer by heart, and didn't need to read them.

My daughter Rebecca had had her first baby shortly after Laura was admitted to hospital, and she came to stay with us for a week when the baby was a month old. Rebecca was keen to see Laura, and for Laura to meet the baby. The baby, Amber, lay on the hospital blanket on Laura's bed while her great-great-aunt stroked her cheek and held her feet in her hand. She said, 'You should be out kicking your legs in the sunshine, not here in this place,' and thanked Becca for bringing her down to see her. We asked a nurse to take a photo of the four generations. Laura died a few days later, and once again Rebecca and I were with her, the baby sleeping contentedly in her mother's arms.

Elizabeth went into a nursing home at about this time, the one that she used to visit daily when Leonard was a resident. Laura had been alert and on the ball right up to the last day of her life; but Elizabeth, like her husband, was beginning to become confused, and was no longer able to live at home with Richard. I didn't hear from her, or of her, until 2007 when she, too, died. I had a letter from Sarah and then saw obituaries in the papers. I had imagined that when she died the secrets and lies would become public knowledge (if indeed the public was the slightest bit interested). But this wasn't the case. I learned from one particular report that all her personal papers, including my father's diaries, had been given to the Mitchell Library, part of the State Library of New South Wales, and that they would remain inaccessible to the public for a further twenty years or until such time as all her children were dead. I have since learned that this report was incorrect, and that it was the library's recommendation that the personal diaries should be restricted for thirty years or until the death of her children, and the correspondence restricted for ten years. However, at the time of reading this obituary, I didn't know this, and thought it macabre; and the more I thought about it, the more I felt impelled to do something about it.

And then, not much more than a year later, in June 2008, Mick died. His death was unexpected. He had been invited by some friends in Exeter for Sunday lunch. He was late, which was most uncharacteristic of him. They phoned, but there was no answer. So they drove round to his house to see if anything was amiss. He lay on the dining-room floor, the radio playing and an unfinished meal on the table. An ambulance and the police were called, but it was too late. The body was taken away for a post-mortem, and his friend Joy left a message on our answering machine at home for me to call her. As soon as I heard her voice, I knew Mick was dead.

Mick was a very well-organised man, and all his papers were filed and ordered, and his will in the filing cabinet. He had already told me, on one of our pub lunches, the contents of the will, and it was very straightforward. With him there were no personal papers to be shut in a locked vault; there were hardly any personal papers at all. As I went through the grim process of clearing everything out, I had hoped to come across some of Joyce's letters — such as the one to her from Leonard asking her to tell me he was dead. And maybe others in the box I had found tied in yellowing tape at the bottom of the trunk in the bathroom. I was also hoping to find the sketchbook with drawings of me as a baby. But all this had gone. There was, however, the letter from Joyce's sister saying that we could no longer meet. There was no correspondence between my mother and Mick, either, just one Valentine's Day card she'd made with witty and touching verses for his birthday on 14 February 1974. Some letters from me to Joyce were in the bottom drawer of her desk, and some to her from my children. There were also two more packets of black-and-white negatives.

Now there was no need to go through the lengthy magic of black-and-white printing. I scanned them on my computer.

These were photographs of Elizabeth and Joyce with Sarah and me. We are no longer babies, but toddlers. Sarah (Sally) is on the move, her dress a streak of white as she runs away from me (or I chase her) with a toy wheelbarrow. We are photographed from behind, throwing soil into the wheelbarrow; then we are with our mothers; again, Sarah is trying to escape. I stand with Joyce's arms about me, holding a golliwog, and I am focussing on Sarah — perhaps impressed by her determination not to stand still and do what she's been told.

Then there are the two women. Once again, I was struck by how similar they looked. Was one copying the style of the other? Medium-long hair drawn back from the face, short-sleeved dresses with buttons down the front, and round collars. This time, a dog lies on the ground between them, a dark wriggling ball, which I recognise as our Scottie, Jock. I'd forgotten all about the dog — oddly, it was more of a shock to see him and recognise him than it was to see Joyce and Elizabeth. I had got so used to their images. The women's hands are almost touching as they fondle the dog, smiling down at him. Was Leonard with them? Was he the photographer? Possibly he was, because tucked into the back of the folder I found one further negative, which showed Elizabeth and Leonard, arms around one another's shoulders, gazing lovingly at each other. I couldn't match Elizabeth's clothing with any of the other photographs, either from this latest lot, or the ones I had discovered years before when Sarah and I were newly born. Did Joyce really not know what was going on? I can only suppose not. I printed copies of the pictures of myself and Sarah, and sent a set to her.

*Elizabeth and Joyce with Sarah and Susan
in the garden in Birmingham*

*Sarah and Susan in the garden in Birmingham*

*Leonard and Elizabeth*

I missed Mick, but wasn't troubled by the feeling of guilt that I felt after my mother's death. Over the years since she had died, Mick and I had got to know each other better, and neither of us, I think, was wary of the other. It had taken me years to get over my childhood jealousy of him, and he, being a reserved man, had not made any presumptions of intimacy with me. I had told him that I'd met my father and he said that, yes, he thought I probably would have done so, but Joyce preferred to think I hadn't. I think that he, too, would rather I hadn't gone to Perth, but understood why I had. I guessed that in the weeks that followed Joyce's death, when he had obsessively got rid of all her clothes, he probably also destroyed all those things that connected her with Leonard

Mick would have hated to move away from his house and to feel that he couldn't live independently, and so his sudden death was a blessing. The coroner assured me that one minute he'd have been listening to the radio (Saturday's *World This Weekend* on Radio 4), and would then have been gone, everything switched off like a light.

There was a lot to do, dealing with all the hundreds and hundreds of books that lined every wall in the house, and I felt his absence each time I went down for another session of clearing, but ultimately I felt liberated. I didn't have to worry about hurting Mick's feelings; I didn't have to worry about not being close by should 'something' happen. It had happened, and I hadn't been there.

It was time for me to return to Australia.

# CHAPTER 15

October 2008: I was on my way to Australia, flying over the oceans that Leonard and his family had first crossed on board the *Orion* nearly fifty years before. It was almost twenty years since I'd first come to Perth to meet my father and Elizabeth, 'the wrong wife'. Now all the main characters in this story were dead: first Harry, then Joyce, followed by Leonard, and, at ninety-one years of age, his sister, Laura. In February 2007, after five years in a nursing home, Elizabeth died. And then Mick, just a few weeks before I set off on this journey.

Having turned down Brian Dibble's request for a meeting when he was researching his biography of Elizabeth, I had now contacted him and arranged to meet him. The biography, *Doing Life*, had just been published and was due in the bookshops any day now. It was twelve years since I had the request from Elizabeth to *afford them* (Brian Dibble and Barbara Milech) *access to any information and records you might have*. Dibble knew both Elizabeth and Leonard well, and I was looking forward to reading his book, hoping it would reveal to me what it was about their characters and their relationship with each other, as well as the dynamics of the Leonard, Monica/Elizabeth, and Joyce relationship that made them all behave as they did. It wasn't necessarily the question that most readers of a biography would ask, and probably wasn't a fair one for me to ask, but this is what I was hoping to get from meeting Brian and reading his book.

He had told me there was another book, not to be published, that he started before he got going with the biography of Elizabeth. The subject of this book was my father, and it had been in connection with this book that he had initially contacted Laura. Brian wrote that he'd leave the draft manuscript for me at the hotel to read before we met. This was even more interesting for me than the published work on Elizabeth. Because not only were Brian and Barbara close friends of both the Jolleys, but Brian held an important key, unavailable to the general public: he had been given permission (by Elizabeth) to read her private papers, now locked in the vault of the Mitchell Library in Sydney.

Since learning of their existence, I became increasingly intrigued by the contents of that locked vault. Why did Elizabeth go to such lengths to ensure that her papers were not seen by her children, or the public at large? What was this control from beyond the grave all about? To me, it sounded like something from an Edgar Allan Poe story — secrets hidden away in a dark vault, ink fading, paper becoming brittle and turning to dust at the touch of a warm, living hand. Having worked in archives, I knew that the letters and diaries would be stored in acid-free files or envelopes in boxes on shelves in a controlled atmosphere: they would be either catalogued or awaiting cataloguing. I couldn't help but wonder if Leonard had confided his thoughts and feelings about leaving me and Joyce to his diaries. I longed to know how he really felt — not how Elizabeth had told me he felt about me. Before leaving home I had contacted the senior curator at the Mitchell Library to make an appointment to meet with him when I travelled on from Perth to Sydney.

Laura had written *I believe in bringing all the skeletons out and giving them a good shake* ... Were these hidden documents Elizabeth's skeletons? Many writers, such as J. D. Salinger, go to great lengths to maintain their privacy; and others have left instructions for their private papers to be destroyed after their death (instructions which have not always been kept). Perhaps Elizabeth wanted to have her cake and eat it, posthumously. From all that I had heard of her, she was a modest person who guarded her privacy. So, was it some kind of literary arrogance on her part to imagine that her novels and stories would still be read in 2020, or thereabouts? Whatever the future of the literature might be, I'd have thought that if you don't want your current readers or your children to know about your personal life, you burn your secrets or feed them to the shredder. But those letters between Elizabeth and Leonard — maybe she couldn't bring herself to destroy the evidence of her emotional life. I'd understand that. Maybe this was her equivalent of Joyce destroying the prints of the photographs of the two women, their two babies and their father in the suburban garden, and yet keeping the negatives.

As I travelled closer to my destination. I began to wonder if it might not have been better to leave the skeletons in their dark cupboards. Merely by talking to people Leonard used to know, it was possible I would discover things that I'd rather not know. And if I managed to get a glimpse of his diaries and the correspondence between him and Elizabeth, who knows what uncomfortable or even painful effects these might have on me? But I had made the appointments to see Brian Dibble and the curator, and I was speeding towards Australia — I'd passed the point of no return.

There were something like eighty films to choose from on the flight entertainment menu. I chose *When Did You Last See Your Father?* It was too ironic a coincidence to ignore, and although I'd read Blake Morrison's memoir, I hadn't seen the film. I was soon absorbed, oblivious of the cramped space and stale air of my surroundings. In the film (and the book), Morrison, played by Colin Firth, recalls both his fury with his father and their close bond, all the things they did together, the embarrassment the father caused the son, the pain of the boy's not understanding what was going on in the adult world. At one point, without any warning at all, I felt tears wet my face. Embarrassed, I wiped them away. The moment that triggered this unwanted emotion was when father and son hug. I never hugged Mick, not once. The closest we got was a peck on the cheek. It was never Mick I wanted, but 'Daddy', the man who spent so many years refusing to see me.

After the film ended I tried to sleep. An elderly man on the other side of the aisle to me was sleeping noisily, dribble snaking a track down his stubbly chin. The girl next to me leaned on her partner's shoulder; a blanket covered them both. I was wide awake and lonely. I dug out from my bag a book, Elizabeth's *My Father's Moon*:

> 'Why can't the father, the father of your — what I mean is why can't he do something?'
>
> 'I've told you, he's dead.'
>
> 'How can you say that, he was on the phone last night. I could tell by your voice, that's who it was.'
>
> 'He's dead. I've told you.'

Monica told Joyce the father of her baby was dying of TB. Unlike the character's mother, Joyce believed her. I'd read the book before. It was a mistake to begin it again now, so I closed it and stared at the map of the world on the screen, the altitude and the speed of the aircraft, the hours from our last stop and before the next. I tried to banish the apprehension and loneliness that grew stronger as the rest of the passengers, it seemed to me, slept and dreamed. I reminded myself that this journey was a fantastic opportunity and made a mental list of the pluses, convincing myself that although it might throw up challenges, there would be nothing I couldn't deal with.

I was looking forward to meeting my half-sister Ruth for the first time. Brian Dibble was immensely helpful to me: after checking with her, he gave me Ruth's email address, and also asked Richard if he'd like to meet me. Unsurprisingly, he wasn't at all interested. Brian and Barbara even invited me to stay at their home while I was in Perth, and offered to meet me at the airport. I turned down their kind offers, as I preferred to be independent: I'd booked myself into a small hotel. Another thing to look forward to was that I'd be spending ten days out in the bush at Bundanon, in New South Wales. Exciting but a bit daunting, too — I wasn't sure what to expect. Bundanon was the home of the artist Arthur Boyd, the place where he came to paint, and where now, through the trust he set up, artists in all disciplines are invited to apply to stay and work. I would be staying in the 'writer's cottage'. I had a stash of books to take there with me — including *My Father's Moon*, *Central Mischief*, and the other two novels that are considered the most autobiographical of Elizabeth's work. I also had my camera, but as yet no clear idea of what I might do there.

I was the only person from my flight who had booked a place on a minibus that took travellers from the airport to any of the hotels in the city. It was midnight. The driver, a middle-aged man with long, tangled hair and tattered jeans, had that mixture of Australian outspokenness and mateyness that borders on being intrusive but isn't intended that way. Although I longed for nothing more than to slip between cool sheets and stretch my limbs, he insisted on taking me on a tour of the deserted city, enthusiastically recounting its history and telling me all the sights I should visit. He asked me whether I had been to Perth before and why I was here now. I said something about doing some family research. He asked the name of my family. I told him Jolley, and he immediately said, do you mean Elizabeth Jolley? He'd read several of her books; she'd been a local celebrity and a national treasure. He'd heard she was a really nice lady. He, too, was a writer. He was writing a novel; he'd get away from the city to the bush, and camp under the stars and write for a week or so at a time. It was a novel based on his own experiences. 'We all have a book inside,' he said, 'and I'm getting mine down on paper.'

The beaten-up minibus rattled and lurched along the wide, empty streets; I held on tight to the side of my seat and wondered if this guy was okay. Maybe a regular, if more expensive, taxi would have been a more sensible option. Or perhaps I should have taken up Brian Dibble's offer of a lift from the airport. We crossed the Swan River, gleaming in the starlit night. 'That's you,' he gestured ahead. 'Nice little hotel. Popular.' He swung to a halt. He took my case up the steps to the hotel door, shook my hand, and refused a tip. 'Good luck with your researches,' he said and climbed back into the minibus. He made me smile and I thought, *It's fine. Everything's going to be fine.*

The night porter told me that he had a note to say that someone had come by with a packet for me — a shoebox of stuff, he said, but he couldn't find it. I knew what it would be: Brian Dibble's account of my father's life. It could wait until the morning. I fell into a deep, dreamless sleep.

On Tuesday 14 October 2008 I woke to bright sunlight and unfamiliar birdsong. The air was clear, the sky a bottomless blue. I sat by a sparkling pool and began to read Brian's manuscript about Leonard, which he described in an accompanying note as:

more a series of notes from long ago and not reconsidered since I started to devote more attention to Elizabeth, rather to Elizabeth and Leonard, from which you will receive a somewhat different picture of LJ.

As the morning wore on (and I would be seeing Ruth soon), I became increasingly bewildered and upset. It seemed to me that the portrait of my father that Dibble was painting was one of a weak, self-deluding, egocentric intellectual snob; a man who was vain and lazy. My father's intellectual snobbery was a characteristic that Joyce had spoken about (and warned me against). However, here there seemed to be no compensatory wit or charm in my father's character to lighten the picture. According to Dibble's analysis in this draft, this man required women to look after him: first, his mother (and from what Laura had told me, he had been my grandmother's favourite, physically weak and vulnerable), and then Joyce (perhaps her crazy promise not to tell any of his family about their separation was a kind of looking after, a fear that if she didn't do this for him, he really would kill himself), and then Elizabeth, who had trained to be a nurse.

I was interested in his attitude to women. Apparently he surrounded himself by attractive women at work, which suggested he was a bit of a womaniser, or at least a flirt, but I was also interested to learn that he employed people with problems (some with physical disabilities, and some with psychological problems) — a practice that revealed a side of him previously unknown to his colleagues. I noted with some pleasure that he had organised an exhibition for International Women's Year in 1975 (which wasn't popular with his male colleagues).

Extracts from his juvenile diaries showed that he was a romantic: he wrote poetry; he saw himself as different. As I read, I thought, *You can't judge a person from what they write* (to themselves) at any age, least of all when they are adolescent. For me (and I have never kept a diary consistently), this is the place where people can tell themselves all kinds of things — it is a space in which they are free to create their own identity. It allows for fantasising, and in Leonard's case this was falling in love with unattainable women or girls. Extracts from the diaries also indicated that Leonard loved to walk alone, to study birds and trees.

It was a relief to stop reading after three hours. I was about to meet Ruth. At least I wouldn't have to view her through any other eyes than my own. I had never seen a photo of her, so didn't know what to expect; but, as I came down the stairs from my room on the first floor to the hotel lobby where she was waiting for me, there was no doubt: this was my half-sister. She looked just like her mother: the same-shaped face, the same hair, but with a candidness about her eyes that I hadn't seen in her mother. Maybe this was wishful thinking, because I really wanted to like her. We hugged, and I felt immediately at ease. She was genuinely pleased to see me. She'd brought me presents — biscuits, a tea towel, a pretty ironstone bead bracelet. We decided to walk through Kings Park, which rose behind the hotel.

As we walked we talked, easily. Mainly we talked about our lives now, our children (she had three boys), and my grandchildren. I was wary of asking her too much about the past. I didn't want to criticise her mother, whom she clearly loved and had been close to. But, gradually, she told me things. I asked where Leonard's grave was — I hoped to visit it, but there was no grave. His ashes had been buried out in the country, at Wooroloo.

We sat in a café in the park. Ruth told me more. She had lived in England with her family for a whole year, in 1966. They had been in Tonbridge, in Kent. Perhaps that was why

Leonard hadn't written to me when I told him I was going to get married. Perhaps he was scared I might suddenly appear on his doorstep. I wondered if he had ever told Laura that he'd been living so close to her (she was in Essex at the time), and doubted it. Richard hadn't been happy at school in England. It seemed that he and Leonard didn't get on at all well. Was this fairly typical antipathy between a middle-aged father and an adolescent son?, I wondered. Too much testosterone flying around the place? Or was it more to do with characteristics Dibble saw in Leonard? Were Richard and Leonard at loggerheads because Leonard saw Richard as a rival — for Elizabeth's affection and attention? Dibble suggested that Leonard suffered from arrested development, that he had been infantilised by women. I was fairly sure that Ruth hadn't read Dibble's notes on her father, and in any case I felt that these weren't the kind of questions I could possibly ask her, or not at our first meeting. But I did ask her what sort of father Leonard was to her. They got on well, apparently.

Ruth had never shone at school; and, given my assumption of Leonard's lack of sympathy for people who struggled academically (based, I must admit, on the frequent references to him not suffering fools gladly), I asked her if he used to get impatient with her. Not at all: he helped her with her homework, and often the two of them, father and daughter, would go up to the house in the country. They'd stay alone up there. She liked that, she said.

The more Ruth and I talked, the more convinced I became that I was dealing here with someone quite unusual, someone so different from me it amazed me that we had any genetic connection. It wasn't merely that we looked so different (whereas when I first met Sarah I'd immediately seen physical similarities between us); Ruth and I had very different characters. Where I was sceptical and circumspect, she seemed trusting and transparent. Unwittingly, she made me feel that I was taking advantage of her; I wasn't being quite honest with her. Back at home, in my filing cabinet, I had those fraudulent letters that damned either one or both of her parents, and I omitted telling her about them; and it was this knowledge of her parents' duplicity that had motivated my journey to Australia and to this meeting with her (although, ever since I knew that I had two half-sisters and a half-brother, I'd longed to know them). I realised it would be hurtful to tell her at this point about those poisonous letters, and decided to put off the decision. In any case, my quest was to understand, not to accuse, and by meeting Ruth I hoped that I would discover more about her parents.

Ruth and Elizabeth had been close, they talked a lot, and when Elizabeth had worked as a cleaner, Ruth would go with her mother and help. Sometimes Ruth would tell her stories about incidents at school, which Elizabeth turned into short stories that were later published. Ruth said she had begun to write some stories, too. I said I'd like to read them, but she seemed shy about showing them to me.

Back at the hotel, I showed Ruth some photos of my home and children and grandchildren. I also had some of our father's family, photos that had belonged to Harry and that Margaret now had. There was one of Leonard when he was about seven, at school in Bow. It was a group photograph, taken out on the street: Leonard was a little boy in the back row, with straight, shiny hair, staring seriously at the camera with his eyes the shape of my own. There were others of our grandfather and grandmother, of Leonard and Laura when they were older; one of Ruth's mother, my mother, and me and Sarah as babies in the Birmingham garden. Ruth said that she thought she'd seen a photograph of my mother once, at her parents' house. Perhaps it was at Joyce's graduation ceremony? I remembered that at my graduation Joyce had told me that Leonard hadn't told his parents about his own graduation ceremony: he was ashamed of them, she said, even though they would have been tremendously proud of his getting a First. But perhaps he was there, at his own graduation and Joyce's, with his camera, snapping his girlfriend.

Ruth left to go home, and I went up to my room to read the rest of Brian Dibble's manuscript. I found the place where I'd left off earlier that afternoon, but I couldn't concentrate — I needed to get out and think. I walked along the Swan estuary for an hour or more, photographing my footsteps in the sand, watching wading birds go about their business of feeding and pairing (it was the Australian spring) while traffic roared along the freeway next to the river. I went over what Ruth had told me, trying to fit the picture I had from her, of Leonard the father, to that I had from Brian Dibble, of Leonard the man who couldn't relate to children; disliked them, even. This chimed with Elizabeth's first letter to me, when she told me that he didn't take much interest in any of his children, and implied I wasn't to take it personally(!). I decided not to carry on reading about my father that night. I was too confused and tired to give it my proper attention.

The following morning I spent by the pool again, reading Brian Dibble's manuscript. People came in for a quick swim before setting out on another trip. They sometimes asked if I'd seen some interesting sight, or recommended a restaurant. I felt a bit of a wimp, and wondered if I was wasting my time here, sitting by a small swimming pool, reading, writing some notes, and occasionally cooling off by dabbling my feet in the turquoise water, as if this were all there was to do in Perth. *Think of this as a very pleasant office*, I told myself. *You're not on holiday*. I wanted to finish that manuscript. There was still a big pile of pages to get through. I would be seeing the author for lunch and this wasn't the sort of thing you could speed-read. This might have been a draft manuscript, but it was thick with detail — much of it, for me, riveting. I noted where I'd got to and skipped ahead until I reached the last chapter. Here were Dibble's conclusions, his analysis of Leonard's character, his summing up of my father's life. According to Dibble, Leonard displayed the characteristics of a narcissist: he had a grandiose sense of self-importance, believing himself special (no doubt encouraged by his mother's 'spoiling' of him, I thought) and demanding of attention; he exploited people (he certainly exploited my mother's generosity of spirit and yet accused her, in a diary entry, of self-absorption); he lacked empathy; he was envious of others; and he was arrogant. Each of these points was expanded by examples, some of which came directly from diary entries. This seemed to me unfair, especially as there were other diary entries that contradicted some of this selfishness and showed a clear-sighted self-knowledge.

I turned back the pages of my notes to where I'd copied a diary entry written in 1940, where Leonard said that he recognised his burning desire for the impossible while he neglected what he had. Following this admission is a declaration of his true feelings of loyalty to Joyce.

The overall conclusion to Dibble's draft manuscript was that Leonard was a person stuck in childhood. He was a fraud, and a good deal of his behaviour was an attempt to hide it. He feared intimacy; he was left frozen at the point of commitment.

I carefully placed the papers back in order in their box. I felt as if I had swallowed something disgusting that stuck in my throat and was making me choke. I drank some water and then jumped into the pool, and swam fast up and down, not pausing at the end of each short length, concentrating on keeping going, attempting to drown my disappointment and hurt. What had I expected? I knew Leonard had lied and gone to great lengths to avoid censure. I saw him as weak — but a fraud? I turned over onto my back, closed my eyes against the beating sun, and floated, and as my heartbeat slowed I felt myself calm down. I thought Leonard was probably more agonised by his moral quandaries than Dibble implied. He obviously felt Leonard was an out-and-out bastard and Elizabeth a victim, even if a self-appointed victim. I climbed out of the pool onto the burning hot tiles. *Don't be so hasty,* I thought. This was hardly a reasonable response to what I'd read, and in any case it wasn't fair of me to look ahead to his conclusions without first reading the reasons that led him to them.

Brian Dibble couldn't have been more considerate and generous. I said that I was finding his biography of Leonard very interesting, although rather alarming, but didn't want to talk about it until I had finished reading it properly. He reiterated what he'd said in his note, emphasising that it was something he'd written long ago, and that I might well find a rather different picture of Leonard in his book on Elizabeth, which was written later (and by implication, based on much more detailed research). I looked forward to seeing this later picture of my father, and hoped that he would appear there as a more likeable character. After all, people I knew, such as the Wheelers and Lesley Lam, my aunt, and, of course, my mother, had all liked him and enjoyed his company. In the event, I didn't finish his manuscript until just before I left for Sydney, and as yet we have not discussed his conclusions.

He took me to lunch in a restaurant in Kings Park. He told me that he'd asked a friend of Leonard's if he'd be prepared to meet me and talk about my father, as this man would give a different perspective on Leonard than Brian's. I said I'd like that. Brian had other ideas, too, of what he might do to give me an idea of what my father had been like. He would take me for a drive, through the streets where he'd lived and to the library where he'd worked. I was cautious in what I said, and felt increasingly guilty that I had refused to see him when he was researching his biography. He had either been led to believe, or had chosen to believe, that when Leonard left Joyce my mother had known that it was Elizabeth he was leaving her for, and that she also knew that Sarah was Leonard's child. She had no idea, I told him. Whether Brian accepted this alternative possibility, I don't know. This wasn't the time or place to argue whose version was the correct one. I would have to wait until I'd read what he'd written in his biography of Elizabeth.

The university library was modern and spacious, set amongst wide sweeps of lawn and shady trees. Brian told me how influential Leonard had been in building up the collection and expanding the library in the years he was university librarian. He took me through a vast room where students sat at desks working, to where a portrait of my father hung on a wall. Sarah had previously sent me a photograph of the painting, but to see it in situ in a public building was a very different experience. Leonard looked very much as I remembered him from twenty years before: he sat in a chair with wooden arms, leaning into the back, with his head thrust slightly forward, a thoughtful yet impenetrable expression on his face, his blue-grey eyes focussed on a space just beyond the viewer's (or the artist's) own point of view. His high forehead and straight, dark, floppy hair, greying at the temples, the wispy beard, and sunken cheeks were skilfully rendered; his hands lay in his lap, the fingers twisting around each other (only the artist had been kind to his hands — they were not deformed by arthritis). He wore a red shirt, a purplish-grey tie, and what looked like a soft leather or suede honey-coloured jacket — hardly the academic librarian in his book-lined study. I took a photo of the painting. Thousands of students must have passed this painting in the years since it was commissioned and hung. I suspect that they hardly noticed it on the wall, or, if they did, they perhaps thought, *Funny-looking old guy*, and looked more closely at the inscription beneath. However, seeing it hanging in such a public space gave me a feeling of pride — one that I needed after the deadening effect of reading Brian's account of my father.

After the library we drove around some more, along the street where Leonard and Elizabeth had lived, past the house where my half-brother Richard still lived. I remembered the house vividly, and would have liked to stop and say hello to Richard, but this wasn't an option. As he drove, Brian spoke warmly of Leonard, about his wit and scholarliness, the acidity of his written pieces in comparison with the charm and gentle humour he showed in social relations and between friends. The more I learned about this man, the more complex he appeared to be. He teased and he made things up, writing in his own profile in an illustrated *Who's Who* in 1979 that he had been University Librarian, University of Western Australia since 1959 (true), followed by a list of positions that he hadn't held. He also said that he was born in Königsberg in 1884 (which would have made him thirty years older than he was), and had married Elisabeth von Hellingrath in 1926 (when he was twelve and the Elizabeth he did eventually marry was three years old). And, to cap it all, he added a photograph of a man who was nothing like him in appearance. Why do it? I suspect he was poking fun at such publications. Apparently he also told different people he'd been born in different places, ranging from New Zealand (to Elizabeth), Diss (where his father had been born — to his friend Ken Gasmier), and Essex (to the editor of a Scottish newspaper). Why say these things? Because it doesn't matter greatly where one is born? Or because he still suffered from the 'shame' of his poor East End origins? Or, more painful to contemplate, that my father was a pathological liar? I would like to think the first is the most likely explanation.

Brian took me back to my hotel, and we arranged to meet again the night before I was to go to Sydney. He and Barbara would like to take me out to dinner. The biography of Elizabeth was still not in the bookshops, but it would be very soon, he said. No chance to nip out and buy it, then. Meanwhile I finished reading his manuscript about Leonard. He had called it *An Allegory of Love*. I particularly enjoyed reading the extracts from Leonard's adolescent diaries. What he says is often insightful, and although the language is at times ponderous, I was impressed by the sophistication of his thought. In one entry, he writes about the value of keeping a diary, noting that although one's self-definition changes as one grows older, his diary will tell him how he used to feel, what he hoped for, even though it won't necessarily make him understand his younger self. Then, still a schoolboy, he falls in love — with a nurse at Moorfields, the eye hospital — and endures the agonies of unrequited love. After that he gets into university (he and Joyce met at the interviews for open scholarships, but he doesn't mention her or any of the other candidates). Before he actually starts his course, he writes of his fears that he will have to stop reading for pleasure, and instead have to study particular texts and read about what others think of the work. I understand that entirely — it is the way I felt when I began my university education.

Later diary entries form the basis of much of Dibble's work — and for me added a dimension to a story I already knew: I had heard Joyce's version of events and of his personality; and

Laura's. Now I had his own perception of what was happening to him and how he responded in the crucial years when he was engaged to Joyce and falling for other women, or having crushes on them — such as Lesley Lam and Louie Wheeler, the nurses at the hospital where he was a patient. (The two became both his and Joyce's close friends.) As far as I could see, these were more of the nature of romantic fantasies than full-blown affairs, and I doubt that they even went as far as a kiss and a cuddle, let alone any real sexual encounters. This, of course, happened with Monica/Elizabeth, but not until after Leonard and Joyce were married.

I telephoned Ken Gasmier, the man who Brian Dibble had told me about, and who had been a fellow librarian and friend of Leonard's, and we arranged to meet for lunch on Friday, my last day in the city.

Before then, though, Ruth had invited me over to her place to meet her husband and her sons, and have supper with them. So, on the Thursday, I decided not to do any more reading or writing, but to go for a long walk in Kings Park and spend the rest of the day in the city. There I wandered around the modern city looking at galleries and shops, glad to escape from the hotel and the park, no matter how comfortable the hotel and how beautiful the park. The busy city also provided an escape from the past, where my thoughts and imagination had been roaming for the past few days.

A commuter train ride out to the suburb where Ruth lived felt almost like an adventure. I met her family: the first thing her husband said to me was, 'You look the image of Leo.' I wasn't sure that I wanted to be immediately recognisable as my father's daughter, although I knew that when I had first seen him I'd recognised something of myself in him. We chatted easily — Bert (who was much older than Ruth, and had had two previous wives and an eventful life before he met her) was entertaining, and the boys drifted off to do their own things.

Friday 17 October was my last full day in Perth, and I was to meet Ken Gasmier for lunch and then have supper with Barbara and Brian.

Somehow, because he'd been described as a friend of Leonard's, I expected Ken to be a very old man. He wasn't. He was younger than me, and drove an old sports car. We drove up to Kings Park. Over the past few days this vast park had become the backdrop to meetings and conversations about my father. I had walked up there on other occasions, too, when I was alone and wanted to think. The day before I'd spent the entire morning exploring the parkland, which ranged from almost wild bush to stunning plantings of native flowers and trees, themed gardens, and miles of pathways. Parrots flitted about the trees, fountains played, students and families hung out, and workers escaped to the restaurants and cafés for lunch breaks.

Ken was, I think, a bit like Leonard in his reserve. He told me that he hadn't been at all sure he wanted to meet me, but then he thought, why not? Whether curiosity or kindness got the better of him, I'm not sure. I immediately warmed to him. He knew Sarah and her husband from the time they were students, and had been a frequent visitor to the Jolley household and still kept in touch with the younger members of the family. He told me how fond he was of Elizabeth — she was like a second mother to me, he said. Leonard, I think, had been supportive of him both at work and personally. When I told him about the secrecy that Leonard and Elizabeth had maintained over the real situation from 1950 onwards, he was quick to defend Elizabeth, explaining it as her shielding Leonard from the reactions of his family to what had happened. I wasn't convinced. I didn't tell him about the letters signed from my mother and myself that were sent to Harry and my grandfather, and that Laura had kept. (I wasn't at all sure that I wanted anyone beyond family members and close friends to know about them as yet.) I did, though, talk about how Elizabeth had controlled the situation when we'd met twenty years before, despite having insisted I should feel free to ask the questions I wanted to ask.

Ken Gasmier said that he thought that what I saw as Elizabeth's tactic of controlling the situation on that occasion was her way of avoiding 'the inevitable fallout' of Leonard's reaction to my questions (which I imagine would manifest itself as irritability and upset that she would have to deal with after I left). For Ken, Elizabeth seemed to be above suspicion, and such was his conviction that I was almost won over to this point of view. It was, after all, feasible: her desire was to protect Leonard while at the same time shielding herself from his anger, however this might be expressed — I imagined in acid words or sulky silences. Leonard was needy, and depended heavily on Elizabeth, who always responded to people's needs, he said. Ruth also had told me about how she wore herself out looking after students and others who she felt needed her. Here Ken seemed to be agreeing with Brian Dibble's assessment of at least one aspect of Leonard's personality — that of the child demanding care.

However, there was another thing that struck me afterwards about Elizabeth's desire to exert control, as I saw it. I said to Ruth what a pity it was that we hadn't been able to meet when I came to Perth back in 1989. She seemed puzzled. She hadn't known I'd even been to the city and visited her parents at their home twenty years before. So, I concluded, the proposed meeting between us must have been a possibility that Elizabeth considered and rejected.

Both Leonard and Elizabeth, Ken said, were supporters of the underdog and of the outsider, and as an example he told me how determinedly they had supported a colleague of Leonard's in the German Department who had shot and killed his little son. Leonard had campaigned to have the man's sentence reduced from life imprisonment, and used to visit him frequently when he was in prison, bringing him books and spending time with him. I had read about this in Brian Dibble's account of Leonard's life, where he attributed Leonard's motivation in this regard to his feelings about children (he felt alienated from them) and his outrage at the lack of humanity of a system that treats people in such a way as this. We then talked about some of Elizabeth's books. I said that I'd found *The Sugar Mother* disturbing.

'Yes,' Ken said, 'that triangular set of relationships occurred time and again in her fiction.'

I didn't voice my next thought, which was that the thing that had upset me about the book was that I interpreted it in very specific personal terms: Leonard wanted Monica and her baby, not Joyce and me.

Ken had to go back to work, and we agreed to email one another if there were other things I might think of asking him later. Or just to keep in touch. Back at the hotel, I looked up the passage that had struck me so forcibly in *The Sugar Mother*:

> The great test for two people was whether they wanted to meet and, having met, whether they wanted — needed — to be together for the rest of their lives. The final part of the test was: could they exist without each other, did they want a life each without the other?

Dinner with Brian Dibble and Barbara Milech was in a very smart restaurant by the yacht club on the estuary. Brian presented me with a copy of his biography of Elizabeth, and while we talked of her and of Leonard, of Richard, Ruth, and

Sarah, I still kept quiet about the letters. I wanted to read what he had to say in the second version he'd written about those times before I said anything else. We moved from the Jolley-centred conversation to my plans for the rest of my stay in Australia — Bundanon, Gordon's family in Sydney, the fact that I had made an appointment to go to the Mitchell Library, and from that to more general topics — books, films, politics, education — the usual sort of chattering classes' dinner conversation.

I was flying out to Sydney on the Saturday afternoon. In the morning I went back into the city to meet one more person. This man, Marco, had nothing to do with Brian Dibble, Barbara Milech, or the Jolleys. He was a curator and a friend of an artist I had worked with back at home, and to whom I had already told my story. The artist, Neville Gabie, had spent several months doing a residency in Western Australia. I thought the work Neville had done here was fascinating, and was interested to know about other projects Marco had developed, and so we met for coffee at the city's Art Gallery. We filled each other in on our work, talked about the problems of maintaining permanent gallery spaces, and the need for international links when you're stuck out at the edge of a huge country, as they are in Perth. He knew all about Bundanon, and had been out there (a long way from anywhere!). And then, like the minibus driver on my arrival at Perth, he asked me what had brought me to the city. I told him.

'Oh, Elizabeth Jolley,' he said. 'She was a lovely person. A friend of mine knew her — she had time for everyone. She used to be everywhere, but in recent years she faded from view. She's dead, now, isn't she?'

# CHAPTER 16

The Mitchell Library in Sydney is an impressive stone building, classical in style, with wide, arched windows looking over parkland to the harbour below and fronted by a portico complete with Corinthian columns. It reminds me of the National Gallery in London. At the time it was clad in scaffolding, which hid its grandeur, but inside a cool and ornate vestibule with a marble floor and high ceiling recalled the weight of learning and the preciousness of the collections held within the walls. And in its vaults.

I was welcomed into the senior curator's office. He sat behind a massive desk piled with books and papers, and was charming and urbane. It was a short meeting. He told me that, as I already knew, Elizabeth's private papers were not available to the public, but that if I wished to see her other papers — drafts of novels, radio, and film scripts, correspondence with her publishers and her agent — that would be easy to arrange. Of course, he understood that this was not what might interest me. He suggested I make an appointment for when I returned from Bundanon, and he would see what he could do.

I thanked him and left the building to walk across the park to Sydney's own national gallery. I was a little disappointed, but hardly surprised by what I'd been told. There was nothing I could do about it, and so I turned my mind to the next stage of my Australian journey: Bundanon. I wanted to look at some paintings of the artists who had worked there: Arthur Boyd and his family, and particularly the work of Sidney Nolan, who had married Arthur's sister, Mary, and who spent a lot of time at Bundanon, painting with Arthur. I had met the Nolans in England, shortly before Sidney died, and then visited Mary Nolan at her home in Herefordshire where they had begun to set up an artists' community similar to the one at Bundanon.

The first time I went to Australia, in the late 1970s, I had visited the Art Gallery of New South Wales and been disappointed in the Australian landscape paintings I saw there. To me, they lacked a distinctive antipodean quality and didn't reflect the experience of being in Australia. It was several years later that the Angry Penguins exhibition of the Melbourne-based group of artists came to the Hayward Gallery in London (this was my first introduction to work by Boyd and Nolan). *This is more like it*, I thought. Here were the colours, the light, the vibrancy and the culture of a different country; here was something that felt very Australian and that engaged with its history. Now that this more recent period of Australian art hung in the galleries, I was looking forward to seeing the place where some of the work had been produced.

As soon as you turn off the road from Nowra to Bundanon, and onto a dirt track that leads to the homestead, you enter another world. And for me this world felt very alien. The sky was dark; it had been raining, and the car slid down deep gullies and scrabbled up impossibly steep climbs. The forest closed in on us. We passed a gate with a rusting sign: Bundanon. From here on, the track was metalled; it straightened and dipped down. A streak of sunlight lit a wide stretch of water through the trees on the right — the Shoalhaven River. Then the landscape opened out, and I relaxed: here I could breathe more easily. There were fields on the river side, and a herd of huge black cattle looking more like bison than cows, gathered in the middle distance.

The director of the Bundanon Trust is an old friend of mine, Deborah Ely, and it was she who took me there and showed me around. My home for the next ten days was the 'writer's cottage', a simple single-storey clapboard building, where farm workers, drovers, maybe, would have lived in years past. Beyond it, up a track and closer to the edge of the bush, was another similar building, the musician's cottage. Every window of this cottage was covered in tin foil that glinted in the stormy light. Not a ray of light could penetrate into the building. The artist who'd painstakingly blocked out the light was known as Y, and his proposal was to live in the dark with no human contact and no food, and see what happened, what he might make or do while in this self-imposed isolation. I wondered if I had a madman as a neighbour.

A couple of hundred yards away from my place was a quadrangle of modern buildings, which faced inwards to a grassy square. These were the purpose-built studios with living accommodation for up to eight people, and a store.

I unpacked and sorted out my supplies. When I was a child I would go to great lengths to make even the most temporary place my own — arranging ornaments on the chair by my bed in boarding school, rearranging the furniture in the spare room at my grandmother's house, insisting on unpacking all my clothes and putting them away, even if we were staying in a hotel or bed-and-breakfast for just one night. Nowadays this nest-making activity has been reduced to a matter of arranging my books and perhaps picking some wild flowers and putting them in a jug. I wandered through the rooms, drinking a cup of tea. I liked the feeling of the little house; the sitting room/

writing room was light and simply furnished: a wooden table, well scratched and ink stained, a leather sofa, and easy chairs. The kitchen and bathroom were well equipped. There were two bedrooms, the larger of which had a double bed and windows on two sides; the smaller one, a single bed and a piano. The bungalow also had two verandahs: one at the back of the house, facing east, looked up to the bush and to the musician's cottage, and the other looked over the river valley. Wooden supports held up the west-facing verandah, and swallows were building nests in its roof. That night I discovered that it wasn't just birds that made their home here; there was a snuffling and a grunting and a bashing about under the floorboards of my bedroom. The writer's cottage was also home to a noisy wombat who left his droppings in neat piles outside the kitchen door.

The sky had lightened, and I decided to explore. I'd read the warnings about going out into the bush on your own, so thought I'd just investigate the immediate surroundings. The track that led to the musician's cottage curved around and up a hill into woods beyond. The bush was quiet; I heard a leaf fall, a buzzing of insects, my own steps. I kept my eyes skinned for any kind of animal or bird that might be dangerous, but as I didn't know what I was looking for, I probably missed any that were about. The forest floor and the trunks of the trees, the enormous ferns, the lianas, and the rotting stumps must provide plenty of camouflage for creatures to hide from a clod-hopping human.

There was evidence of much human activity, just no humans right now. The path bent around some thick bushes, and then the trees thinned and the air seemed to lighten: in front of me was a natural amphitheatre, an amazing curved backdrop of grey rocks dripping with hanging ferns and orchids, and at the foot of the cliff lay large mossy boulders. Logs had been placed on the forest floor to seat an audience. Through the towering trees I could now see a deep cerulean sky, and innocent, fluffy white wisps of cloud drifting by. The place felt magical.

I lay in bed that night, listening to music on my laptop to drown out any weird and scary night sounds from the bush. I needed a plan, otherwise my time here would be spent enjoying the magic of the place, taking the odd photograph or bit of video, and daydreaming. Of course, I had Brian Dibble's biography of Elizabeth to go through. I'd read it quickly during the few days I was in Sydney, but I wanted to read it more thoroughly and make notes. And then I had my stash of Elizabeth Jolley books. Obviously I'd be doing some reading. But I could read anywhere. Here I had the luxury of time and isolation, with no demands other than those I imposed on myself. I should use the place itself to work out how I would begin to make sense of all the information I now had, and to develop an approach to this account.

The first day at Bundanon, I read and read. When I first opened Dibble's biography of Elizabeth, I had done what I imagine anyone who thinks they might feature in a biography does, and looked myself up in the index. I wasn't there. I was pleased, because it meant that he hadn't tried to tell my story. But Joyce was — 'Jolley, Joyce Ellen Hancock', with about thirty page references, and immediately below her, 'Jolley, Leonard', with a list of subheadings and page references that began with 'arrogance', went on to 'controlling nature', 'estranged from family', 'as flirt', 'intolerance', 'marriage to Joyce', and so on until the last but one entry was 'visitors discouraged' (the last 'at Wooroloo'). It wasn't hard to see how Dibble viewed my father — there was not a single positive subheading, unless you were to count his employment and a major publication (on cataloguing).

For my second reading I concentrated on the chapters

that involved Joyce, which mainly occurred in the period I knew most about — not only from what she had told me, but also from what I remembered. I began by writing notes, but soon abandoned that and wrote my reactions in the margins of the book. I started with the time when Elizabeth (at that time Monica Knight) re-met Leonard and Joyce, now married and living in Birmingham. I already had read Dibble's account of Leonard first meeting Monica at the hospital at Pyrford where he was a patient and she a trainee nurse. (Note that, here, Dibble refers to Elizabeth Jolley as Knight, her maiden name. I will refer to her here as Monica, because that's the name she was known by at the time and the name that Joyce always used for her).

> To Knight, Joyce and Leonard were an ideal couple — modern, educated, cultured, socially committed. She was overwhelmed by the Jolleys' responding so positively toward her, to the point where eventually they seemed to orient their own lives around her and her visits.

Did Joyce really begin to orient her life around Monica? From Joyce I had the impression that she liked Monica, and I guess that she was probably flattered by the attention the younger woman paid her, but this view of Joyce and Leonard seemed to me to be more wishful thinking on Monica's part than anything else. I have no doubt, though, that Leonard found her sexually attractive and that she fancied him, too. This is confirmed by Dibble saying that Leonard persuaded an unwilling Monica to go skinny-dipping in the river with him and Joyce. The skinny-dipping experience is recreated in *My Father's Moon* (narrated by Vera). I looked up the relevant passage:

Magda's body is beautiful.

'You are beautiful.' I tell Magda. She is standing naked on the river bank and Dr Metcalf is pouring buckets of water over her. She seems taller without her clothes and I am surprised at her hips. I am surprised too about the size of her breasts. She is sunburned, a lovely golden brown, all over. The bodies of rich people are always suntanned and handsome. Dr Metcalf is brown too. It is because they can be in places where they can take off all their clothes. They do not have to look out of tall windows and see the sun and not be out in it because they have to work. People like me are always white. Even if there is a sunny day and I can lie in the sun I simply get hot and I stay white. My face is gaunt with the dark circles of night duty for ever round my eyes.

It would be naive of me, or of any reader, to make a direct translation of this particular triangular relationship; it was more the situation that was taken from life and put into fiction. Leonard and Joyce weren't rich, and neither did they come from backgrounds where nude sunbathing and skinny-dipping was the norm. Nevertheless, it is just this kind of passage that I initially found upsetting when I read Elizabeth's books: I see her painting the picture of an innocent led astray by selfish and manipulative sophisticates, and can't help but relate what happens in the fiction to the facts of her experience, and in the process of writing, her distortion of those facts. But isn't this what all novelists do? Maybe it's because I see the reason for her distortions as self-justification.

Whatever my personal take on fact and fiction, this doesn't stop me maintaining, somewhat hypocritically, I admit, that a novel should stand on its own and be judged by what happens between the covers of the book rather than relating it back to the author's life.

The other books in the Vera Wright Trilogy are *Cabin Fever* and *The Georges' Wife*. Together with *My Father's Moon,* these three novels are recognised as the most autobiographical of Elizabeth's novels. The books are intimately connected one to another, but they do not follow in strict chronological order. In *Cabin Fever,* Vera reflects on memory:

Memories are not always in sequence, not in chronological sequence. Sometimes an incident is revived in the memory. Sometimes incidents and places and people occupying hours, days, weeks and years are experienced in less than a quarter of a second in this miraculous possession, the memory. The revival is not in any particular order and one recalled picture attaching itself to another, is not recognizably connected to that other in spite of it being brought to the surface in the wake of the first recollection.

This, I think, is a key to seeing how Elizabeth structured her fiction: incidents and even passages are revisited and repeated — for example the opening of *My Father's Moon,* which I read on the plane coming over to Australia:

'Why can't the father, the father of your — what I mean is why can't he do something?'
    'I've told you, he's dead.'

This is repeated word for word in *Cabin Fever,* with just one additional line in the second version. It isn't so much a case of 'What Vera Did' and 'What Vera Did Next', more how Vera remembers those same events again and again. And many of those events or characters would seem to connect to Elizabeth's experience and her own memories.

Although I find them interesting, it isn't my purpose here to trace the parallels between Elizabeth Jolley's life and her fiction, but some are so startling that I can't ignore them in trying to see how Elizabeth felt about my mother and my father. The detailed analysis of the facts of Elizabeth's life and how they are dealt with in her fiction is something her biographer explores. I was fascinated by his conclusions. Using her diaries and letters as his source material, Dibble tells us that Monica felt guilty about her relationship with the Jolleys, guilty about going to see them in preference to visiting her parents. For several weeks during the year before my birth, it seems that her feelings of guilt were such that she resolved not to see any more of the Jolleys. But then she gave in to her need to see them and went to visit. According to Dibble, Elizabeth records in a diary entry how:

> Leonard told her that she was repressed, they both said she had been brought up too strictly, and Joyce explained to her how some friendships end but in others the interest increases and surprises and so the friendship continues. After that Knight prayed that the Jolleys would never reach the end of her.

These feelings find expression in the fiction. For example, in Monica's life and in her fiction there was a real person called Gertrude who reappears as Gertrude in her fiction. The fictional Gertrude seems to be extraordinarily close to the real one. Not only do they share a name: each Gertrude is an older woman, each is a friend of Vera's/Monica's mother, each provides the family with black-market eggs and chickens, and each listens to the young woman's problems and offers her advice. The real Gertrude didn't trust Joyce and Leonard. She called them 'the Jolley boys'. In *Cabin Fever,* Vera thinks about Gertrude:

When I think of Gertrude now and how she, in her own honest way of thinking, tried earlier to draw me away from the fascination and the excitement of my new, in her words, wild and extravagant, friends, I also remember (I can never forget) how she, as she put it, tried then to go along with me, to humour me as if allowing me a full taste of the Metcalfs as if to tire me with them ...

I imagine that the real Gertrude had just this attitude to Leonard and Joyce, and thought that having failed to persuade Monica to break off her friendship with them, she changed tack, realising that to condemn them would only make Monica want to see them more, while hoping that overexposure to Leonard and Joyce would dull her appetite for them. It didn't work. As her diaries reveal, Monica became increasingly obsessed.

The theme of Vera's fascination with other couples is revisited in *The Georges' Wife*. Vera is now a single mother (with Helena, Dr Metcalf's child) living in Scotland, where she has found work as housekeeper to an older man, Mr George, and his sister (a couple of a different kind). At this point in the narrative, she and Mr George have become lovers and she has had a second child (by Mr George). She has left both children with Miss George and moved back down to Birmingham, where she is working as a hospital doctor and staying with her parents. She has made friends with another couple, Noel and Felicity. Her mother isn't happy about this:

'Why do you always have to have some other place to go when you come home for a day off from the hospital and why always a couple?' My mother's indignation shows between her shoulders as she bends over the sink. 'Have you forgotten already how easily people make use of you? And what is it about these people? This couple?'

But like Elizabeth with the Jolleys, Vera can't get enough of this couple. She is drawn (or sucked) into their unconventional world — they live in a dilapidated farmhouse and appear to live off nothing but what they scrounge from other people and, now, Vera. They are both Oxford graduates playing at being bohemians. They call Vera 'Persephone' (referencing her fertility and her bringing in of the harvest?). One night, a friend of theirs comes to visit while Vera is there. She goes upstairs to sleep in the small, damp back bedroom, but overhears Felicity and Noel talking to their friend about how useful she is to them. She hears their huge artificial laughter and wishes to escape, but is caught by Felicity at the kitchen door. She is taken up to bed, to lie between them:

'Come on,' Felicity says, 'you first, in the middle.'
Unable to stop shivering, I feel their nakedness on both sides of me. I feel their warmth and their ardour.

These of course are just short scenes from Elizabeth's novels, written long after the time when she was visiting Joyce and Leonard at their flat in Birmingham (and feeling guilty about it). But it seems to me that they position Vera, the innocent, as being taken advantage of and patronised by an older, more educated couple, and they suggest that these people were a sham; and these two characters were based to some extent on Joyce and Leonard, that 'educated, cultured and socially committed couple'.

Triangular relationships occur time and again in Elizabeth's fiction, and it is all too easy to conflate and confuse fact with fiction, to make assumptions about the novel from knowledge of the life. However, I wonder if Elizabeth was attempting in her writing to make 'her' part in the fictional equivalents of the Joyce/Leonard/Monica triangle that of innocent victim.

To return to Dibble's biography—what with the skinny-dipping and the hints of three in a bed, it is no surprise that he reaches the conclusion that Joyce was aware of the sexual relationship between Leonard and Monica, and, by implication that possibly Joyce joined in. I personally doubt that Joyce had any sexual relations with Monica and Leonard (together), otherwise she would have realised that Leonard was Sarah's father and, later, that Monica was the woman he was leaving her for. She said to me several times that had she known, she would never have agreed, firstly, to let him go without a struggle and, secondly, to make that promise to him to keep quiet about their separation. I speculated on who knew what, who thought they knew who knew what, and whether Joyce was completely in the dark. I came to the conclusion that whatever the two women thought, the only person who knew exactly what all three of them knew was Leonard, and he wasn't going to tell Joyce he was having an affair with her friend, or tell Monica that Joyce knew, because then Joyce might have done something about it, disturbing the precarious harmony of the friendship between him and his two women. He was having his cake and eating it, too.

According to the Dibble biography, after her declaration of her desire that the Jolleys would 'never reach the end of her', Elizabeth went on to write in her diary that she was certain that Joyce knew about her affair with Leonard, because she and Leonard had been seen hand in hand. In fact, Joyce told me this had happened. Someone had reported to Joyce that they'd seen Leonard 'with a young woman'. She challenged her husband, asking him if the young woman the neighbour had seen him with was Monica, and he swore it wasn't. He had been seeing someone else, but it was a casual thing. It was over now, and Joyce was the woman he loved. Whether Leonard loved her or not, he was making love to both her and Monica, and whether it was a matter of failed contraception or no contraception at all, both women became pregnant at about the same time. Monica told her mother that the father of her child was a patient at the hospital dying of TB, but she elevated his status to being a doctor when she told Joyce that she was expecting a baby. Clearly Leonard colluded in this story.

I continued to read, marking what I considered factual mistakes, dotting the pages with question marks. A particularly large question mark (and exclamation mark) comes when Dibble states that when Leonard left Joyce and me in 1950, he had told Joyce all about his affair with Monica, that it was all out in the open.

*What?* I thought. *What a load of rubbish! He had done no such thing!* She found that out months later, during that first Christmas holiday after we'd gone to St Catherine's and were staying with her cousin Gwen, and she'd been incensed by Leonard's treachery. I looked back at the transcript I had made of Joyce's letter to Laura written in 1967, and to me its integrity was transparent:

> I saw less and less of her — and L wouldn't talk about her — so I didn't question him or know where she had gone. He had become very gloomy and physically distant with me, though he said that he loved me — and I believe that he did. Needless to say I — unfortunately for me — loved him deeply — and was totally under his influence. You know what a dominant personality he has. He always made me believe that he was right and I was rather silly (though perhaps he didn't intend to do this) and I utterly believed every word he said — I mean that I couldn't conceive that he would lie to me.

I couldn't *not* believe what she wrote there. I was sure Joyce had no idea what was going on. But then what Dibble had said about Monica's insisting that Joyce knew what was going on gave me cause to doubt, and I wondered again about the Joyce/Leonard/Monica triangle.

I returned to the Noel/Felicity/Vera triangle in *Cabin Fever*, which is referred to at the beginning of *The Georges' Wife*. Vera is on her way to Australia, and on the ship meets another woman, a widow:

> 'Tell me about yourself, Migrant,' the rice-farm widow says to me. So I tell my widow things about myself. When I tell her about Felicity and Noel her mouth is so wide open, as she listens, I can see her gold fillings ...
>
> ... 'You mean to tell me!' she says. 'Oh, I can't believe ...'
> She says, 'that they, I mean, <u>together</u>. You can't mean <u>that</u>.'
> 'Yes, that's right,' I tell her.
> 'Oh Migrant. You poor child, poor poor child.'

Vera puts the widow right. No, it wasn't as she thought. The sex, she implies, was consensual.

Like much of Elizabeth's writing, I find this passage very funny. I love the rice-farm widow's salacious expressions of shock and Vera's apparent ingenuousness in her response, but still it made me think about the possible parallels in Elizabeth's and my parents' lives. Might Joyce and Leonard and Monica have had sex together? If they had, Joyce wouldn't tell Laura, or indeed anyone, least of all me. She was no prude, and I'm certain she had several relationships with men between Leonard and Mick, and for all I know she had relationships with women, too. Her best friend when she was at school was undeniably gay. So maybe they had ... in which case ...

I put aside my books; I had to get out of the house. Most of the day had passed without my realising it, and the thought of not having made any further explorations of my surroundings was shameful, rather like my sitting by the pool in Perth. I set off up the path I'd taken the previous afternoon. This time, someone was sitting on the verandah of the musician's cottage. He waved at me and invited me up. He told me that he'd been plagued by thoughts of food all the time he'd been in the dark house, and was enjoying himself, gazing over the valley planning a menu for a big meal for the following night. Would I like to come? He was making a shopping list. But, hey, why not come for a walk with me if I were going up into the bush? He'd been in the dark so long.

I was glad of his company, and we walked for an hour or more, going further into the bush than I would have done on my own, climbing off the path, up slopes covered in ferns and rocks, some of which were massive formations looking like ancient creatures. (One in particular looked to me like a giant tortoise.)

While we walked and talked, I mused over the questions that my reading had thrown up. Who was who? Was Vera the character in Elizabeth's novels her younger self, Monica? Were the various older male characters in her fiction Leonard? Edwin in *The Sugar Mother*, Dr Metcalf in *Cabin Fever* and *My Father's Moon*, Mr George in *The Georges' Wife*? If I wanted to know what sort of man my father was, would these portraits help me understand him? If the latter three are considered her most autobiographical books — and Dibble discusses this very interestingly in his biography — the place where Elizabeth does speak with less ambiguity about herself and her writing is in the collection of essays, *Central Mischief*. That would be the next book to look at in more detail. Tomorrow.

Elizabeth wrote about England from Australia. Her sense of place and of period is acute and detailed; it's as if the physical and historical distance sharpened her vision. During my stay at Bundanon, I was spending a lot of my time in the past — my imagination was full of it — and in my dreams I returned to a house that had never in reality existed but was familiar to my dreaming self, and has been for years and years. I've never been able to will myself to go there; it just happens. The house is like St Catherine's School with its staircases and underground passages, but is incomplete — staircases lead to emptiness, things I know to be familiar are just out of sight. It's disturbing but not frightening. When I am in the dream house, I know I'm dreaming, but at the same time I know I can't escape the dream. In the writer's cottage, I returned to it night after night.

In the daytime I lived in a completely unfamiliar environment, and I wanted to document the experience of being there, so every day I went out with my camera. And without realising exactly how it happened, as the days passed, a method of working developed. When I wasn't reading I rambled through the bush, taking photographs of the landscape and odd 'found' objects. I downloaded them onto my computer, putting them with scans of old photographs, ones that had come from my mother's and my father's families and from my own childhood. The words weren't there yet, and if not the actual structure of the story, an approach to telling it emerged through my playing about with images on the computer.

I discovered that my fellow residents at Bundanon would all be leaving on the same day and that I would be there on my own for several days. This bothered me: although I had got used to being in such an isolated place, I knew that there were people around should 'anything' happen. The 'anything' wasn't so much a practical disaster, like a snakebite or an ankle twisted while climbing a rock — I had a telephone in my cottage with a list of numbers to call in such an emergency. The 'anything' was more to do with the unseen fears embodied for me when I was a child by the White Lady of St Catherine's. The residents didn't see much of each other — apart from some evening socialising, but knowing that there were friendly human beings close at hand was reassuring.

I put my fears to the back of my mind and continued to read *Central Mischief*. This was the book that both Lesley Lam and Laura had been given by Brian Dibble when he came on one of his trips to the UK to do his research into Elizabeth's life, and both had passed their copies on to me. It is a collection of articles, speeches, and essays assembled and edited by Elizabeth's literary agent Caroline Lurie. It makes a revealing companion to her fiction. Coloured markers bristled from the pages of my copy, making it almost an artwork in itself: each sticker marking sentences and paragraphs that were particularly significant to me.

The subtitle of the book is *Elizabeth Jolley on writing, her past and herself.* Elizabeth comes across as a modest woman with an engaging personality, and funny, too; a good public speaker, I imagine. Although she declares in an early piece that *writing about myself and my work, this self-examination, disturbs me*, she nevertheless gets on with it and, as her editor notes in the introduction:

> Elizabeth reflects on her life and ideas in precisely the same way that we all reflect on this. Perhaps with a sharper eye, a keener wit, a more unblinking honesty than most of us can manage.

I raised my eyebrows at the 'unblinking honesty', but I did find such admirable honesty in her essay, 'The Changing Family — Who Cares?'. Here she describes the mother's fear for her child, and hints at her own problems with her son, her need for help in dealing with his problems.

> Perhaps the mother guesses the length of the child's suffering, perhaps she has suffered herself from fears and compulsions ... all kinds of miseries unspoken. It is not possible somehow to talk of them with the child ... Because of the lack of communication the mother has to turn to someone for help. Sometimes mothers and fathers are unable to help each other, both sink into a kind of gloom and it is better if they don't see each other too much.

I could imagine the frustrations of trying to help her child and deal with Leonard, who, it seemed to me, was perhaps no better at communicating and empathising with the children with whom he lived than he was with me (although Ruth hadn't given me that impression at all).

The question of autobiographical writing is, to me, the most interesting of the issues raised in the essays. The book is thick with possible quotes: *For me, fiction is not a form of autobiography*. And elsewhere:

> On the whole I prefer to write the imagined than the autobiographical. I have to understand that the one cannot be written without the other.

Inevitably, Brian Dibble tackles this question. The discussion occurs in the chapter that focuses on the last decade of her writing life, her exceptional popularity at that time, and her current absence from the consciousness of both the wider world and the Australian media. (It was as Marco had said to me in Perth, no one hears anything about her any more. Only one of my fellow 'residents' at Bundanon had read anything by her, and although the others thought her name sounded familiar, they weren't quite sure why it did.) Dibble quotes Elizabeth as saying both that *My Father's Moon* was the most autobiographical book she had written, and that it wasn't an autobiographical novel by any means.

I feel that there is a strong autobiographical element in this novel, and near the end of the book there is a passage that I think must reflect Monica's feelings about her relationship with Leonard and her feelings about my mother. Dr Metcalf has left both Magda and Vera. The gossip in the hospital about where he is and what has happened to him gets more and more outlandish, and a distraught Vera has to listen to it. She is very much in love with Dr Metcalf and has written a love letter to him; and now that he is apparently dead, she is terrified that the letter will have been returned to Magda, along with all his other belongings. And that Magda will have read the letter.

She imagines speaking to her lover, reminding him of how he was with her and how he explained his predicament:

> But it was hurting Magda you were really afraid of and it was sweet when you said you wanted to protect me from your own feelings. Behaviour, you said. When we talk about Magda you explain so well that if Magda was a perfectly horrible person it would be easier. I understand because I love Magda too but it is you I want to be with for ever. You wanted me and you thought you should not. I feel very happy knowing how much you wanted me.
>
> Magda needs you, you explained. I understand that too.

There is nobody at Dr Metcalf's house, and Vera turns away. There are people dancing in the street. *This dancing in the street is how the war has been ending these days*, she tells her imagined lover, and the passage ends with Vera watching a skinny black cat vomiting at the edge of the crowd of dancing people. *Whatever shall I do with my life without you.*

Eventually, she finds Magda at home, and Magda hasn't read the letter and returns it to Vera unopened. She also tells Vera that she doesn't think her husband is dead. He has gone to join Smithers, a man he'd fallen in love with. Magda is in tears:

> 'I'm waiting,' she says. 'One thing I'm certain of, when he comes back, if he comes back, I'm never going to let him go ever again. I simply can't live without him.

Elizabeth wrote many love letters to Leonard. Whether there was an occasion when she wanted to retrieve one from Joyce, I have no idea. I don't think it's important because, unlike the skinny-dipping scene, which was based on a real event, this, I imagine, was based on an emotional reality. Joyce didn't want to lose Leonard, and neither did Elizabeth. The solution for the novelist is that Dr Metcalf runs off with another man, and by thus revealing his sexual preference shows both women he's done with them: time for Magda to make her exit and for Vera to forge a future for herself and her unborn child.

Once everyone had gone I felt very alone. I watched the farmer herd the cattle from one field to another with his pick-up truck; they were a breeding herd — monstrous creatures. The sale of their semen helps fund the Bundanon Trust. I'd intended to go down to the river to swim, but on the two occasions I started off, I could see the big black bulls between me and the shining water, and turned back. In the evening, wallabies, one with her joey tucked into her pouch, came bouncing out of the bush to feed outside my kitchen door. They were like something out of a children's storybook, and rather cute. But I thought of the deep silence of the bush at night and began to get nervous.

Deborah had told me that if I wanted to sleep at her place they had a set of keys to her house in the trust office over at Riversdale (twenty kilometres away, across the bush), and her assistant, Tracie, would come over to Bundanon and give me a lift into town. I rang Tracie.

On our way back down the dirt track, the first time I had been out of Bundanon for over a week, Tracie suddenly stopped the car. She'd spotted a goanna. I stepped onto the track to have a proper look. It was the biggest lizard I had ever seen — a couple of feet or more long. The goanna and I stared at each other. Careful, she said, it has very sharp claws and teeth. I didn't stop long. I'd heard how they can mistake a human for a tree and try to climb up you. This sighting of Dangerous Wildlife was enough to convince me that I was doing the sensible thing in hurrying back to civilisation. Nevertheless I felt a pang of loss as we came off the dirt track onto the road and eventually to the outskirts of the town.

The following morning I returned to the writer's cottage. I'd already decided that I wasn't going to spend a night up there on my own, and had arranged for a lift back down to town in the evening, where I'd be seeing Mike, Deborah's husband, who was coming down from Sydney to do some work on their garden. Now, knowing that I wouldn't be spending the night here, I revelled in the glorious isolation of Bundanon. There was a strange atmosphere. It was very hot and very quiet; colours shone with an almost pulsating vibrancy, shimmering in the heat. Above the bush there was a greyish haze — perhaps the eucalyptus oil evaporating in the hot still air. I felt restless, and decided to walk in the bush. This was a self-imposed challenge, particularly after seeing the goanna the evening before. I took my camera and my mobile phone — although there was little likelihood of there being a signal if I needed to use it.

I walked along the track towards the entrance to Bundanon. There was an area I hadn't yet explored, down towards the river, and a path that veered away from the fenced fields into scrub. It wasn't very overgrown, and from there I thought I'd be able to keep the track more or less in view. I was enjoying the feeling of being a (very tame) adventurer and taking some nice pictures — the light was incredible. Suddenly, without any warning, a hot, violent wind sprung up from nowhere. The bush came alive. The trees shook and creaked, the wind roared, and yet the sky remained a quiet and silent blue. To begin with it was very exciting, and I switched my camera onto video mode and started shooting, but the wind didn't let up — not for a second did it falter — and I began to feel nervous. The air was like a dragon's breath. It was so hot I quite expected it to ignite the oily eucalyptus trees, and that thought sent me retracing my steps, then breaking into a run back to the open ground by the buildings, away from the swaying, moaning, creaking trees. I watched from the safety of my verandah and waited for my lift to come by to pick me up in his truck and take me down to Nowra.

I spent one more night at Bundanon — not on my own. Two friends from Sydney came to visit. While they did the Sunday tour of the homestead and Arthur Boyd's studio and gardens, I packed up. I didn't want to leave the place — in just ten days it had become mine, a refuge, not for hiding in, but a place where I had felt as if I'd been given permission to explore my own thoughts and feelings without being hampered by any other considerations, and with no reference to the needs of others — self-indulgent, possibly, the mental equivalent of a spa treatment, but far more restorative. As one of the artists, Tim, wrote in an email after we had all resumed our normal lives (and I was back home): *I hope you got home ok and are adjusting to life outside the cosy bubble that was Bundanon.*

It was in some ways a cosy bubble free of the usual daily pressures; but, to extend Tim's analogy, it was also a bubble which outside that environment could burst or shatter.

For my first day back in Sydney I had made an appointment to see the senior curator at the Mitchell Library. It was he who held the key to the locked vault where Leonard and Elizabeth's correspondence was kept. On my earlier visit (before I left for Bundanon), he had promised to see what he might be able to do about allowing me to look at some of this material. I felt that this last stop of my Australian journey might well be where I would find the remaining clues to the mystery of what had motivated Elizabeth and my father to tell all those lies, and to keep my father's family in the dark.

# CHAPTER 17

My first night back in Sydney was not restful. I missed the bush noises that had become familiar, and although my brother-in-law's house was spacious and quiet, I felt hemmed in. I lay in bed and worried, revisiting the doubts that had weighed on my mind as I travelled from England to Australia a month before. Now, having read so much of Elizabeth's writing and feeling familiar with her life through Dibble's biography, I was no longer entirely sure I should be even asking to look at the correspondence between Elizabeth and Leonard. If there were things there she felt might be painful for her children to read, might it not also be painful for me? What would I gain? Was it right for me to look at this stuff? Wouldn't I be better off not knowing what passed between my father and his lover?

But this was an important, even crucial, step in my journey. And although I was tempted, albeit briefly, to opt out of my self-imposed task and spend a few days enjoying the city, lazing around here on the beach at Bronte, 'doing' the new downtown galleries, and seeing friends, I knew that to give up at this stage wasn't an option. I had three more days in Australia — I should use every minute of them, and if a way had been found to allow me to read some of the material in the Elizabeth Jolley archive, I should take that opportunity.

The next morning I got the bus to Bondi Junction, and from there the train into the city centre. My middle-of-the-night doubts about the moral validity of looking at other people's private letters began once again to snag at my conscience.

There is a passage in Jane Austen's *Persuasion* where Anne Elliot is shown a letter that was not intended for her eyes:

> She [Anne] was obliged to reflect that her seeing the letter was a violation of the laws of honour, that no one ought to be judged or to be known by such testimonies, that no private correspondence could bear the eye of others ...

I forgot about violating any laws of honour as soon as I was told that although I couldn't look at either Leonard's or Elizabeth's diaries, I would be able to read their correspondence. There were ten boxes of letters, and the curator had selected some he thought would be of most interest to me: those spanning the years 1945 (when Elizabeth and Joyce both became pregnant) and 1950, when Elizabeth and Leonard moved to Edinburgh.

I was shown to a desk by a window. A blind diffused the bright sunlight, and my back was to the rest of the room. A large cardboard box was already on the desk. I couldn't photocopy any of the material, but I could take notes (in pencil, so that there would be no risk of ink damaging — or a reader defacing — the archival material), and if I needed any help, all I had to do was ask. The box contained a mix of papers: individual letters, larger envelopes on the outside of which were pencilled dates and who they were from — EJ or LJ; there were also some bundles of letters in stiff, grey envelopes, addressed in Leonard's distinctive spiky spaced-out words or Elizabeth's looping script.

I sharpened my pencil, opened my notebook, and wrote

*Box A3; EJ/LJ 1948, mostly May–Sept.* This was the year in which Sarah and I were two years old. Within minutes, I was taken into the maelstrom of the affair between Monica and Leonard. It was unlike any other research I'd done in archives, but I tried to put aside my emotions and keep my researcher's hat firmly in place. As I read and wrote my notes, keeping my handwriting as clear as possible, I felt myself gradually dissolve inside. Here were two people passionately in love, and adoring their child. I shall call Elizabeth 'Monica' here, as this is how I think of her at that time. Leonard's pet name for her was 'Fish' and hers for him 'Stix' or 'Styx' (apparently from Cleversticks). By this time she was working as a housekeeper for a doctor, whom she calls 'Piggy' and who I recognised from Brian Dibble's biography as Peggy Frazer. In the first letter I read, written in October 1948, Monica is dreaming of the future when they will live together. Leonard writes back in language that suggests he is consumed by his love for her. Monica, it seems, was often upset and ill. She promises that she will be 'a different sort of mother' when she has Leonard with her all the time. Leonard is solicitous, saying how he wants to look after her. They both adore their baby, Leonard asking if they are merely conceited parents thinking Sally is so wonderful.

I felt like shouting, *What about me, then? Did I fail to elicit any paternal feelings in you?* But then, absence makes the heart grow fonder, I suppose, and he could see his lover and her child only occasionally (although they wrote almost daily), whereas I probably kept him awake every night, making demands. I remembered how, at about this time, if Joyce were out at night (she taught evening classes), I would wait to hear the front door close and then tiptoe downstairs, where he'd be listening to the wireless or to gramophone records, or reading, and I'd climb onto his lap and get him to read me stories. Joyce would have sent me straight back to bed. Did he like this time with me, or did he wish it were his other daughter who snuggled up to him? Or no child at all, but Monica sitting on his knee?

He writes to Monica to reassure her that he is never as happy as when he is with her and Sally, and how it pains him to learn that his little girl misses him, but once they are all living together she won't miss him. *No*, I reflected as I read my father's familiar handwriting, *Sally shan't miss you; I shall*. I understood that he had to choose one child over another, one woman over the other, and reading this correspondence it was clear that Joyce and I would not be the chosen ones.

With each letter I read I felt increasingly that this was a mistake, I should stop, I'd only end up horribly hurt. And, in any case, these letters weren't written for my eyes; but then, they weren't written for a biographer's eyes either. I wondered how Leonard would feel about other people, particularly me, reading his outpouring of passion. Incandescent, I imagined. And yet, I suppose that he knew Elizabeth had kept his letters to her, and somehow he had kept hers to him. But where? At our home in Chadwick Avenue? Or at the library where he worked? I felt both guilty and embarrassed reading my father's love letters, and yet I felt impelled to continue.

On one occasion he writes to say that Joyce and I have gone blackberry picking, and if only he'd known, he could have seen Monica that afternoon. I imagined Leonard at his desk in the library, supposedly working, writing these notes to his lover, daydreaming that he could be with her while my mother and I were safely out of the way. Where did we do our blackberry picking? Did we get the bus and go into the Lickey Hills? Or walk down to the allotments? If he'd nipped out to spend the afternoon with Monica, what excuse would he have made to his colleagues for his absence? The two of them met at a café, went for walks together, wrote letters all the time, and yet

Joyce apparently was unaware of what was going on so very close to home.

The morning passed by in the company of these two lovers, who were crazy about each other. I wondered whether, had Joyce known the strength of their passion, she would have behaved differently.

Monica was depressed — hardly surprising, as she had been given so many promises of future happiness that didn't translate into action. Leonard says he can't bear to think of her alone and unhappy. He longs to rush to her side, presenting himself as Monica's protector and carer, reassuring her that one day they'll be together for always.

I tried to put myself in Monica's position — it must have been delicious to read these words and know that Leonard loved her so deeply, and so very painful that she was denied the domestic security she craved.

At one point we — Joyce, Leonard, and I — are staying with my grandmother at Deal. There's a photo that I have of a family gathering on the pebbly beach at Deal: Grandma and Great Auntie Millie, and my grandmother's cousin, Grace (on a deckchair) are decorously dressed in straw hats and coats; Joyce looks glamorous in a white two-piece swimming costume; her pretty elder sister Elsie is there, and their cousin Gwen, with me and two of my cousins at the front, sucking on ice lollies. In the past I'd wondered who took the photograph, and now, as I read Leonard's descriptions of cycling into Sandwich (the next town along the coast) to collect letters from Monica at the post office and to write to her, I couldn't help but think he might have been the photographer. The adults look very happy, laughing, as if they've just been told a funny story. We children are concentrating on our lollies, probably itching to get back into the water. In the letters from Deal there is no mention of anyone outside the charmed circle of *Fish, Stix,* and

*Sally.* But then he wouldn't want to make Monica feel excluded even further by chatting on about his wife's family — not that he ever *chatted* — or mentioning them at all. However, I can't think that he was utterly miserable while holidaying at the seaside, but I can see that he probably felt bad about being surrounded by a happy group of people when she was alone with her daughter, and he no doubt wished he and she were holidaying together.

*A family outing to the beach at Deal*

He sends a couple of books to Sally, mentioning that he's bought the same ones for me. (More duplication—I can't think which books these might be. He gave me many books, and I suspect Sally was given books, too. I doubt that Monica had spare cash to buy books, and this would have been a way of helping both mother and daughter.)

Ever the literary scholar, he sits in the churchyard at Sandwich and writes to her, quoting Blake: *What is it men in women do require? The lineaments of Gratified Desire.* She wants them to have lots of babies. He says how he would die happy having lived with her; how he, too, wants children, her children, lots of them.

The sex is clearly very good: the letters are peppered with sometimes coy, sometimes explicit, references to what they did or are fantasising about doing. I didn't linger over that kind of detail. Leonard is torn (hence I guess Dibble's assessment that he is frozen at the point of action) and continues to prevaricate for two more years. Monica wanted people to know they were lovers, that they belonged to each other, and that Sally was Leonard's baby. It was almost as if she wanted to be 'caught out', but Leonard, as we'd say today, couldn't commit. Monica is pleased when a neighbour sees them out together (I wonder if this is Mrs Griffiths, who I remember lived next door). She just can't wait for them to be married. Then she is full of regret and remorse, telling him he mustn't waste his time on her.

The situation was intolerable and continued thus for a long time yet.

I went out into the sunshine and reality of the present, and walked in the park below the library, where joggers jogged, office workers sat in the shade of trees eating their sandwiches, and a girl and a boy kissed, and then strode on down the path, hand in hand.

When I returned to the library I had just a few more letters to read from this box. The next lot I got out were from a year earlier, 1947. In these, Leonard is very loving, full of physical longing and remembering their precious time together. The realities of his position vis-a-vis myself and Joyce are totally ignored. Joyce is the elephant in the room, and I'm her lumbering calf. How could he not address the very real problems he faced? Was this, I wondered, as I read his words, a man who has a grip on the situation, or one who is wallowing in romantic notions of love? Playing with Monica's feelings, promising her the earth and then saying, sorry, can't, not just yet? When he wrote that there should be no guilt associated with their relationship (although in more elevated language), I snorted aloud in disbelief at the extent of the self-delusion, so much so that a woman working at the next desk looked over at me in surprise. The atmosphere in the special collections room was one of quiet and sober study. It was not a place to exclaim aloud, or swear under one's breath. To me, my father seemed to be living in some kind of escapist literary romantic fiction, and I was reminded of Joyce telling me that she thought that Leonard had unreal expectations of a relationship between a man and a woman, based on literature more than anything else, and on D.H. Lawrence's writing in particular.

Other letters from 1947 show me a side of my father I hadn't even begun to imagine. Not only was he a prolific letter-writer (when did he find time to work, I wondered) and I had always thought of him being, as Elizabeth described him often, 'not a letter writer', but in his voluminous correspondence with Elizabeth he uses the most unlikely language: baby talk and silly spellings such as *stoopid* (stupid) and *tikkit* (ticket). The two lovers often write in the third person, as if they're telling stories about themselves.

Monica both flatters him and makes demands. In May 1948 they are both on holiday (although this letter was in a separate box, I suspect that this is when Leonard was in Deal and writing to her from Sandwich). Monica says she hopes he won't fall into the clutches of any other woman. Thinking back to that photo taken on the beach, I am reminded how very pretty Joyce's sister was, and how all the women are laughing, charmed perhaps by this flirt. But this is speculation and, no matter how tempting, I shouldn't read a situation into a photograph. Monica flatters him, telling him she is jealous because he is so attractive, and not just to her. Doubtless Monica did find him very attractive, and so did Joyce, but when I look at photographs of him I can't imagine what it is they saw in him. It wasn't his face or his body, as far as I could see. He must have had some kind of charisma. And he was good in bed.

I went back to my brother-in-law's at Bronte, emotionally drained. Nick wasn't at all interested in what I'd been doing, which was fine by me because I didn't want to talk about it. It would involve too much explaining, and I wasn't sure how I felt about reading these letters. Rather grubby, I suppose. We walked along the cliff path to Bondi beach to eat there. We discussed non-personal things — the world financial crash and its effect on his industry (he is a geologist and works freelance for mining companies), and how Mick's investments had plummeted since his death. We then moved on to family gossip: his and Gordon's brothers, and his younger sister and her family, who also live in Sydney. The evening passed pleasantly, and it was dark by the time we walked back along the cliffs. I went to bed as soon as we got back, not even looking at the notes I'd taken in the library.

The following morning I was back at the library. I had decided that I should take a more chronological approach to my reading, but, because of the way in which the material had been put together, I soon gave up and read whatever came to hand.

Monica was frequently depressed during the late summer and autumn months following Sally's birth. I came across no letters that belonged to the time immediately after Sally was born, possibly because Monica was at that time seeing Leonard every day, as she and her baby were living at our house in Chadwick Avenue. Later she writes a great deal, longing for him, saying she can't live without him. She seems very lost and needy. If I hadn't known the degree of deception she and Leonard were practising on Joyce, I would feel very sorry for her, and I sympathised greatly with her situation. It must have been extremely difficult to be a single mother at that time, and to know that the father of her child was with another woman and another child. Even if she also knew that he wished he weren't.

On one occasion, he writes to her to say that if Sally comes to play in the sandpit (I gather, with Susan, although I am not mentioned by name), then he will see Monica before she receives this letter. This must have been about the time of the photographs of Sally and me as toddlers playing together in the garden. Monica becomes desperate; she absolutely adores him. Leonard's replies are loving and seem to hold out promises, but still these don't lead to any action on his part.

In April 1949 she writes to him from Bournemouth. She talks about their having had a child together as an *impossible dream* that came true, and of the many difficulties they had overcome together since the conception of Sally. Was the dream to have a child with Leonard Monica's alone, or was it a dream they shared? The letter does not make this clear. But I could only interpret the *impossible dream* to mean that Monica's pregnancy was no accident, for her at least.

I stood up, pushed my chair away, and strode past my puzzled neighbour in the library and out to the toilets. I splashed cold water on my face and stared at my reflection in the mirror. Monica's pregnancy was no mistake. And then she'd told Joyce she could easily get an abortion if she wanted to, but she'd decided against that; she'd do the right thing and have the baby. And Joyce had admired her for that brave decision. *Go on, Elizabeth*, I thought, *make the woman you've betrayed feel sympathy for you! Make her admire you! And Leonard. Where the hell was his brain?* (I refrained from making a crude comment to myself as I stared at my own face in the mirror). From the letter I had just read it seemed to me unlikely that Leonard was *unaware* that Monica was hoping to become pregnant. But even if he was unaware, he was no innocent, surely, when it came to the mechanics of conception. Did he, then, like so many men, leave the whole business of contraception up to the woman? Or was he complicit in this, turning up to have sex with Monica at the right time of the month? Was Joyce also trying to get pregnant at the same time? Did he know that both of his women were feeling broody, longing for his babies? I washed my face and carefully put on my make-up. It was important not to look shattered.

I read a lot more, and slowly became inured to it (and yet have been unable to look at the notes taken at the Mitchell Library until now, a year later, almost to the day). I finally came to the correspondence around the time that Leonard left. I don't know if he had told Joyce he was leaving at this point, but since he refers to Joyce's pain, I think they must have had some discussions about their future. Not long before this, I had inadvertently helped set events in train. Like any three-year-old, I loved drawing and 'writing', and a favourite game when I bounced about on my parents' bed in the mornings was to write letters and 'post' them. The postbox was the hollow end of their brass bedstead, where a knob had come off. Apparently, one day, wondering why I was so quiet upstairs, Joyce came to look for me and discovered me playing at letter-writing (ironic that my father at this time was spending so much of his time writing letters). I had found Leonard's diary and started scribbling on the pages, tearing them out ready to 'post' into their bed. I remember this clearly, as Joyce told me off about it and said that Daddy would be cross. Years later, in one of our occasional conversations about my father, I recalled this event, and she told me that as she smoothed out my scribbled pages she saw that Leonard seemed to have appointments with an initial she didn't recognise (might it have been 'F' for Fish?). She asked him who this person was, and he admitted that he had met and fallen in love with another woman. This was after the neighbour had reported seeing Leonard with a 'young woman', and again Joyce asked if the woman he was in love with was Monica. No, he insisted; she was someone else entirely, someone Joyce had never met. Joyce hadn't seen or heard from Monica for more than a year; she didn't even want to know the identity of this other woman, and Leonard didn't offer to tell her. He was leaving her, he no longer loved her — that's what mattered to my mother.

By this time, the spring of 1950, Monica had left Birmingham and taken a job as a matron in a progressive boarding school, called Pinewood. To begin with, Sally was with her, but, according to Dibble's biography of Elizabeth, Sally was unhappy there, and an outbreak of gastroenteritis led to her being sent to stay with her grandmother (her maternal one, naturally). Leonard had applied for and been offered a job in Edinburgh, where Monica and Sally would join him. That, apparently, was the plan. But Leonard was hesitating. It seems that he had been thinking, or talking, about trying to make a go of his marriage. On 29 May 1950 he sent a letter to Monica, saying that he was torn with pity for Joyce right now, but that this pity would vanish should he try to make a fresh start with her. He acknowledged that there were things he valued, and would miss (including me), but it wouldn't be enough. If he stayed with me and my mother, everybody would suffer, and in the end it would be worse for me.

*He's doing a good job of convincing himself*, I thought.

I see now where Brian Dibble got the idea that Leonard had told Joyce about Monica. In a letter to Monica, he says that it was going to be wonderful when everything was out in the open and there were no more lies and no more deception. But he didn't do it. He didn't tell Joyce. He continued to vacillate. On 2 June (the day before my fourth birthday), he writes to Monica that he is utterly torn — which I don't doubt. It must have been a very difficult decision for him to make, and I can only think now that it would have been so much easier for all of us — Joyce, Monica, Sally, and myself — if he had told the truth. Monica replies the next day to say that she wants him to make a complete break and that if he doesn't, their life together — their mutual happiness — will be spoiled. And then, I think probably in response to this letter, Leonard agrees that he must make a total break, and won't be writing regularly to Joyce, but adds that he will have to take some financial responsibility for me. In the event, he made very little financial contributions to my care, beyond the annual five pounds birthday money and the parcel of warm clothes sent to Mattaincourt. Joyce received no further money once he had moved to Australia, although, of course, I received occasional quite large cheques from Leonard (really Elizabeth) after that first time she wrote to me when I was eighteen. I think it was probably Joyce's pride that kept her from asking him for money for my care. She clung to her independence, and once she started working in Exeter was earning a reasonable salary.

I had to leave the library at lunchtime because all the staff would be out watching horseracing on television. It was

Melbourne Cup Day. The streets were crowded with excited punters, a huge television screen hung above a pedestrian precinct, and everybody, it seemed, was having a flutter. Girls paraded in their hats and party dresses, teetering along in high heels, waving glasses of champagne in gloved fingers, and men in suits swung along the pavements, arms over shoulders, drunk on either beer or excitement. When I came back to the library there was a hum of chat. It was a world away from the chilly and austere postwar English world that I'd been living in all morning.

I returned to that world, the one that Leonard left in 1949 to go to America, where he bought me and Sally dresses and toys — the dresses for American three-year-olds, who were so much bigger than their skinny English counterparts. Monica sent him a sketch map on which she'd drawn all the routes of the walks they took together. What happened to Sally when Leonard and Monica were wandering along lovers' lane, I wondered. Was Joyce looking after her? Or perhaps she was at a nursery or with her grandparents.

I could have gone back to the library for a third day of letter reading, but I'd had enough. The staff were very helpful — if there was anything I wanted checked, all I had to do was write with the box number and whatever reference I could find. I didn't want to read any more. I had more than enough to be dealing with in my notebook.

# CHAPTER 18

On my last full day in Sydney I had a holiday. The sun was hot and the sky clear; Nick went off to the city, so I went down to the beach for a swim, pushing through the surf until I could swim beyond where the waves broke. I lay on my back in the water, thinking maybe I could take the bus into the city, but as it was such a beautiful day and I knew that back at home it would be dark and grey and cold, and there would be months of such miserable weather to endure, I decided to go for a walk instead, and take the coastal path in the opposite direction from Bondi beach.

The path took me through a vast cemetery, Waverley, which overlooks the ocean. Here were the graves of hopeful émigrés from all over the world. How many of them had escaped a dark and difficult past in Europe to find happiness, or the promise of happiness and prosperity in this country? And what, I wondered, had Leonard and Elizabeth hoped for as they set out from Tilbury Docks? A complete break with the past? The possibility of creating a new life for themselves and their children?

According to Brian Dibble, Elizabeth had been working on novels and stories for many years, in Birmingham and later in Edinburgh and Glasgow, but it was only once in Australia that she achieved her ambition to be a published writer. And it seems to me that in this country she found her voice. And Leonard? If he'd stayed in the UK he probably would have made a successful career as a university librarian, but I suggest it was at least in part escape he sought. And did they think they'd achieved this break with the past (apart from the annoying reminders in the form of cards and parcels for me in June for my birthday and at Christmas every year)? That is, until the day in 1967 that Harry came to Perth, to be greeted by Elizabeth instead of Joyce. Nowadays, of course, this disappearing act would be well nigh impossible. In the 1950s they — we — used to communicate by letter, and only on rare occasions would the telephone be used. Cheap air travel, email, and the internet have made the kind of deception carried out by Elizabeth and Leonard upon his family virtually impossible.

I'd be flying home the next day. I sat down on a low wall next to an overgrown plot with a double white marble headstone, and gazed out over the unbelievably blue ocean. It was a very peaceful place to be. 'In Loving Memory' was carved in Gothic script on the headstone, but tall, delicate grasses obscured the names of those so lovingly remembered, of whom I had no knowledge; blood-red geraniums spilled over it from the adjacent grave. What, I asked myself, had I achieved coming all this way, digging around in the past, pulling Laura's skeletons from their dark cupboard? I think the most important thing was my understanding of the strength of my father's feelings for Elizabeth and of hers for him; this was a big love story, and perhaps that is why she couldn't bear to get rid of the letters I had spent the previous two days reading. As I sat in the sun in the graveyard, I tried to put the facts I had learned both from talking to people and from Brian Dibble's biography of Elizabeth into some kind of order. I needed to write it down, so I took out my notebook and a pen from my bag and began to write — not this story, but a list of everything I now knew, or thought I knew. It was rather like the 'timetable of events' Laura had sent me when she wrote to say she would dig out the letters she had from Australia.

There were many crossings out and insertions, and I later typed it all up and expanded it, turning it into a timeline to refer to during the writing of this story. I began with Leonard's illness in 1940 and his meeting the trainee nurse, Monica Knight, and continued up to the previous day when I had read the love letters and reached the conclusion that Elizabeth was trying to get pregnant. As I made my list, I thought, *These are merely things that happened. Why did it upset me so much?* Nothing tragic had occurred; I hadn't suffered. What you don't know (my father's family), you don't miss; in fact, I'd had a good and interesting education, and was brought up in a sometimes unconventional but always loving environment.

But then I thought again about that first meeting with Laura when I was twenty-one, and recalled the horrible feeling that somebody had stolen my identity; that someone had created for me a life and experiences that didn't match my own. I was made to feel invisible. It didn't bother me greatly that my father had had an affair — or that he had left my mother and me. That was all fairly run-of-the-mill stuff. Even having a half-sister five weeks older than me was ultimately no big deal, and I was very glad that I now had found my half-siblings. However, as well as this question of identity, there was another thing that bothered me now, as I listed the 'facts'. This bothersome thing was that I had so long maintained my father's position on his pedestal, refusing to acknowledge what must have been clear to anyone else, that this man was self-deluding and selfish. I now had no doubt that he must have been a very difficult man to live with, whether as his wife or his child. But still I missed him. I think that a child's love for a parent must take an enormous amount to destroy, and despite everything I had learned, I couldn't let go of this childish love.

He had been loved, too, by both Joyce and Elizabeth. The love between him and Elizabeth was so overwhelmingly powerful, I wondered where it came from. Was it born from a mutual need? The idea — as it now appeared — that Elizabeth had deliberately become pregnant, with the cold-hearted intention of stealing Leonard from Joyce, left me shocked and angry. Was this what a grand passion can lead a woman to do? Or was the whole thing not thought out? Was Elizabeth (Monica) a young woman passionately in love with a man, and wanting to have his baby, so that this mattered more than anything else? Did she imagine that once he clapped eyes on the baby, he'd be smitten? That he'd have to leave his wife for her? That he would take his responsibilities (to her and their child) seriously? Did she not consider that Joyce, too, might be wanting to have a baby? I was, and am still, unable to find answers to these questions.

My thoughts now turned to Laura, who had encouraged me to make my metaphorical, if not my physical, journey. *All dead, now*, I mused: the three East End kids — Harry, Laura, and Leonard — who'd done so well academically and professionally; Joyce, the wayward daughter of Exclusive Brethren parents who had brought me up on her own; and Elizabeth, a daughter of an unusual family who became one of Australia's most acclaimed authors.

I happened to find myself in this cemetery — I hadn't known it existed before coming across it, and it seemed an appropriate place to finish my journey, in the company of the dead. The picture wasn't perfect, though. There were repairs going on here, as well as at the Mitchell Library — red plastic fencing cut off some of the paths that were cracked and disintegrating. A little further on from where I was sitting was a very elaborate monument on a family plot. Two angels with swirling dresses and elegant sweeping wings held in their arms a young woman, as if offering her to the heavens above. The top angel's head had fallen off, or had been knocked off. I wasn't looking for a metaphor, but there it was: Leonard had finally fallen from his pedestal.

Back at Nick's place, I returned to *Central Mischief*. Elizabeth writes about being in Toronto for a writers' conference in 1983 and coming across, by chance, in a bookshop, a woman she had known when she was at Pinewood (and waiting for Leonard to leave Joyce and me). It is another Elizabeth, Elizabeth Smart, who was the lover of the poet George Barker. He was still married, but he and Elizabeth Smart had four children, who were all boarders at the school. Elizabeth Smart would pick up the children every weekend in a taxi and take them to London. Elizabeth Jolley was very impressed by this woman — she was lovely and confident, whereas clearly Elizabeth Jolley was feeling insecure and unsure of her future. (At the time she was working at Pinewood, Elizabeth had changed her name from Monica Knight to Monica Fielding. She had yet to change her name again to Elizabeth Jolley.)

In this piece, 'By the Waters of Babylon', Elizabeth Jolley writes:

This other Elizabeth, Elizabeth Smart, I watched her as she came and went. She belonged, I thought then, to a life which was quite beyond my reach. I thought, at that time, that this handsome woman was loved, was wealthy and was chosen. True, the poet had a wife, but all the same, Elizabeth Smart must have been the wanted, the wished for lover. I never imagined then, that she was lonely and alone. Lonelier than I was ...

There is no mention here of the reason for her being at Pinewood, or that she, too, was the chosen one, or desperately hoped that she was.

Elizabeth Smart gave Elizabeth Jolley a copy of a book she'd written in 1945: *By Grand Central Station I Sat Down and Wept*. In her piece in *Central Mischief*, Elizabeth tells how she opened the cover of the book and read that

> their relationship [between George Barker and Elizabeth Smart] provided the impassioned inspiration for one of the most moving and immediate chronicles of a love affair ever written ...

She hadn't known about the book, but read it that day. However, having met Elizabeth Smart the once, and having her telephone number, she didn't contact her before leaving Canada:

> I am unable to force myself once more to relive a time which was too difficult for her and for me.

When I read Elizabeth Smart's book I realised just why Elizabeth Jolley found it so painful to contemplate reliving that time in her life. Their situations were remarkably similar, except that George Barker didn't leave his wife. In her long prose poem, Smart reflects all those feelings that Elizabeth must have been experiencing while she was at the boarding school, waiting for Leonard to finally leave Joyce. Like Leonard, Barker was torn; he wavered. Smart writes, of Barker:

> He did sin against love, and though he says it was in Pity's name, and that Pity was only fighting a losing battle with Love, he was useless to Pity, and in wavering, injured Love,

which was, after all, what he staked all for, all he had, ungamblable.

Smart, too, had felt great affection for her lover's wife, and terrible guilt.

My feeling is that guilt caused both Elizabeth and Leonard to suffer from then on, although the burden must have lightened as time passed. I believe theirs was a grand passion, which probably later became weaker as, sadly, most grand passions do, with the tedium of everyday family life. I also believe that they might have been happier had they not continued to lie and deceive. As Joyce said in her letter to Laura:

I know that Leonard suffered terribly because of the situation in which he put himself — or allowed himself to be put. And I think he would have suffered less if he had been able to admit or confess everything.

Joyce chose to believe that Leonard had 'allowed himself to be put' in the situation, thereby implying that it was Elizabeth who was the prime mover.

The question of who was to 'blame' for the events I have recounted here is not, as far as I am concerned, the main issue. It is more a question of what motivated people to behave as they did — Leonard, Elizabeth, Joyce, Laura, and, of course, myself in embarking on this quest.

When I look at those letters written in mine and Joyce's names, I still don't understand what motivated Elizabeth to put pen to paper. Did Leonard stand behind her, metaphorically if not physically, and *make* her do it? As he had *made* Joyce promise not to contact his family? Did he force her to do the lying for him? And why did I not come out with it and ask Elizabeth and Leonard my questions when they were alive and sitting in the same room as me? Was it cowardice on my part? A desire not to rock the boat? A fear that my father would hate me and tell me to go away and leave him alone? Ken Gasmier said he thought that Elizabeth's controlling the situation on that occasion was her way of avoiding the inevitable fallout of Leonard's reaction to my questions. But might he be wrong? Might it have been a long-established desire to control that led to her (independent) perpetuation of Leonard's initial lies to his family? The novelist has ultimate control over her characters, and as Laura said to me: *Elizabeth was probably living a novel rather than writing one!*

There's another feasible explanation. As Elizabeth herself pointed out in her essay 'What Sins to Me Unknown Dipped Me in Ink?', she had taken the role of placator in the family since childhood:

> I became by nature and circumstance a placator and learned to read every change in the eye, every crease in the brow. I am still a placator.

She was trying to keep the peace at home and, at the same time, by pretending that Joyce and Leonard and their children were living first in Scotland and then in Australia, she was trying to keep my grandfather happy back in London. Perhaps she hid from Leonard the letters and gifts for me that the postman delivered to their home every six months for seventeen years. I think Leonard was the sort of person who wouldn't enquire, even if he had an idea of what was happening — it would have been easier to ignore such irritating problems. It would be interesting to see Elizabeth's diary entries for October 1963 to January 1964 to see if she was aware of what she was doing, or if, when she appeared to lose the plot, she was in fact suffering some kind of mental breakdown.

Those few letters written during those months merely provide proof of what Laura had told me — of a deception that continued for many years — and yet it wouldn't really matter if they no longer existed. The fact was that Laura was hurt and angry at the deceit practised on her and Harry and her father, particularly her father. And she asked me to do something about it. *The final end of all artefacts is the waste-heap but I am passing the decision to you.*

Elizabeth's decision not to destroy the letters that she and Leonard exchanged, but to bequeath them to the Mitchell Library, could be perceived as exercising control from beyond the grave, which had been my immediate response upon learning about the embargo. But now, realising that limiting access was part of the arrangement with the library, and having read some of those early love letters, I am glad that she didn't feed them to the shredder. Reading them made it clear to me that if Leonard had compromised and stayed with Joyce and me, none of us would have benefited — neither adults nor children.

For Joyce, the pain of losing Leonard continued for a long time. As well as writing to Laura as soon as I told her about the cards and cheques from my newly found relatives, she wrote to Leonard's brother, Harry. This letter was written on 19 January 1968. My cousin Margaret found it amongst her father's papers and gave it to me.

Joyce first of all apologises for the long silence:

It grieved me very much not to contact your father, but I had promised not to do so, and though tempted — especially when Susan asked about him and wanted to see him — I didn't know whether Leonard had revealed the truth, or, in fact, what story he had told. Strange to say, Susan was convinced that he was still alive when I argued that in all likelihood he had died.

Dear Harry,

Thankyou for your card at Christmas.
I too, am happy to be in touch with
you and Laura again, and to be
able to rectify some of the mis-
conceptions that I knew you must
have formed of my behaviour in the
past.

It grieved me very much not to
contact your father, but I had
promised not to do so, and though
tempted — especially when Susan
asked about him & wanted to see
him — I didn't know whether Leonard
had revealed the truth, or, in fact,
what story he had told. Strange to
say, Susan was convinced that he
was still alive when I argued that
in all likelihood he had died.
I believe that she asked Leonard in
a letter about this, but as he never

answered her letters - only very brief notes came from Monica (Elizabeth) - we did not know what had happened.

Laura will have told you what has happened to us over the years. I did meet, by chance, two people who knew you, at a Youth Hostel in Devon - Bigbury. Mick and Susan and I were on a brief walking holiday - and I had lost my spectacles, & was explaining to the Warden that the name in the spectacle case was Tolley, not Mitchell, as I hadn't changed it. The lady who overheard this asked me if I knew you, & explained that her daughter and Margaret were great friends & that Margaret was at the University. I explained who I was, but asked her not to mention it, as it might cause distress to the family. But I was very tempted to allow her to tell you of our meeting.

The real purpose of my letter, however, is to express my sympathy with you in the loss of Lilian. I know what it is to be deprived of one who has seemed a very part of oneself, and I think that no human being can understand how it feels who has not himself suffered in this way. I know that there are consolations, but they are little compared with the sense of loneliness that so often and for so long oppresses.

I must also thank you for your kind thought in sending a present to Susan & Gordon. Quite apart from the fact that they are starting a home without having had a chance to save the gift was most welcome. Susan has always seemed to feel actively deprived of her father, although she has not had an unhappy childhood - and she is happy now to feel some real recognition from his family. Monica's letters have been no substitute for the absence of letters from Leonard, even though I have never, until now, revealed to her the extent of Monica's duplicity - and indeed guilt - in the whole matter. Susan herself did remark to me upon the ease with which 'Elizabeth' wrote so affectionately to me whom she had caused to suffer. If you are inclined to judge Leonard very severely in this matter I would like to say, in his defence, that it was she who tried by every means in her power to make him leave me, and who caused him such torture (as I now understand it) that made any chance of happiness with me totally impossible. I only hope that he has now found happiness, and that his children will not suffer from the pressures that his sense of guilt may create within him. But perhaps that is over with him; as to Monica, she seems to be able to create — up to a point — the world she wishes to believe in.

I am very glad indeed that your chance meeting with Leonard has caused all this to be revealed. Surely he will feel happier to be free of the necessity to cover up the truth?

I hope that you will feel free to stay with us if you think of spending a holiday in this area — (which as you know is very beautiful) We have room and the desire to entertain you, so please take advantage of it — either at Whitsun or in the summer. I shall be away

*Yours sincerely, Joyce Mitchell*

*at Easter, on a course.*

*Letter from Joyce to Harry, 19 January 1968*

She goes on to say this:

The real purpose of my letter, however, is to express my sympathy with you in the loss of Lilian. I know what it is to be deprived of one who has seemed a very part of oneself, and I think that no human being can understand how it feels who has not himself suffered in this way. I know that there are consolations, but they are little compared with the sense of loneliness that so often and for so long oppresses.

Leonard had been the person who had seemed a very part of herself. Although she was happy with Mick, I'm not sure that she ever got over Leonard's leaving her.

As for me, to return to Elizabeth's reference to the story of Clytemnestra in her essay, 'What Sins to Me Unknown Dipped Me in Ink?':

But when people judge someone, they ought
To learn the facts, and then hate, if they've reason to
 And if they find no reason, then they should not hate.

I've learned the facts and have found no reason to hate, but only to be sad that it has taken so long to unravel the story. Even now, I don't understand why it all had to happen as it did. I have been given clues by others. Ken Gasmier, for example, sent me some photos of Leonard taken around the time he retired; in one (at a retirement lunch), a woman stands behind him (he's seated), her arms circling him, his hand grasping hers. I find the photo sad — an old man who still harbours ideas of his sexual attractiveness; or maybe it's a picture of a childlike man who requires the protection of a woman (her arms circling him), a petulant child who could be scathing and critical. But perhaps these are unfair responses to this photograph. However, Ken said Leonard could be quite rude to this colleague, and both Laura and Joyce told me what a sharp tongue he had and that he 'didn't suffer fools gladly' (a view supported by much in Brian Dibble's biography of Elizabeth).

It was my desire to find out what sort of man my father was that fuelled my search and has led me to re-examine my memories and revisit past events. And still I'm not sure why Leonard failed to face up to the realities of the difficult but hardly uncommon situation he was in.  There might, of course, yet be further details that would add to my understanding — anecdotes from other friends and colleagues, people who loved him, and those who disliked or despised him. It could be that any of my half-siblings would give very different explanations for the lies and deception — they knew their parents, and I didn't, not in any real sense of the word. But I'm not writing Leonard's biography, and while what I have learned of his character has scarred the image of the man I held so long, it hasn't obliterated it.

I agree with Brian Dibble that my father could be egocentric and arrogant, and he did indeed vacillate between choosing to stay with Joyce and me, and joining Elizabeth and Sally. But wouldn't anyone in his position be torn? I'm also sure that his mother fussed over him when he was a child, which might explain his later reliance on women to look after him, and make allowances for bad behaviour. It's interesting that both Elizabeth and Joyce told me that they wanted to protect him — Elizabeth from the effects of reading my letter (*from a reawakening of the pain*), and Joyce from him having to witness and deal with the inevitable pain his leaving us would cause me — hence her collusion with him in concocting the story that Daddy was going away for just a short while to find a new house for us in Scotland. But it wasn't only a matter of protecting Leonard; both women were to some extent trying to protect themselves: Elizabeth from dealing with this reawakened emotional pain in a man already suffering from severe physical pain, and Joyce because once he'd left us, it would be she who had to deal with my misery as well as her own.

Leonard was the youngest child of the three (three years younger than Laura), and he was frequently ill. Throughout his adult life he was rarely free of pain for any extended period, and had to undergo surgery time and again. When he wrote to me from Sheffield to say that he didn't want to see me, I was hurt and disappointed. I thought he was weak and unwilling to face up to his responsibilities. Now, though, I have changed my mind. I think he was being honest, not cowardly, when he wrote:

> I have just learned what breaking old physical scars can mean. Emotional scars may perhaps contain just as much a threat if disturbed.

And then he signed off with these words: *With very much real, if distant, love.*

And although I was sceptical when Elizabeth told me that he was glad that he had met me in Perth, I believe now that he probably was. Both she and Joyce, at different times, assured me that my father loved me.

I will never know who was the instigator of the 'theft' of my identity, whether Elizabeth or Leonard. It most certainly wasn't Sarah, who, unknown to her, was passed off as Susan — and in this respect she, too, was denied her own identity. From all I have read and seen, from the notes I have taken, and the conversations I have had, I have come to the conclusion that it was not a coldly deliberate decision to deceive, but that it just happened, and, like a car slithering down an icy hill, the story ran out of control.

# AFTERWORD

I was a baby boomer, one of that generation which, according to Philip Larkin, 'discovered sex' in 1963. I also read *Lady Chatterley's Lover* (concealed behind a brown-paper cover) and danced to the Beatles. From tastes in music, to attitudes to sex and marriage, ours was a very different world from that experienced by our parents in their youth.

This story has an Australian aspect, and it's one for which Larkin was perhaps partly responsible. Like my father, Leonard Jolley, he was a librarian, and the two men met when they applied for the same job at Hull University. Larkin got the job; but had Leonard been the successful candidate, this story might have taken a different direction. As it was, he left the UK to become librarian of the University of Western Australia in Perth. And so began the Australian connection in a story of sex, love, family secrets, and deception.

Although it was 1967 when I first discovered that a web of lies had been woven around the facts of my life, it wasn't until 40 years later, after further discoveries, that I felt ready to tell it. To begin with, I thought I would write an objective account of events, weaving my story into the wider context of changing social mores. However, I quickly discovered that this approach wasn't going to work. This wasn't an exploration of social history — it was about my life — and I felt I needed to write in a more personal and emotionally engaged way.

Laura, my father's elder sister, was instrumental in propelling me to write this book. Leonard had led her and his brother and father to believe that his marriage to my mother, Joyce, was fine, and that when we left our home in Birmingham it was to move to Scotland and later to Australia; and that, while still in Scotland, he and Joyce had two more children. This was simply not true. The fact was that he'd left me and my mother in 1950 to live with his lover, Elizabeth (whom he later married); their daughter, Sarah, who was just a few weeks older than me; and 'my' younger siblings. Laura was horrified at the level of deceit practised on the Jolley family, and when I told her I was thinking of writing about it, she encouraged me to take the skeletons from their closet and 'give them a good shake'.

Something else that made me feel I should get on with writing my own account of events was that a biography of Elizabeth Jolley was being researched by Professor Brian Dibble. To my enormous astonishment, Elizabeth suggested I might like to contact him. I assumed that Professor Dibble knew the truth; but whether he did or not, I decided I would prefer to keep control of my own story, so I turned down the offer to meet with him. It seems he was unaware of some salient details, because in his biography, *Doing Life,* he suggests that my mother, Joyce, had known all about her husband's affair with Elizabeth, and had accepted it, and that Leonard's family had been in touch with Joyce after she and Leonard split up. This was so far from the case that I wanted to put the record straight. The biography was published in 2008, shortly after Mick, my stepfather, died. Leonard himself had died by this time; and both his sister and his brother, my mother, and Elizabeth were all gone. I travelled to Australia to do some further research and began to write.

Elizabeth Jolley was a highly successful and celebrated author of fiction in Australia — indeed, her fame and reputation spread worldwide. Both she and my father were well known in their professional fields, and it is no surprise that Elizabeth's fabrication of letters that purported to be from people who couldn't possibly have written them adds a piquancy to the story. But, as I found when *The House of Fiction* was first published in Australia, mine wasn't so uncommon a tale. Time and again, the people I met at literary events, and those who interviewed me, told me their own stories of family secrets, and many said how my story resonated for them; others at book signings told me they were buying the book for relatives or friends who had experienced similarly confusing events in their lives.

It was also interesting to meet people who had known Leonard or Elizabeth, and who had no idea about their past in England. These reminiscences were fascinating for me, and added to my understanding of both my father and stepmother. I had expected to be taken to task for my revelations, and had prepared answers to tricky questions, but in fact I was overwhelmed by the sympathy I was shown.

There are skeletons, whether scary or benign, in most families' closets, and sometimes it might be wisest to keep them there, locked away, doing nobody any harm. If they're taken out and given a good shake, they might well upset people's ideas about friends they thought they knew, or those they loved; but if the secrets the skeletons represent have caused hurt or harm that could have been avoided, my feeling is that it may help to let them out and give them some air.

Social mores in England have changed enormously during my lifetime: people talk more readily about their private lives. My father, by all accounts a private and reserved character, unsurprisingly didn't like what he saw as intrusiveness.

He wrote in a letter to me, commenting on a publisher's biographical notes on Elizabeth, 'I do not care for this silly personal publicity ... it was not done, I think, say forty years ago.' And that was in the 1980s! Now, with easier communications — email, cheap telephone calls and air travel, Skype and social media — those biographical notes would be commonplace. But, more to the point, this story couldn't happen in the way it did.

A desire to put the record straight was a catalyst for writing the book, but my main purpose was to try to understand what had motivated the older generation to behave as they had: for my mother to keep a promise that meant I was deprived of a grandfather, aunts, uncles and a cousin; for Leonard to delude his family and to refuse to see me for forty years; and, lastly, for Elizabeth to concoct the extraordinary 'evidence' of a fictional Susan and Joyce living in Australia when the real ones were living in Europe, in circumstances totally different from those imagined by Leonard's family.

Was this silence and concealment to do with these particular people with their individual histories? Or did their behaviour reflect a more widely accepted social atmosphere? Some readers have been disappointed that I have been unable to answer these questions with any certainty. But although this book is written like a detective story, where I present the evidence and gradually unravel the mystery, in the end I don't blame any of the people who appear in my story. Their motives were rarely straightforward, and I feel their actions were not driven by a desire to hurt or damage, so much as to protect, whether themselves or others.

To return to Larkin: in 2012, soon after I came home from Australia, I was in Chichester, where I came across the tomb that inspired Larkin's poem, 'An Arundel Tomb' with its famous last line, 'What will survive of us is love.' What Larkin meant by this is debatable — was he being ironic? But the words made me wonder about Leonard and Elizabeth's letters written with such passion 60 or more years ago, preserved not in stone as a public memorial, but in the environmentally controlled atmosphere of a public archive. These letters revealed to me an all-consuming love that left no room for me and my mother in my father's life, and provided answers to some of the questions that had bothered me for most of my life. One might reasonably conclude that, ultimately, the characters in my story were motivated by love, albeit a wilfully blind love.

# ACKNOWLEDGEMENTS

The author gratefully acknowledges the following:
© Elizabeth Jolley, from *Central Mischief*, Penguin Australia, 1992, reproduced with the permission of The Estate of Monica Elizabeth Jolley;
© Caroline Lurie, from *Central Mischief*, Penguin Australia, 1992, reproduced with permission;
© Elizabeth Jolley, from *The Sugar Mother*, Penguin Group Australia, 1988, reproduced with the permission of The Estate of Monica Elizabeth Jolley;
© Elizabeth Jolley, from *Cabin Fever*, Penguin Group Australia, 1990, reproduced with the permission of The Estate of Monica Elizabeth Jolley;
© Elizabeth Jolley, from *My Father's Moon*, Penguin Group Australia, reproduced with permission;
© Elizabeth Jolley, from *The Georges' Wife*, Penguin Group Australia, reproduced with permission;
© Brian Dibble, from *Doing Life: A Biography Of Elizabeth Jolley*, UWA Publishing, 2008, reproduced with permission.

Additional material is drawn from: *eroticism, pedophilia and obsession*: Nikki Barrowclough, 'Secrets and Lies', Good Weekend, *The Sydney Morning Herald*, 28 June 1997; *stretch thy wings/ And quit this joyless sod*: Emily Brontë, 'Retirement',

Susan Swingler

*Bronte Poems*, John Murray, London, 1915 (poem by Anne
Brontë, wrongly attributed in early publications to Emily);
*What is it men in women do require*: William Blake, 'Several
Questions Answered', *William Blake Selected Poetry*, Oxford's
World Classics, OUP, 1996; *He did sin against love, and though
he says it was in Pity's name*: Elizabeth Smart, *By Grand Central
Station I Sat Down and Wept*, p. 97, Panther, 1966, Great Britain.

I should also like to thank Caroline Lurie, Elizabeth Jolley's
literary executor, for permission to quote from Elizabeth's
correspondence; Paul Brunton, senior curator of the Mitchell
Library, Sydney, for permission to read letters passed between
Elizabeth and Leonard Jolley; and Brian Dibble for permission
to quote from his note to me of October 2008. I am grateful to
the Bundanon Trust and Deborah Ely for the opportunity to
spend time at Bundanon working on this book.

Other people who have been immensely helpful are my
half-sisters, Sarah and Ruth, and I thank them for their
understanding and generosity. My cousin Margaret Edmonds
has also been very helpful, particularly with information about
my father's family. Thanks also to Sara Davies, Helen Taylor,
and Patricia Harewood, who have read and given feedback on
the manuscript, and to fellow writers Rachel Bentham, Sarah
Duncan, and Linnet van Tinteren, who have seen the whole
thing through, offering valuable criticism and encouragement
along the way. In Australia, the help and support of my agent,
Lyn Tranter, and the wise suggestions of Georgia Richter,
my editor at Fremantle Press, have been crucial and much
appreciated. To these I should like to add my thanks to Henry
Rosenbloom and Scribe for bringing my story to the UK.